The publication of *Cornwall Railway Stations* brings a worthy close to Mike Oakley's remarkable series of books on the railway stations and halts of the West Country. The project has taken some ten years to complete, during which time he has researched the story of over 800 stations and halts from Tewkesbury in the far north of Gloucestershire to Britain's most southerly station at Helston in Cornwall. Mike was born and brought up in Dorset before moving to Bristol in the mid 1960s where he had a career in town and country planning until retirement in 1996. His keen interest in the history and role of stations and halts in the evolving social and economic life of the West Country has resulted in an extensive collection of photographs, a selection of which have appeared in this series of books. All the stations and halts now open have been viewed, together with the sites of the vast majority of those long since closed. Well received by local historians and railway enthusiasts alike, the five other books in the Dovecote Press series are 'Discover Dorset' *Railway Stations* (2001), *Somerset Railway Stations* (2002), *Gloucestershire Railway Stations* (2003), *Wiltshire Railway Stations* (2004), and *Devon Railway Stations* (2007).

Devon Railway Stations 'is a comprehensive work and a format that could well lend itself to other counties'. *Steam World* March 2008.

'For enthusiasts it (*Devon Railway Stations*) makes for a fascinating account of the facilities provided for the travelling public using the "permanent way".' *Exmouth Journal* December 2007.

'Mike's text (in *Somerset Railway Stations*) is, as ever, exemplary offering as full a history of each stopping place as possible with anecdotes and more formal details like passenger numbers, designs of buildings and everything else. A delightful slab of industrial history.' *Bristol Evening Post* 2002.

Following page:
Luxulyan. Looking north-west in June 1958 (see page 71).

CORNWALL RAILWAY STATIONS

Mike Oakley

THE DOVECOTE PRESS

Penzance. Steam railmotor No 45 stands at the 1879/80 side platform under the roof in about 1908.

First published in 2009 by The Dovecote Press Ltd
Stanbridge, Wimborne Minster, Dorset BH21 4JD

ISBN 978-1-904-34968-6

Printed and bound by KHL Printing, Singapore

All papers used by The Dovecote Press are natural, recyclable products made from wood grown in sustainable, well-managed forests.

A CIP catalogue record for this book is available from the British Library

1 3 5 7 9 8 6 4 2

CONTENTS

Cornwall Stations and Halts

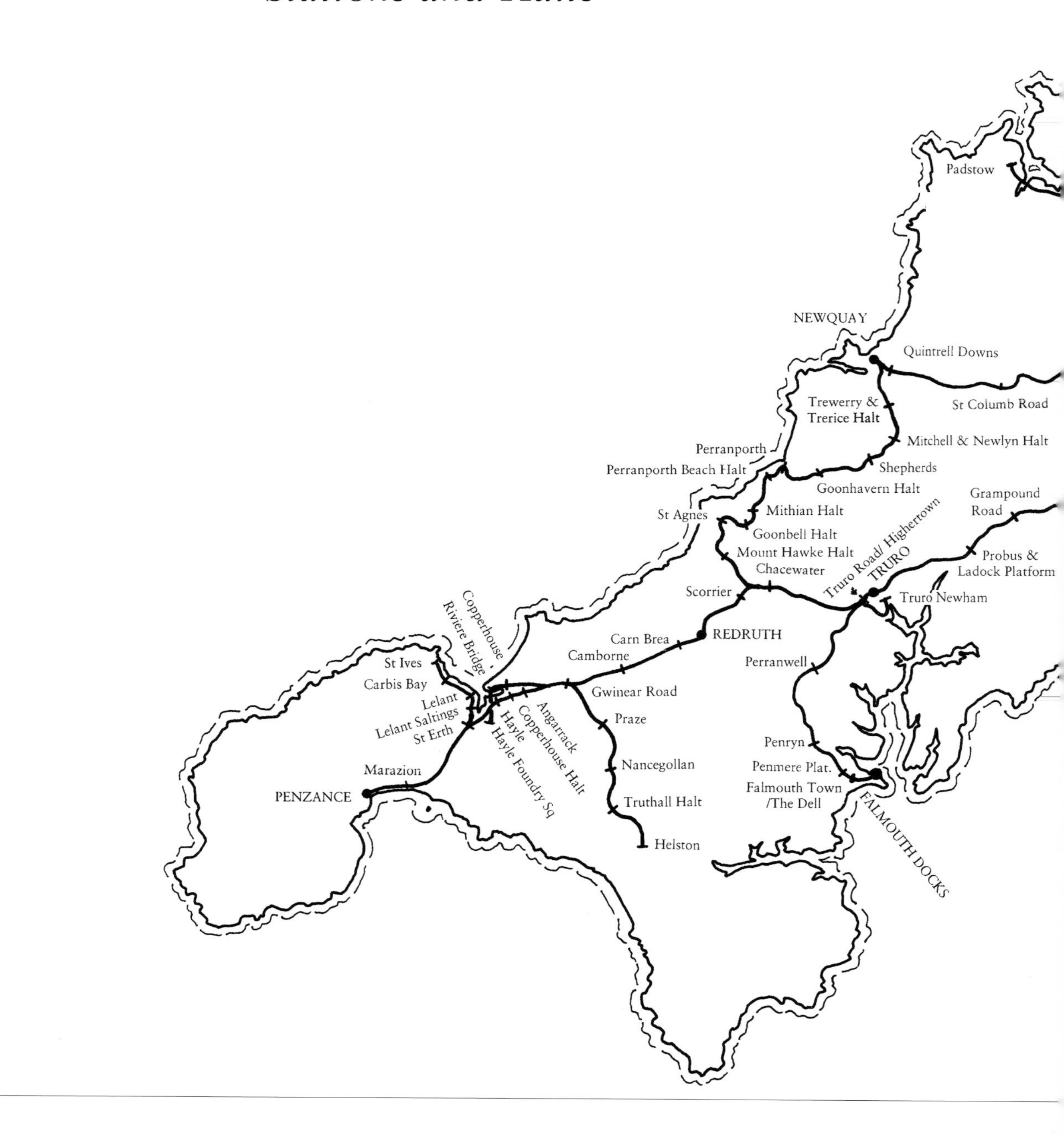

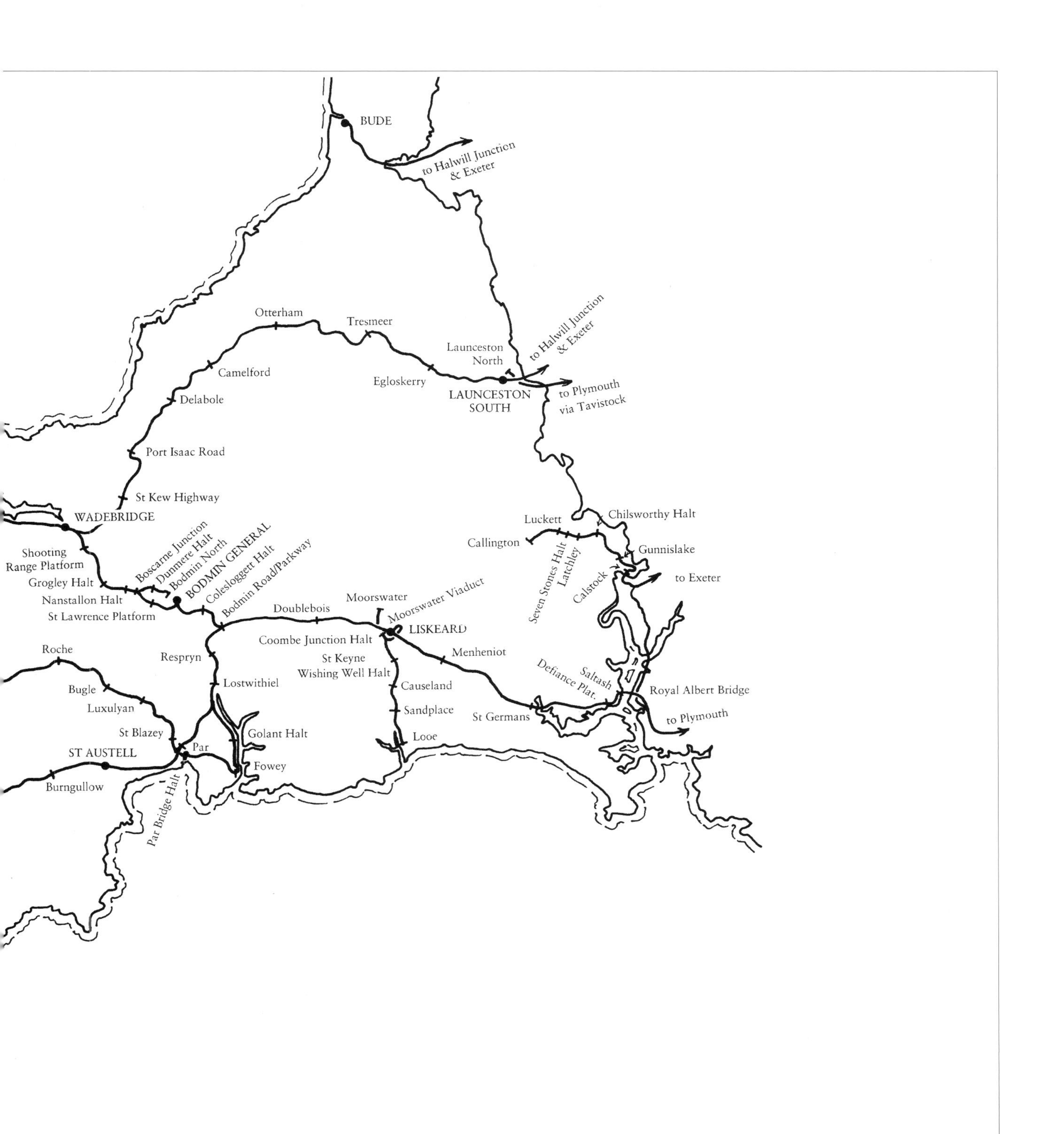

BUDE
to Halwill Junction & Exeter
Otterham
Tresmeer
Launceston North
to Halwill Junction & Exeter
Camelford
Egloskerry
LAUNCESTON SOUTH
to Plymouth via Tavistock
Delabole
Port Isaac Road
St Kew Highway
WADEBRIDGE
Shooting Range Platform
Grogley Halt
Nanstallon Halt
St Lawrence Platform
Boscarne Junction
Dunmere Halt
Bodmin North
BODMIN GENERAL
Colesloggett Halt
Bodmin Road/Parkway
Luckett
Chilsworthy Halt
Callington
Gunnislake
Seven Stones Halt
Latchley
Calstock
to Exeter
Doublebois
Moorswater
Moorswater Viaduct
LISKEARD
Coombe Junction Halt
Menheniot
Roche
Respryn
St Keyne Wishing Well Halt
Defiance Plat.
Saltash
Royal Albert Bridge
Bugle
Lostwithiel
Causeland
Luxulyan
Sandplace
St Germans
to Plymouth
St Blazey
Golant Halt
Looe
ST AUSTELL
Par
Fowey
Burngullow
Par Bridge Halt

INTRODUCTION

THE COMING OF the railway heralded a new chapter in the economic and social life of the county. Mining and quarrying had been major activities throughout Cornwall for centuries but by the early 1800s it was becoming vital for new faster modes of transport to be developed to convey heavy loads of minerals to the coastal ports for export. This was the catalyst for the development of the county's earliest railways (eg Hayle Railway 1838). As some of this mining activity faltered, passenger services were introduced on the early freight lines, some seeking to exploit the tourism potential of the county (eg Cornwall Minerals Railway 1876). A further impetus was the desire of Cornwall's commercial and industrial interests to have improved transport links to the rest of the country. To meet this need a major route was developed through the spine of the county linking Penzance and Truro to Plymouth. Further developments included the branch lines from this spine route and the construction of new lines to serve north Cornwall. Both of these opened up large areas of rural Cornwall and isolated sections of coast.

Much of this early development of the rail network was undertaken by locally based companies but these were soon absorbed, or taken over, by either the Great Western Railway (GWR) in the south and west of the county or the London & South Western Railway (LSWR) in the north. These two larger companies often operated the lines from the outset. The county's railway stations and halts played a significant role in these developments with station buildings constructed to meet the needs of passengers and goods yards and sheds provided for the use of local industries and agriculture. Built in the style of the various companies, the structures contributed greatly to the local scene, particularly when local materials were used (eg stone and slate). The station master was a key figure in the local community, in many cases provided with a house that was larger and grander than the station facilities!

Details regarding the evolution of Cornwall's railway network and the services provided have been well covered in many publications (see Further Reading) but in most cases only limited reference is made to the just over 100 stations and halts that at one time or another have met the needs of the county's residents, workers and holidaymakers. This book sets out to fill this gap, setting out in alphabetical order their history, features and role. Each has been researched, mainly from published sources, and most sites have been viewed either in autumn 2008 or early 2009, particularly where no recent information has been available regarding their current use. Where the term 'Halt' is included in the name it can be assumed that normally no facilities for the handling of freight have ever been provided. Where the terms 'up' and 'down' platforms are used they normally refer to that used for travel towards and away from London. When this is not clear further indication is given by reference to the nearest main station along the line or a compass point is given stating the siting in relation to the line. The date given for the closure of a station or halt to passengers is that of the first day when services would normally have run but did not. In the majority of cases this will have been a Monday with the last train running on the previous Saturday. The photographs are drawn from a collection built up in recent years. They have been selected primarily to illustrate the principal features of the station or halt; thus few include engines or trains as they can mask details of the buildings!

DEVELOPMENT OF CORNWALL PASSENGER SERVICES 1834 – 2009

The Bodmin & Wadebridge Railway had the honour of running the first passenger trains in Cornwall. Unlike most early Cornish railways whose objective was to convey ore or china clay to the coast, the initial purpose of the Bodmin & Wadebridge was to convey sea sand from Wadebridge to farms in the Camel valley. In October 1834 the first passenger trains ran between Bodmin and Wadebridge. In 1846 the London & South Western Railway, in order to frustrate the ambitions of the Cornwall Railway (see later), bought the Bodmin & Wadebridge Railway, though at that time the line was some 200 miles west of the London & South Western Railway system.

Mining activity was the initial reason for the development of the Hayle Railway from the port of Hayle to Redruth. The line included two inclines with rope assistance. Passengers had sometimes travelled in the open mineral wagons but the first solely passenger trains between the two towns ran on 22nd May 1843 with about 200 people travelling in two passenger coaches and three wagons. The full passenger service began the following day.

The West Cornwall Railway was established in 1846 with the aim of taking over the Hayle Railway and extending it east from Redruth to Truro and west from Hayle to Penzance. The Hayle Railway was closed in February 1852 for reconstruction and some realignment, the latter including the elimination of the two rope assisted inclines. Passenger services commenced between Redruth and Penzance in March 1852 and between Redruth and Truro in August of the same year. The West Cornwall Railway at first intended to lay track to the broad gauge planned by the Cornwall Railway but eventually adopted the standard gauge of the earlier Hayle Railway with the trackbed wide enough to accommodate broad gauge.

In the mid 1840s plans were made by the newly established Cornwall Railway to construct a major route through the spine of the county linking the major towns to Plymouth and thus the rest of southern England. This was seen as essential for the economic prosperity of Cornwall. On 4th May 1859 the Plymouth to Truro section of the broad gauge Cornwall Railway opened, including the famous Royal Albert Bridge over the River Tamar. In August 1863 came the opening of the Truro to Falmouth section. At Truro passengers could transfer to the standard gauge West Cornwall Railway for travel on to Penzance. This break of gauge at Truro brought considerable delays and inconvenience and in 1864 the Cornwall Railway insisted, as an earlier Act had ruled, that the broad gauge be laid from Truro westward. The West Cornwall Railway did not, however, have the necessary finance to fund this work. In 1865 the West Cornwall Railway was leased jointly to the GWR, Bristol & Exeter and South Devon Railways and from 1st January 1866 they became the owners and laid the broad gauge,

Falmouth Docks. The opening of the Truro to Falmouth section of the Cornwall Railway on 24th August 1863 showing the arrival of the first train.

though the standard gauge was retained for some years used by local goods traffic and limited passenger services. The first broad gauge freight train to Penzance ran on 6th November 1866 and the first broad gauge passenger service four months later on 1st March 1867.

With the aim of restricting costs and to eliminate sharp curves and steep gradients in often challenging terrain, a number of towns on the spine route were served by stations some distance away (eg Bodmin). A special feature of the route was the impressive timber viaducts where the lines crossed the very deep valleys. All of these were subsequently replaced by masonry structures, though in some cases not for many years.

Following the establishment of the major spine route through the county further passenger services were introduced often using earlier freight and mineral lines. The aim was, in many cases, to link the coasts to the main line and also exploit the tourism potential. A good example of this was the Cornwall Minerals Railway, based upon a number of lines built by J.T. Treffry of Fowey, a major landowner with interests in several mines. His aim was to link the north and south coasts of Cornwall. On 1st June 1874 a single track north – south line was opened for freight traffic. Two years later, in June 1876, a passenger service was introduced between the two ports of Newquay and Fowey.

Over ten years earlier in July 1865, Launceston, at the eastern end of the county, joined the rail network

Bude. Many stations in the south west received evacuees early in the Second World War. Crowds gather outside the station in 1939 to see the new arrivals in the town.

with the opening of the Launceston & South Devon Railway from Tavistock. At the other end of Cornwall the St Erth to St Ives branch opened in June 1877. Two years later, in September 1879, the Liskeard & Looe Railway opened for passenger traffic. At first isolated, it was linked to the main line at Liskeard from May 1901. Further lines to open for passenger services were the Helston branch (May 1887), Lostwithiel to Fowey (September 1895) and Chacewater to Newquay (July 1903 – January 1905). Bodmin itself was linked to the main spine route with the opening of the branch from Bodmin Road (May 1887). The development of these branches was undertaken both by independent companies and the GWR but all eventually came under the control of the latter either by acquisition or amalgamation.

In parallel with these developments in south and west Cornwall, further passenger services were introduced in the north of the county, these being undertaken either by the London & South Western Railway itself or by smaller companies subsequently taken over the London & South Western Railway. These northern lines had the primary aim of bringing tourists to the coastal resorts. The North Cornwall Railway opened in stages over a period of 13 years: from Halwill Junction (Devon) to Launceston (July 1886), to Tresmeer (July 1892), Camelford (August 1893), Delabole (October 1893), Wadebridge (June 1895) and Padstow (March 1899). At Wadebridge the London & South Western Railway finally linked with the Bodmin to Wadebridge line acquired nearly 50 years earlier. In the far north of the county the last section of the Devon & Cornwall Railway opened from Holsworthy (Devon) to Bude in August 1898. Finally the Plymouth, Devonport & South Western Junction Railway opened its branch to Callington from Bere Alston (Devon) in March 1908. Reflecting the earlier pattern, this line used much of the earlier trackbed of the East Cornwall Mineral Railway.

During the two World Wars there were some reductions in passenger services and the isolated closure of halts. During the Second World War many evacuees were conveyed to the county by train.

Withdrawal of passenger services in Cornwall began early – in July 1929 on the St Blazey to Fowey line. No further closures came however for over 30 years, the first being the Helston branch in November 1962. This was followed by the Tavistock to Launceston line (December 1962), Chacewater to Newquay (February 1963). Lostwithiel to Fowey (January 1965), Okehampton to Bude and Halwill Junction to Wadebridge (October 1966), Gunnislake to Callington (November 1966) and Bodmin Road to Padstow and Bodmin North to Boscarne Junction (January 1967).

Today the Bodmin & Wenford Railway reminds us of the GWR steam era. In April 1987 short trips within the confines of the former Bodmin General station were run and the first steam hauled passenger services commenced on a section of line between Bodmin General and Bodmin Parkway (former Road) on 1st September 1989 with regular passenger trains all the way between the two stations starting in June 1990. Extension of the services from Bodmin to Boscarne Junction commenced in August 1996. The Launceston Steam Railway is another steam operated line running 2½ miles west from Launceston on the trackbed of the former London & South Western line, the initial short length of line opening on 26th December 1983. The Lappa Valley Railway is a 15 inch gauge line along part of the former trackbed of the line between Perranporth and Newquay. This railway opened on 16th June 1974.

THE STATIONS AND HALTS

ANGARRACK

OPENED: 11th March 1852 (with the opening of the Penzance – Redruth section of the West Cornwall Railway).

CLOSED: After October 1853.

When the West Cornwall Railway re-routed the original alignment of the Hayle Railway, east of Hayle to avoid the rope assisted incline at Angarrack (see Hayle text), records indicate that a small station was erected. No details are available and it only lasted until late 1853 with the last reference in a timetable being in October. Some sources suggest that an earlier station was provided on the original Hayle Railway. Although trains would have had to stop for ropes to be attached to the engines to assist with the ascent of the 1 in 10 incline, there is no contemporary evidence of a specific structure. Use of this incline route covered the period June 1838 to February 1852.

BENNY HALT

OPENED: 16th June 1974

CLOSED: Remains open as the northern terminus of the Lappa Valley Railway.

Following closure of the Chacewater to Newquay line in 1963, plans were made to reopen a section and this came about eleven years later on 16th June 1974 when the Lappa Valley Railway opened along a mile of the trackbed. This 15 inch gauge line runs from Benny Halt south to the site of the East Wheal Rose mine just to the east of the former Mitchell & Newlyn Halt. At the former mine there are a number of tourist attractions including two miniature railways, an exhibition of mining history, the former mine engine shed and chimney, a boating lake and woodland/nature trails. At Benny Halt itself there are a turntable, run-round loop, workshop and a ticket office/shop. The railway has a small fleet of steam and diesel locomotives. Benny Halt is a new facility on the Lappa Valley Railway and did not feature on the original line.

BODMIN GENERAL

OPENED: 27th May 1887 (with the opening of the Cornwall Railway/GWR branch Bodmin Road – Bodmin).

CLOSED: Passengers – 30th January 1967.
Goods – 1st May 1967 (except for private sidings later closed).

REOPENED: 19th April 1987 (for brake van rides in the Yard).

When the Cornwall Railway opened its line through the spine of the county in May 1859 Bodmin, because of its elevated location, was by-passed to the south. The residents of the town had to travel three miles by road to the aptly named Bodmin Road station. The absence of a direct rail link undoubtedly hindered the

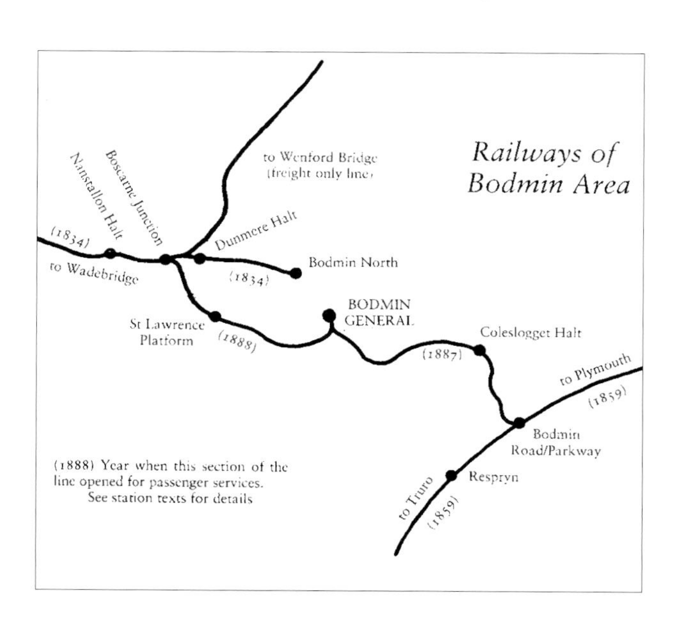

development of the town. Some thirty years later, the situation was remedied with the opening of a branch line north from Bodmin Road to a new station a short distance south of the town centre. Services started in late May 1887. This was some fifty years after the opening of Bodmin's first station on the north-west edge of the town linked to the line north to Wadebridge and Padstow (see Bodmin North text). Some fourteen months after its opening as the terminus of the branch from Bodmin Road, the station became a junction on 3rd September 1888 with the opening of a link line south and west joining the Bodmin & Wadebridge Railway at Boscarne Junction (see diagram). The GWR had running powers on the earlier line from Boscarne Junction to Wadebridge. The suffix 'General' was added from 26th September 1949; on the same date the earlier station was renamed Bodmin 'North'.

On a north – south alignment, Bodmin General was a classic GWR style terminus station. The main stone building with four chimneys was of an L shape around the north and west end of the tracks. This structure, with a wide platform canopy, contained all the main waiting, booking, office and toilet facilities. The one single face stone platform was on the west side of the tracks; towards its southern end was a metal structure acting as a store. Parallel to the platform track was a further track with an engine release close to the buffers. To the north of the station building was a spacious approach road and to the west, at a higher level, Harleigh Road was linked to the platform by a long flight of steps. In 1903 38,669 passenger tickets were issued at the station; by 1933 this figure had dropped to 27,077. The large barracks, immediately east of the station, generated a considerable volume of traffic.

Opposite the platform was the goods yard which included a large stone goods shed through which ran a siding terminating adjacent to the north section of the station building. The yard facilities included a 6 ton capacity crane and an agricultural merchants' store. An outer siding on the east side of the yard ran alongside cattle pens. Agricultural produce, fertiliser and farm equipment formed a large proportion of the goods handled at Bodmin. In 1936, a peak year, it was recorded that 505 trucks of livestock passed through the yard. A stone one road engine shed (1887) stood on the down (west) side of the line, accessed by a trailing siding from the main running line; close by were a tall conical water tank (30 ft high) and a covered coal stage. Bodmin signal box was also on the down side between the south end of the platform and the engine shed.

As with many stations in Cornwall, decline and rationalisation came in the 1960s. The engine shed closed in April 1962. Nearly five years later, at the end of January 1967, passenger services ceased. Goods facilities were withdrawn some three months later and the signal box closed on 17th December 1967. However, lines in the station area continued to be used by china clay goods traffic until 26th September 1983, trains reversing here en route from the Wenford Bridge area to Bodmin Road and the south coast ports via Lostwithiel. In 1969 the engine shed, which had closed seven years earlier in April 1962, was occupied by the south-west group of the Great Western Society (GWS). This lasted until 1977 but, soon after, the shed and the signal box, despite

Bodmin General. A group of staff stand beside a Class 517 0-4-2T in about 1910. The lamps were later moved nearer the rear of the platform.

Bodmin General. A view north in June 1956. The wide canopy provided good shelter for waiting passengers. The signal box operated until 17th December 1967.

much opposition, were demolished. The main goods shed had been demolished in about 1974.

The seed for a major revival at Bodmin General was sown on 28th June 1984 when a public meeting was held 'to formally set up the Bodmin Railway Preservation Society'. In December 1984 the Bodmin & Wenford Railway plc was formed. The first open day at the station was held on 1st June 1986 and on 19th April 1987 brake van rides began. In that year the Cornish Steam Locomotive Preservation Society moved its stock from Bugle to Bodmin. In June 1989 the Bodmin & Wenford Railway formally occupied the station buildings and on 17th June 1990 regular services began between Bodmin General and Bodmin Parkway (formerly Road). Finally on 15th August 1996 public services recommenced between Bodmin General and Boscarne Junction where a concrete platform had been erected (see Boscarne Junction text). In parallel with the development of train services, other developments took place at the station. The first essential step was the establishment, on the site of the old goods shed, of an engine workshop moved from St Austell in 1987. During the winter of 2000/2001 an extension was built. Other work has included the re-erection in 1997 of a signal box on the site of the original, using parts gleaned from demolished boxes, the erection of a water tank in 1998 to replace the earlier one which had been moved to the GWS Didcot site and the construction in January 1999 of a two road engine shed on the site of the original shed.

Today the Bodmin & Wenford Railway continues to run services to and from Bodmin Parkway and Boscarne Junction. The eventual aim is to extend the line towards Wadebridge alongside the Camel Trail, the first phase being the short distance to a site close to the old Nanstallon Halt (see text for that halt). In the 2009 maximum summer timetable there were three return journeys to both Bodmin Parkway and Boscarne Junction from Bodmin General. Special events are held throughout the year, in particular the popular Santa Specials. When visited in March 2009, the opening day of the year's operations was proving very popular, the offer of half price over the weekend being a particular attraction. The original terminus building has been beautifully restored with the aim of reflecting the 1950s era. In 1996 a new souvenir shop and booking hall were built in a traditional style and, during the winter of 2000/2001, the buffet was renovated. Work on the locomotives can be seen in the new engine shed. Services to Boscarne Junction provide a good link to the popular Camel Trail foot and cycle way.

BODMIN NORTH

FIRST STATION

OPENED: 1st October 1834 (with the commencement of passenger services on the Bodmin & Wadebridge Railway).

CLOSED: 1st November 1886 (for line re-building by the London & South Western Railway between Dunmere Junction and Bodmin).

SECOND STATION

OPENED: 1st November 1895.

CLOSED: Passengers – 30th January 1967.
Goods – 29th November 1965.

A small terminus station opened north-west of the town centre at the beginning of October 1834 when passenger services started on the Bodmin & Wadebridge Railway from the north coast port of Wadebridge. Known then as Bodmin Wharf, it was at the eastern end of a spur line running east from Dunmere Junction. From this junction the original freight only Bodmin & Wadebridge Railway line continued north to Wenford Bridge. On its approach into the station the single track ran south of, and adjacent to, Bodmin Jail to which, records indicate, train passengers went to view executions in the late 1830s! This original Bodmin & Wadebridge spur line followed a steep and winding alignment and the new owners, the London & South Western Railway (LSWR) decided to reconstruct and re-align it, work being undertaken between late 1886 and 1891. The LSWR also decided to build a new station, this opening close to the original at the beginning of November 1895. The long absence of a station for nine years was of much concern to Bodmin residents.

Bodmin North. A view east in about 1910. Note the typical large LSWR apex platform canopy and the ventilator in the roof of the gent's toilet.

The layout of the 1895 station comprised a main running line alongside the south facing single face platform terminating at buffers. Parallel to this line were two long sidings also ending at buffers and a short spur from the outer siding terminating alongside a loading platform and cattle pens. South-west of the station building was a medium sized goods yard, a long siding running through a stone goods shed. To the west of the yard a siding trailed into a 50 ft turntable. This was little used as tank engines predominated over the years. The station signal box was at the west end of the goods yard on the south side. A two lever ground frame, at the east end of the platform, also controlled points.

The main granite built single storey station building, with a slate roof and three chimneys, stood on the east end of the platform. It contained the principal facilities including the booking office, a general waiting room, a ladies' waiting room and toilets. The gent's toilets were at the west end of the building with a ventilator in the roof. A large apex style canopy supported by pillars covered the platform in front of the building. An early map indicates that a small canopy once covered the main road side entrance to the building but later photographs show that it had been removed. A further stone building at the rear of the platform stood to the west of the main structure. Passenger use of the station was relatively high in the 1920s and 1930s. In 1928 20,822 passenger tickets were issued and 30,152 collected; by 1936 the figures had fallen to 14,191 and 22,838.

From 26th September 1949 the suffix North was added to the name. The station remained relatively busy until the through service to and from Wadebridge and Padstow was withdrawn as from 15th June 1964. From that date a shuttle service, operated by a four wheel rail-car ran along the spur to Boscarne Junction. At the junction two wooden platforms were erected to enable Bodmin North passengers to transfer to through trains running from Bodmin Road and Bodmin General to Wadebridge and Padstow. For three weeks in April 1966, as an experiment, these through trains ran into Bodmin North but this routeing involved reversals both at the station and at Boscarne Junction. Not surprisingly the experiment did not succeed! The shuttle service resumed until the end of January 1967 when passenger services on the Bodmin Road to Wadebridge/Padstow line and the Bodmin North spur ceased and the station closed. Freight services had been withdrawn some 14 months earlier at the end of November 1965; the sidings opposite the platform had been lifted in 1964. The station was unstaffed as from 3rd January 1966 and, unusually for a terminus, was designated a halt from 18th April 1966. The signal

Bodmin North. From the buffers looking west in 1962, some five years before the station closed. The stone goods shed is in the distance beyond the lorry.

box closed with the station at the end of January 1967.

Following closure, a road (Railway Terrace/ Brownlow Place) was constructed along the alignment into the station. The site has now been redeveloped including a supermarket and Bodmin Fire Station. No trace of the railway remains. A small car park marks the location where the station building once stood at the east end of the site.

BODMIN ROAD/PARKWAY

OPENED: 27th June 1859 (nearly 2 months after the commencement of services on the Plymouth – Truro section of the Cornwall Railway through the site on 4th May).

CLOSED: Passengers – remains open for services on the Plymouth – Penzance line and also as the southern terminus of the privately run Bodmin & Wenford Railway.
Goods – 4th November 1963 (except for private sidings later closed).

The station is sited in the valley of the River Fowey, some three miles south-east of the former county town, which, because of its elevated position, was by-passed when the Cornwall Railway was opened through the spine of the county in mid 1859.

When services commenced through the curved site early in May 1859, Bodmin Road station was not quite complete and passengers were required to use Respryn, a private station some three quarters of a mile to the west serving Lanhydrock House. The initial facilities at Bodmin Road, which opened at the end of June, comprised two platforms on a passing loop and three sidings, all track laid to broad gauge. The absence of a station at Bodmin itself handicapped the development of the town compared to other Cornish settlements with rail facilities and to remedy this, a three and a half mile branch line was opened north from Bodmin Road to Bodmin General on 27th May 1887. This branch was laid at the standard gauge and thus, until conversion of the main line from broad gauge in May 1892, no physical connection was possible. The connection was made in October 1892. During the period of mixed gauges at Bodmin Road there was an exchange platform west of the station to facilitate the transfer of goods.

To service the main and branch lines, the station was rebuilt by 1896 with a single side platform on the down side of the main line and an island platform for the up main line services and the branch line trains. The main wooden station building, with the principal facilities, was on the down platform, whilst on the island was a wooden waiting room and large canopy protecting passengers on both sides. A covered footbridge connected the platforms at the east end. A separate porters' room stood west of the main building. These original buildings were demolished and replaced by brick structures in 1989 but the covered footbridge was not replaced and remains in use today. Between the two World Wars twelve staff were based at Bodmin Road.

Bodmin Road. A view east towards Plymouth in the summer of 1958 showing the main timber building and signal box on the down platform.

Bodmin Road. Looking west on 11th June 1966. Note the fine covered footbridge which remains in place today. Trains from Bodmin General and Wadebridge used the outer face of the island platform (right).

Bodmin Road. The road side elevation of the main down side building in the summer of 1958. This building was replaced in 1989 by a brick structure, as was the waiting room on the up island platform.

An original goods shed was sited east of the station on the up side but, following reconstruction, extensive facilities were developed to the west, on both up and down sides. The main yard, on the down side, incorporated two sidings, one of which ran through a large wooden goods shed. A dock siding trailed back behind the west end of the down platform. Alongside were cattle pens; another cattle dock was also built on the site of the earlier exchange platform on the up side. From 1920 until 31st December 1966 the goods siding through the shed continued west for a further half mile, initially serving china clay dries and latterly a Naval store. On the up side west of the station were four parallel long sidings fanning out from a single track. A dock siding trailed back behind the west end of the up platform. Adjacent to it was a large water tank. A further smaller water tank was sited on the up side of the line adjacent to the east end of the island platform. It was fed from the nearby River Fowey. This supplied water to locomotives through a pipe cantilevered over two tracks.

General goods facilities were withdrawn at Bodmin Road in early November 1963; the down siding parallel to the goods shed was lifted in December 1966 and that through the shed in March 1968. This down side goods yard is now in use as a car park. The up sidings were taken over by the Bodmin & Wenford Railway in 2007 and a large carriage shed was erected. Passenger and freight train movements were controlled from 1893 by a 36 lever signal box on the down platform east of the main building adjacent to the footbridge steps. The box ceased to be regularly used on 30 November 1983 and closed on 30th May 1985. Subsequently it was developed as a café which continues today run by the Bodmin & Wenford Railway (see Bodmin General text).

Passenger services on the branch to Bodmin General ceased on 30th January 1967 and the line closed entirely on 3rd October 1983; in the latter years it had been used only by china clay trains en route from Wenford Bridge to Fowey, a journey that necessitated reversal at both Bodmin General and Bodmin Road. From 4th November 1983 the station was renamed Bodmin Parkway. Services run by the Bodmin & Wenford Railway ran through from Bodmin General to Bodmin Parkway as from 17th June 1990 using the north side of the island platform. There is no connection between the Bodmin & Wenford line and the main line at the east of the station, the up island platform having been extended. The sole connection is at the west end via a headshunt.

BOSCARNE JUNCTION

OPENED: 15th June 1964 (see text)
CLOSED: 18th April 1966
RE-OPENED: 2nd May 1966
CLOSED: 30th January 1967
RE-OPENED: 15th August 1996

In mid June 1964 what became known as an exchange platform came into use sited at Boscarne Junction, in the V between the Bodmin General to Wadebridge line and the spur line to and from Bodmin North, via Dunmere. This facility, costing some £2000, enabled passengers to transfer between the DMU services on the Bodmin General to Wadebridge and Padstow line and the four wheel AC railbus service running between Bodmin North and Boscarne Junction. A normal

Boscarne Junction. A close up of the elevated platform serving trains on the Bodmin to Wadebridge line. In timetables it was sometimes called an 'Exchange Platform'.

height wooden sleeper platform, of only one coach length, served passengers on the Bodmin – Wadebridge line. It had a nameboard 'Boscarne Junction – alight for Bodmin North and Dunmere'. Passengers on the Bodmin North spur were only provided with a rail level wooden platform, the rail car having centrally placed retractable steps. A short path, lit by three oil lamps, connected the two platforms. There were no shelters or ticket facilities and only access by rail to the oil lit platforms.

The exchange platform went out of use in mid April 1966 when, as an experiment, trains from Bodmin General to Wadebridge and Padstow reversed at the junction and directly served Dunmere Halt and Bodmin North. This manoeuvre lasted less than three weeks when the exchange facility recommenced. Use of the platforms ceased in January 1967 when services were withdrawn on both the Bodmin to Wadebridge line and the spur to Bodmin North. The wooden platforms were removed.

Some 29 years later a concrete platform and track loop were opened at Boscarne Junction by the Bodmin & Wenford Railway as the northern terminus of its operations. Public services to the new platform, sited just to the west of the original junction, commenced on 15th August 1996. The new station was officially opened a month later. In January 2009 work commenced on the construction of a new waiting shelter on the platform, its design based on shelters of the former North Cornwall line with stone walls and a slate roof. A new running in board was also being made. The new platform provides a good link with the popular Camel Trail foot and cycle path to Wadebridge and Padstow.

BUDE

OPENED: 10th August 1898 (with the opening of the Holsworthy (Devon) – Bude section of the London & South Western Railway).

CLOSED: Passengers – 3rd October 1966.
Goods – 7th September 1964.

Like a number of coastal towns in the South West, the development of Bude in the nineteenth century was seriously handicapped by the absence of a direct link to the evolving railway system. The Devon and Cornwall Railway, absorbed by the London & South Western Railway in 1872, reached the west Devon town of Holsworthy in January 1879. However, it was another 19 years before the LSWR completed the 10 mile extension on to Bude, services commencing in mid August 1898. During the intervening period the LSWR had subsidised what was described as a 'smart coach service' from Holsworthy to Bude to the tune of £2 per week. The arrival of the railway was seen as a lifeline for the town, which at that time had a population of about 800. This was soon swelled by large numbers of holidaymakers in Bude, for day trips and longer stays.

The line entered the town from the south, the station being sited on the southern outskirts. This location, though not ideal, was partly to placate the residents of Stratton, who had campaigned that the railway should serve that settlement which, before the arrival of the railway, was larger than Bude with a population of about 1000. On a north – south alignment the main track ran alongside the west face of the single platform; parallel to this was a long run round loop. A track also ran into a bay platform at

Bude. The staff pose on the platform in this view in about 1910 of the single platform and building. The large canopy is a particular feature. At the far end is a prominent notice advertising the large refreshment room.

Bude. A reproduction of a postcard of about 1910 looking north along the station approach with horse drawn carriages alongside the building.

the south end of the station. Parallel to this bay track, a siding trailed from the main running line and, having run through the stone goods shed, divided in two, one stub serving an end loading dock and the other running by a cattle feed store and terminating alongside cattle pens. On the down (west) side of the site a siding trailed back from the run round loop and ran through the 1898 one road engine shed and across a 50 ft turntable. North of the engine shed was a coal stage and elevated metal water tank. Prior to 1939 this engine shed siding continued south to connect with a branch which left the main line south of the station running west over the River Neet to serve a small wharf at a basin on the Bude Canal. Here coal from South Wales and sand from local beaches for land improvement was loaded on to rail wagons. The traffic declined between the wars with the introduction of chemical fertilisers and growth of road transport but the canal branch survived until the withdrawal of freight services at Bude in 1964. General freight traffic was focussed at the small goods yard on the up side with its goods shed. Goods handled included the usual coal, building materials, household goods, agricultural fertilisers and cattle. An abattoir was sited for some years south of the station on the up side. Adjacent to it was an 8 ton capacity crane.

The main station building, on the north end of the platform, was a very impressive stone structure. At the northern end was a large two storey station master's house, which featured a slate roof, three chimneys, an impressive gable and a large ground floor bay window overlooking the station forecourt. On its northern wall, a door, protected by a porch with a finial, led into the station master's garden. South of the house, a long single storey section, again with three chimneys, contained all the main station facilities, including the booking hall and office, waiting rooms, the station master's office and the ladies' toilet. A particular feature was a large refreshment room at the northern end adjacent to the house. A dormer window in the slate roof over the booking hall gave extra illumination. The gent's toilet was at the southern end of the building with a large ventilator in the roof. A large apex style canopy with a wooden valance ran along the whole platform frontage extending slightly beyond its southern end, attached to a high wall. The canopy was supported

Bude. The impressive station building on 19th July 1963 just over three years before it closed. A particular feature is the large station master's house with its ground floor bay window. The dormer window in the roof gave extra light in the booking hall.

by a number of tall pillars and decorative brackets. Rail movements were controlled from a brick signal box with 36 levers, standing a little to the south of the station on the down side beyond the engine shed and turntable.

When originally constructed, the 570 ft long platform was thought to be longer than required for normal passenger services but it came into its own when excursion trains of eight or nine carriages started to run to Bude. In the 1930s even longer trains were run responding to the demand and thus at Bude changes were made. This involved moving the signals further away from the platform so that the long trains of up to 15 carriages could be split, with the main sector in the longer platform (capacity ten carriages) and the remainder in the bay, both being loaded at the same time. This large volume of holidaymakers was reflected in the number of passenger tickets issued and collected: in 1928 16,159 were issued and 37,710 collected; figures for 1936 were 8,923 and 26,157. During the Second World War a number of trains conveying evacuees arrived at Bude. (see photo page 10)

Passenger services at Bude were never very frequent though they did include, on a daily basis for many years, portions of through trains to and from London Waterloo. Complete trains also served Bude at summer weekends. The level of service declined after transfer of the Bude area to the control of the B R Western Region from January 1963. Indeed, in the summer of 1965 the Saturday through trains to Bude from London were transferred from Waterloo to Paddington, reversing at Exeter St Davids. Services from the mid 1960s became more local with DMUs being introduced. Bude engine shed closed in September 1964, though servicing facilities were retained until January 1965. In the final few months prior to closure of Bude station for passenger services, at the beginning of October 1966, there was only a shuttle service to Okehampton. It was estimated that in this last summer season some 30% of the holidaymakers at Bude travelled by the two car DMU! This closure was a great blow for Bude and the surrounding area of north Cornwall, the nearest rail head being 30 miles away at Okehampton. The situation worsened from January 1972 with the closure of that station, the nearest now being at Exeter. There had been a great local campaign against closure but it was in vain.

Following closure, the station building remained for some years, becoming increasingly derelict. Eventually in the 1980s it was demolished and the whole station area has been redeveloped for elderly persons' housing. The southern section, including the former sites of the engine shed and goods shed is accessed via Ceres Court. The northern section, including the site of the station building itself is served by Bulleid Way. A plaque on a warden's house was placed on 3rd October 1998 recording the centenary of the railway's arrival in the town on 10th August 1898. It states that 'Bulleid Way is named in honour and memory of O.V.S. Bulleid, Chief Mechanical Engineer of the Southern Railway'. On the plaque is a coloured illustration of the West Country class engine 'Bude' designed by O V S Bulleid. To the south of the housing development on the former track alignment is an industrial estate and to the south-west the old bridge, which took the Wharf branch over the river, survives with modern railings alongside a footpath to the canal basin.

BUGLE

OPENED: 20th June 1876 (with the commencement of passenger services on the Cornwall Minerals Railway, Newquay – Fowey).

CLOSED: Passengers – remains open as a request stop for services on the Par – Newquay branch.
Goods – 1st June 1964 (apart from private sidings, later closed).

Named after Bugle, a village a half mile to the south, the development of the station was in two distinct stages, before and after doubling of the track. Sited at the heart of china clay country, it opened in June 1876 when passenger services commenced on the Cornwall Minerals Railway's line from Newquay to Fowey.

The station site was located between Goonbarrow Junction to the south-east from which, at one time, eight different clay workings were served and branches to the north-west to Wheal Rose and Carbis Wharf. The former was opened in 1893 and the latter in 1874. The original Cornwall Minerals Railway station, on an approximate north-west to south-east alignment, comprised a single platform on the up (east) side of the line on which was a low wooden building with an apex slate roof and two chimneys. An iron clad shed was later added south east of the building for storage of parcels. A signal box stood at the south–east end of the platform. There were sidings on both the up and down sides of the station. Alongside one of the two down side sidings was a substantial clay loading wharf where

Bugle. A view in 1906 of the original 1876 Cornwall Minerals Railway station shows the single platform, the low wooden building, the iron clad parcels office and the original signal box. This last was replaced in 1916 by a GWR box south-east of the station.

horse drawn wagons could unload. On the up side there was a two siding goods yard that handled general merchandise. The second siding was added in 1910.

In preparation for the doubling of the line from Goonbarrow Junction to Bugle in 1930, the station was redeveloped into a single island platform with two faces and a wooden building and canopy. Access to the platform, which came into use on 20th July 1930, was via steps to and from a road overbridge at the north-west end of the site. The bridge had been modified to cross two tracks. A GWR 41 lever signal box replaced the original Cornwall Minerals Railway box in 1916. It stood on the down side at the south-east end of the station site adjacent to the level crossing at Molinnis. Bugle station was at its peak in the late 1920s and early 1930s. The number of passenger tickets issued rose from 6,293 in 1903 to 8,679 in 1913 and 11,725 in 1923. The number fell slightly to 11,273 in 1933. Twelve men were based at Bugle for most of the 1930s. Staffing ceased on 12th July 1964.

After the Second World War both china clay and passenger traffic declined and by 1964 rationalization had begun. The Wheal Rose branch closed on 29th November 1964 along with the up goods yard and down side loop alongside the platform. From that time the double track line from Goonbarrow Junction operated as two parallel single tracks with cross-overs removed. Newquay branch line traffic was confined to the up side track and only the up side face of the island platform was used. A surviving down side track away from the platform was used for freight traffic to the Bugle wharves and the Carbis Wharf. The 1930 signal box at Molinnis was reduced to a ground frame only in 1964 and the crossing became open in August 1973 with the box closing entirely. A few years later the Bugle down side wharf

Bugle. Looking south in 1962 at the redeveloped single island platform station which came into use on 20th July 1930. The wooden station building has a canopy on the up side. Access to the island was via steps down from a road bridge at the north-west end, at the foot of which was a wooden fence (bottom right).

and sidings were removed. From the end of 1989 Carbis Wharf and its connecting line also closed. From the early 1990s a wooden hut replaced the earlier wooden station building; photographs indicate that the angled canopy from the latter could have been re-used on the hut.

Today the scene is transformed. The wooden hut has been replaced by an open glass shelter, new lighting has been installed and the now single side platform has been resurfaced, trains stopping at the former up side. The former railway land on either side has been redeveloped for housing.

BURNGULLOW

OPENED: 1st February 1863 (on the Plymouth – Truro section of the Cornwall Railway originally opened through this site in May 1859).

CLOSED: Passengers – 14th September 1931
Goods – Uncertain but pre 1947

Opening at the beginning of February 1863, the station at Burngullow, on a then single track section of the Cornwall Railway, served a hamlet of the same name close by to the south. It was sited at a junction between the main line and the mineral only Newquay & Cornwall Junction Railway which ran north to Drinnick Mill and St Dennis Junction with the Par to Newquay line. The original small station building was on the down side east of a road bridge; a broad gauge one road engine shed (July 1869) stood west of the bridge. This shed closed in March 1906 and was demolished in 1929.

When the main line was doubled in the Burngullow area in 1888/1889, it was not possible to construct a platform on the up side opposite the original platform because of existing china clay dries and sidings. The station was thus re-located, as from 1st August 1901, west of the road bridge, the down platform now being sited opposite the junction with the mineral line and the shorter up platform constructed in the V between the up main and mineral line tracks. A covered footbridge was erected connecting the east end of the up platform with the centre of the down. The main stone building was on the down platform east of the footbridge; a stone shelter west of the footbridge served passengers on the up side. As the mineral line never carried passenger services, no platform was provided at Burngullow to serve it.

There was insignificant population in the area around the station and thus the number of passenger tickets issued was low: in 1903 8,627; 1913 9,590; 1923 6,300; 1931 (part) 1,318. It is of little surprise that the station closed to passengers in September 1931.

The main line was singled west from here to Probus on 5th October 1986 when the down side track was taken out. At this point the 1901 former West signal box (31 levers) on the down platform west of the main building was closed but was subsequently used by permanent way staff until it burnt down. The former

Burngallow. A 1922 view west from the road bridge of the 1901 re-sited station. The shorter up platform is between the up line (towards St Austell) and the line serving several china clay firms. The original 1869 broad gauge engine shed stands alongside the mineral line (right). The shed had closed by March 1906 and was demolished in 1929.

East box (23 levers), east of the junction, opened in 1899 but closed from 24th March 1935. Double track was reinstated by 2004. Today remains of a building on the up side can still be seen close to the mineral line which remains open for china clay traffic.

CALLINGTON

OPENED: 2nd March 1908 (with the opening of the Plymouth, Devonport & South Western Junction Railway branch, Bere Alston – Callington).
CLOSED: Passengers – 7th November 1966.
Goods – 28th February 1966.

Callington. Taken from the station approach, the view shows the corrugated iron station building and the wooden train shed. The station was initially called Callington Road, an appropriate name, being sited at Kelly Bray, one and a quarter miles north of the town.

Callington station opened at the beginning of March 1908 when passenger services began on the Plymouth, Devonport & South Western Junction Railway branch from Bere Alston in west Devon. Some thirty six years earlier on 7th May 1872, the East Cornwall Mineral Railway had opened a 7¾ mile 3 ft 6 inch gauge line from Calstock on the River Tamar to Kelly Bray, one and a quarter miles north of Callington and 640 ft above sea level, to carry tin and other ores from the inland mines. At the east end of the line a long cable assisted incline, with a gradient of 1 in 6, linked to the riverside quay at Calstock. In 1894 the East Cornwall Mineral Railway was fully absorbed by the Plymouth, Devonport & South Western Junction Railway which, in 1890, had opened a line from Lydford to Devonport via Bere Alston in west Devon. Under Light Railway Orders of 1900 and 1905 the gauge of the former East Cornwall Mineral Railway Calstock to Kelly Bray line was converted to standard. The alignment was also changed to eliminate the incline which was replaced by a wagon lift sited adjacent to the 129 ft high concrete block 12 arch Calstock viaduct, which carried track over the river to link with the earlier Devonport line at Bere Alston. The lift operated until September 1934. Col Stephens, the operator of a number of Light Railways, was appointed Associate Engineer to the Plymouth, Devonport & South Western Junction Railway and his hand can be seen in the design and structure of the station buildings on the 1908 line.

Callington. A view east from the buffers in 1962. The single platform and the track alongside are covered by a wooden train shed which, until the 1950s, had a sloping extension covering the parallel carriage siding.

The East Cornwall Mineral Railway, constructed to link the mining area around Kit Hill to the quay at Calstock, terminated in the centre of Kelly Bray close to a crossroads. With the commencement of passenger services the Kelly Bray depot was renamed Callington Road, an appropriate name which lasted less than two years until 1st November 1909 when it changed to Callington for Stoke Climsland, which itself continued until 1949 when the suffix was dropped. Though plans were made to extend the line south to Callington, these never materialised, a road service providing the link. Some thirty years earlier, long before the arrival of passenger trains north of the town, Callington had been served by horse buses running to and from Saltash on the main Plymouth to Truro line. From 1876 the GWR had subsidised a four horse coach between the two towns; this was replaced by motor cars from 1st June 1904.

The east – west aligned station comprised a main running track alongside a south facing one face platform together with a parallel carriage siding. In order to run around trains had to reverse out of the platform to use a loop east of the station. The platform was extended by some 30 yards at its east end in 1927. The west end of the platform and the track alongside were covered by a high wooden train shed supported by a wall along the rear of the platform and ten wooden legs. The platform extended beyond the shed at both ends but particularly to the east. Until the 1950s the parallel carriage siding was also covered by a sloping wooden extension of the main shed roof. Attached to the main shed on its north side was a single storey corrugated iron building with an apex roof which incorporated the station's main booking and waiting facilities. A small open corrugated iron hut stood for some years on the platform west of the train shed. The station house incorporated offices of the Plymouth, Devonport & South Western Junction Railway until 1923.

The early nameboard set out an ambitious claim that Callington station provided a direct route 'for Plymouth, Exeter, Portsmouth & London'. In 1928 20,349 passenger tickets were issued and 27,095 collected; in 1936 the equivalent figures had increased to 23,384 and 32,769. Such an increase was an unusual trend for Cornwall stations.

Callington goods yard, which handled a variety of freight traffic for the town and surrounding rural areas, was to the north-east of the station building. A long siding connected to the main running line east of the station ran alongside the south wall of the corrugated iron goods shed. The rail side entrance to the shed was protected by a large canopy supported on tall legs. Inside the shed was a 3 ton capacity crane. A crane also operated in the yard. A stub off the long siding served cattle pens erected in 1916. Also in the yard were a number of storage sheds operated by local traders. East of the station on the up side was a 1908 two road wooden engine shed; originally this was accessed from the west but track layout changes in the late 1920s, associated with the 1927 platform extension, resulted in shed access only from the east. Further modifications to the shed took place in 1935/36. A coaling stage was sited adjacent to the east end of the engine shed. To the south of the station sidings served a number of local coal merchants. There was no signal box at Callington, points and signals being operated by ground frames.

The engine shed closed in September 1964 and freight facilities were withdrawn at the end of February 1966. The station closed entirely after the withdrawal of passenger services in early November of the same year after services were cut back on the line beyond Gunnislake.

Today the whole station site, accessed from Station Road, has been redeveloped for commercial uses and housing, the former in the appropriately named Beeching Park Industrial Estate.

CALSTOCK

OPENED: 2nd March 1908 (with the opening of the Plymouth, Devonport & South Western Junction Railway branch Bere Alston – Callington).

CLOSED: Passengers – remains open on the branch line Plymouth – Gunnislake via Bere Alston (the Tamar Valley line).
Goods – 28th February 1966.

The village of Calstock stands on the steep slopes of the valley of the River Tamar. Its centre is some 150 ft above the riverside quays alongside which sailing barges once moored, engaged in the import of coal and the export of tin, copper and arsenic, mined inland in the Kit Hill area of east Cornwall. To assist with the haulage of these minerals for export, the East Cornwall Mineral Company opened a 3 ft 6 inch gauge line from Kelly Bray, north of Callington, to Calstock in early May 1872. The last section of the line was in the form of a cable assisted incline from just south of Drakewalls (south of Gunnislake) to Calstock Quay, a drop of some 350 ft at a gradient of about 1 in 6. In 1894 the East Cornwall Mineral Railway was absorbed by the Plymouth, Devonport & South Western Junction Railway and the line was converted to standard gauge (see Callington text). The aim was to connect the Callington mineral line to the LSWR main line between Tavistock and

Calstock. Crowds are gathered on the station's opening day, 2nd March 1908.

Calstock. A train from Bere Alston to Callington approaches the single platform having crossed the splendid Calstock viaduct in mid 1908. To the right a siding in the goods yard leads to the top of the wagon hoist linked to Calstock Quay.

Plymouth at Bere Alston, which had opened in 1890. In order to cross the River Tamar a new line was constructed on a circuitous alignment from just south of Drakewalls through the higher parts of Calstock and on to the famous Calstock Viaduct. This is a 12 arch concrete block structure, each arch with a span of 60 ft, carrying the line 129 ft above the river. This line, which opened at the beginning of March 1908, thus eliminated the incline down to the Calstock Quay. It was however important that the link was maintained and, to achieve this, a wagon hoist was installed at the north end adjacent to the second arch of the viaduct on the down side to which ran one of the sidings in Calstock goods yard. This hoist, with a capacity of 20 tons, operated until September 1934 and was removed the following year.

Unlike most other stations on the Callington branch, Calstock station, sited on a sharp right angled curve at the north end of the viaduct, was thus not on the site of an earlier East Cornwall Mineral Railway depot. On an approximate north-east to south-west alignment, this single curved platform station was on the up (south-east) side of the line. Parallel to the platform track was a short passing loop but no downside platform was ever provided. Beyond this loop was a further goods loop and a small goods yard. An outer siding served a cattle dock and another ran to the top of the wagon hoist noted above. Over the years this yard handled a variety of freight including horticultural produce from the Tamar valley, in particular flowers and fruit. Records indicate that at the peak some 14 vans of strawberries were despatched per day!

Over the years a varied collection of structures stood at the ends of, and on the single platform. From north to south these comprised a ground frame box, a water tower, a metal goods shed, the main building, a brick gent's toilet, a metal lamp hut, a

Calstock. A more recent view over 50 years later in June 1962. The building is little changed from opening day but more structures have appeared on the platform. Note the water tower, seen over the station canopy, a vital feature for trains climbing towards Gunnislake.

Camborne. A steam rail motor stands at the up platform near the level crossing gates prior to its departure for Truro in about 1910. The main station buildings date from late Victorian times. Note the large covered footbridge.

coal stage and another small ground frame hut. The main building, a wooden frame structure with corrugated iron cladding, had a wooden backwards sloping platform canopy supported by three wooden posts. It incorporated the booking and waiting facilities and the ladies' cloakroom. The ground frame, beyond the northern end of the platform, originally only had 4 levers but a 10 lever frame was installed in 1937. At this point the ground frame at the south end ceased to operate. The northern ground frame box closed on 5th May 1968, when the station passing loop was taken out of use. The water tower was a well used facility with most engines taking on water before tackling the steep gradient (initially 1 in 40) en route to Gunnislake. The sidings were taken out of use from the 4th August 1966 although general goods facilities had been formally withdrawn in the previous February.

In the 1920s and 1930s the station recorded good levels of passenger use considering the relatively sparse local population. As at Gunnislake, the numbers increased during this period, unusual at Cornish stations. In 1928 11,991 passenger tickets were issued and 13,615 collected; by 1936 equivalent figures had risen to 12,416 and 14,439. The station became unstaffed in early 1969. Today many commuters use the station for travelling into the Plymouth area on what is called the Tamar Valley line, the road links being very long and circuitous. The early 2009 timetable of nine trains in each direction provided a vital public transport link. All the early buildings on the platform have gone, being replaced today by a brick shelter with a canopy supported by three stanchions of a style now found at many surviving small stations and halts in Cornwall. The former goods yard is mainly in use for car parking in addition to limited housing development in Lang Gardens.

CAMBORNE

OPENED: 23rd May 1843 (with the commencement of passenger services on the Hayle Railway, Hayle Foundry Square – Redruth).

CLOSED: 16th February 1852.

REOPENED: 11th March 1852 (with the opening of the Penzance – Redruth section of the West Cornwall Railway).

CLOSED: Passengers – remains open for services on the Plymouth – Penzance line
Goods: 5th October 1964.

The first station at Camborne opened when passenger services started on the Hayle Railway between Hayle and Redruth in May 1843. Just under nine years later it closed briefly while work was undertaken by the West Cornwall Railway which, by an Act of 1846, had incorporated the Hayle Railway in order to improve it and extend the lines east to Truro and west to Penzance. After just under a month's closure,

Camborne. Detailed view (circa 1960) of the late Victorian up side building with its wide GWR style canopy. The wooden building to the left is probably of the earlier West Cornwall Railway era. The footbridge just visible on the right is now an open plate girder structure dated 1940.

Camborne station reopened in March 1852. Originally of standard gauge, broad gauge tracks were added to give mixed gauge through the station in 1866, when control of the line changed to an amalgam of Companies including the GWR. The gauge reverted to standard in May 1892; the line east of Camborne was doubled in 1898 and to the west in 1900.

The station, conveniently sited just south of the town centre, gradually evolved with the main buildings dating from the GWR late Victorian era, replacing earlier West Cornwall Railway structures. The principal red brick building, with a hipped shaped roof and tall chimneys, was built on the up side. Photographs indicate that in its early days a canopy surrounded much of the building but later a more conventional GWR standard canopy covered the platform only. A projecting extension at the rear of the building was a later addition to the original Victorian structure. The building contained the usual booking office, station master's office, waiting room and toilet facilities. West of the building was a small Brunel style hut constructed of horizontal timbers and with a tall chimney. Its appearance suggests it dated from the West Cornwall Railway era.

A brick waiting shelter with a wide platform canopy served passengers on the down (towards Penzance) platform. The platforms were originally linked by a large covered footbridge at the east end of the station. This was replaced in 1940 by an open plated girder structure. Adjacent to it is a level crossing that, for many years, was operated from the 1890s gable roof style brick and timber signal box (35 levers) standing on the up platform east of the main building. Camborne has always seen high levels of passenger traffic: in 1913 150,288 tickets were issued. In the 1930s the station dealt with an average 113,000 bookings per year in addition to about 400-500 season tickets. Between the two World Wars some 22-25 people were employed at the station.

The goods yard at Camborne was on the down side west of the station. Facilities included a large Brunel style goods shed through which ran one of the sidings and a yard crane of 4 ton capacity in the 1920s, which later increased to 6 tons. The shed was principally used for the loading and unloading of general merchandise. West of the shed a further four sidings fanned out. A number of other buildings used by local firms stood in the yard. For some years there were also two other sidings on the up side, one behind the building and one terminating in a dock at the west end of the platform. The station sidings were mainly used for the handling of coal, minerals and other bulk traffic. The up sidings were lifted in the 1930s and this allowed the 1937 westward extension of the up platform from its original 343 ft. Although general goods facilities were withdrawn at Camborne in October 1964, the main goods yard sidings continued to be used a little until 28th May 1965. The subsequent lifting of these sidings allowed a westward extension of the down platform in July 1981 adding to its original 285 ft.

Today the up side main building remains in use though its canopy has gone. Passengers on the platform are also protected by a metal and glass shelter standing just beyond the site of the old West Cornwall Railway building which has now gone. Also gone is the 35 lever signal box which operated until 8th June 1970. This replaced an earlier 27 lever box. Lifting barriers were introduced at the level crossing from 12th October 1970, operated from the box at Roskear junction east of the station. On the down platform the former brick waiting shelter and its successor, a small bus stop type structure, have been replaced by a modern metal and glass shelter. The former goods shed still stands, used by a firm of builders' merchants. The remainder of the goods yard has been built over. In autumn 2008 plans were announced for improvements at Camborne. When completed the station will have a new waiting room with improved disabled accessibility, new toilets including one which is wheelchair accessible, improved lighting, signage and seating, CCTV, bike lockers and disabled parking. The project is being undertaken by a partnership led by Cornwall Council along with First Great Western and Camborne Town Council, supported with further funding from the Railway Heritage Trust and the Department of Transport's 'Access for All Programme'.

CAMELFORD

OPENED: 14th August 1893 (with the opening of the Tresmeer – Camelford section of the North Cornwall Railway).
CLOSED: Passengers – 3rd October 1966.
Goods – 7th September 1964.

Camelford. Looking west at a passenger train arriving at the up platform hauled by an N class 2-6-0 locomotive No 31834. Note the square multi pane window signal box.

About 700 ft above sea level at a road junction one and a half miles north of Camelford, the station opened as a terminus in mid August 1893 with the completion of the third section of the North Cornwall Railway from Tresmeer. The line on to Delabole opened two months later on 18th October. Its siting, though remote and with little local habitation, was nevertheless helpful in its role as the rail head for a number of other settlements to which road services were established. These included Boscastle to the north and Tintagel to the north-west. Indeed the station nameboard for many years stated 'Camelford for Boscastle and Tintagel'. At its opening it was estimated that some 9,000 people gathered at or around the station to welcome the first train.

On an east – west alignment, Camelford was a passing place on the otherwise single track line, two loops serving up and down stone platforms. These loops were extended at the west end from 2nd July 1911 and at the east end from 30th July 1911 to give a capacity for a 35 wagon goods train or a 12 carriage passenger train. At the west end of the station a road bridge carried the B3266 over the two loops; inter platform movements were via the road bridge or rail level board crossings at both ends of the platforms.

The main station building at the centre of the up platform, was of a standard North Cornwall Railway design comprising a two storey station master's house at the east end and a single storey wing to the west. It was constructed of faced Delabole stone. The house section was clad with slates to give extra protection against the frequent rain in this exposed area. Reflecting its higher status, compared with other stations on the line, a platform canopy, supported by four decorative iron columns, was provided in front of the house and single storey wing. An original plain version was replaced by a more decorative apex style structure by 1900. The station facilities of the booking hall and office, station master's office, parcels office and porters' room were within the single storey wing but the ladies' waiting room and cloakroom were in the ground floor of the house. The gent's toilet was in a lean-to structure at the east end of the house. As with other stations on the line, the station master's accommodation was fairly extensive but with no bathroom and the W C in the backyard. An open front stone shelter served passengers at the centre of the down platform; to its east was a corrugated iron oil and lamp store. From

Camelford. A detailed view of the up side main building in the 1950s showing the two storey station master's house and the single storey wing housing the main offices. The nameboard states 'Camelford for Boscastle and Tintagel'.

1927 Camelford station took over control of the three stations to the west at Delabole, Port Isaac Road and St Kew Highway. In 1928 6,263 passenger tickets were issued at Camelford; by 1936 the total had fallen to 3,504. Over the same period the number of season tickets rose from 8 to 27. Between these two years the number of tickets collected fell from 10,895 to 7,134.

The goods yard located to the south-east of the station was entered via facing and trailing points from the down side loop just to the east of the down platform. The Delabole stone goods shed, in the centre of the yard, had doors on the rail and road sides, the former protected by a large high canopy supported on two legs. The shed had a slate roof and one tall chimney on the north-west corner.

A number of local merchants had stores for agricultural produce and fertiliser in the yard. In 1934 a brick slaughterhouse was opened at the far east end of the yard. This was later used as a fertiliser store. For some years slate from Lambshouse Quarry near Tintagel was loaded in the yard. Goods services ceased at Camelford early in September 1964, though the yard remained rail connected until 30th November 1965. Even after final closure of the station with the withdrawal of passenger services in early October 1966, goods wagons were stored for a short while in the up side loop.

Movements through the station loops and in the goods yard were controlled from a 17 lever signal box, a square structure of stone and brick with multi-pane windows and a slate roof. The brick replaced an earlier wooden section below the windows. Sited towards the east end of the up platform, it had a small porch at the head of the steps. The box and the station loops remained in use until closure of the line.

Occupied for some years by an agricultural merchant, the station buildings are now used as a house and the British Cycling Museum. A concrete structure added to the front of the single storey section across the former trackbed gives extra exhibition space. The platform canopy has gone but its decorated pillars remain in situ. Many of the station's internal features have been preserved. The former down side shelter has gone but sections of the two platforms remain to the west of the extension in an attractive garden. In March 2009 the site was indicated as being a Camping and Caravan Club certified site. Beyond the west end of the station the former road bridge has been demolished as part of a road improvement scheme.

Carbis Bay. A branch line train to St Ives hauled by 'Buffalo' 850 Class locomotive 0-6-0 ST enters the single platform in about 1912. Note the station building high above the waiting shelter.

CARBIS BAY

OPENED: 1st June 1877 (with the opening of the St Erth – St Ives branch).

CLOSED: Passengers – remains open for services on the St Erth – St Ives branch.
Goods – May 1956 (limited, see text).

The station, on an east – west aligned section of the St Ives branch, was built high above the bay from which it took its name. Carbis Bay opened when services commenced on the line from St Erth at the beginning of June 1877, the last Cornish branch to be laid at the broad gauge. Conversion to standard gauge came in 1892. On the down side of the single track, the site was originally sloping and in order to minimise excavation, the facilities were split level with the main building high above the platform. The granite structure with an apex slate roof and two chimneys, contained booking and toilet facilities. A sloping path led down to the long platform at the centre of which was a brick waiting shelter with a decorative platform canopy and a hipped slate roof topped by one chimney. At the west end of the platform was a small goods shed used for parcels traffic until May 1956. At times it also provided storage for passengers' bicycles. No other goods facilities were provided at Carbis Bay. Two men were employed in the 1930s. Staffing ceased from 6th May 1958.

By the early 1990s, the main station building had gone, the site occupied by a small hut and car

parking. On the platform, at that time, a small concrete hut served passengers but the goods shed had gone. Today the concrete hut is still in place.

Carn Brea. Another view west towards Penzance, this time in the 1960s. The main building is on the down platform (left). The footbridge shown is that at the west end of the platforms.

CARN BREA

OPENED: 23rd May 1843 (with the commencement of passenger services on the Hayle Railway, Hayle Foundry Square – Redruth).
CLOSED: 16th February 1852.
REOPENED: 25th August 1852 (5 months after the opening of the Penzance – Redruth section of the West Cornwall Railway).
CLOSED: Passengers – 2nd January 1961.
Goods – 1st May 1967.

In the heart of the Cornish copper and tin mining area midway between Camborne and Redruth, the station was just to the west of Carn Brea Yard, the location of the main depot of the Hayle and subsequently the West Cornwall Railway. Just to the east of this depot was Portreath Junction from which a three mile, goods only, branch ran north to Portreath harbour on the north coast. In the early days of the Hayle Railway the station was known as Pool. At its reopening on the West Cornwall Railway in August 1852 the station was called Carn Brea; from January 1854 until 1st November 1875 it reverted to Pool before its final renaming once again to Carn Brea.

Carn Brea. Looking west in about 1910 on a dull day, an 0-6-0 Saddle tank engine is on the up main line. The goods yard is to the right.

The station opened when passenger services started on the Hayle Railway between Hayle and Redruth in May 1843. Just under nine years later it closed while work was undertaken by the West Cornwall Railway which, by an Act of 1846, had incorporated the Hayle Railway in order to improve it and extend the lines east to Truro and west to Penzance. Unlike at Camborne, however, the station did not reopen concurrently with the restart of services in March 1852, this being delayed until August. Records indicate that the reopened station was not exactly on the same site as the original Hayle Railway structure.

Although it was a small station, Carn Brea had a range of facilities for both passengers and goods traffic. Small buildings served passengers on the up and down platforms, the main facilities being provided on the down side. The platforms were linked by a GWR style covered plated girder footbridge at the centre of the platform. This lost its roof in later years. At the west end of the platforms another, this time open, footbridge across the station site linked two pedestrian ways. The records of passenger numbers handled show marked variations between 1903 and 1938. In 1903 only 9,566

Causeland. Locomotive No 4569 arrives with a train from Liskeard to Looe on 8th July 1960.

passenger tickets were issued but surprisingly there was a great increase to 38,213 in 1913. Thereafter the figures fell to 15,991 in 1923, 8,595 in 1933 and 5,425 in 1938. In 1903 Carn Brea had a staff of 15 but the number subsequently fell to 11 by 1925 including a station master. In the later GWR era 7 people were employed at Carn Brea, the station being under the control of the Redruth station master. In the post Second World War era Carn Brea was the least used of any station between Truro and Penzance and thus it was of little surprise when it closed to passenger traffic at the beginning of January 1961, before the publication of the Beeching Report.

A four siding goods yard, sited behind the east end of the up platform, was equipped with loading banks, cattle pens and a 6 ton capacity fixed hand operated crane. A larger yard at the site of the main depot east of the station had two loop lines from which a number of sidings served coal wharves and the locomotive sheds and workshops originally developed by the Hayle and West Cornwall Railways. East of the station were refuge sidings on both the up and down sides of the main lines. An early two road engine shed was opened in 1838 by the Hayle Railway east of the station on the north side of the line. This was prior to passenger services being introduced. The shed was taken over by the West Cornwall Railway in 1846 and by the GWR 30 years later. Modified in 1896, the shed closed in August 1917. The station signal box (23 levers) at the east end of the up platform operated until 18th October 1953. The station goods yard was gradually run down over the period 1965 to 1967 with final closure at the beginning of May 1967. The large yard to the east also ceased to operate from 1967. Today there is no trace of the former station.

CAUSELAND

OPENED: 11th September 1879 (with the commencement of passenger services on the Moorswater – Looe line).

CLOSED: Remains open as a request stop for passenger services on the Liskeard – Looe branch.

When passenger services commenced in September 1879 on the then isolated Moorswater to Looe line, Causeland was the only intermediate station (for early history of the valley line, see Looe station text). Its siting seemed strange in so isolated a position, with Duloe over a mile to the west and Trewidland a mile to the north-east on top of a hill. On the west side of the line, the original wooden platform face was rebuilt in masonry during the GWR era. An article in the *Railway Magazine* of March 1899 described Causeland as 'merely a platform on which is erected a sleeper hut – like a platelayers – but without even a door, over the entrance to which is placed a board with the name of the station in black letters on a white ground'. As well as a shelter the only other items on the platform were two oil lamps.

When Sandplace station opened in 1881 and St Keyne in 1902, closure of Causeland was proposed but, on both occasions, petitions from local residents led to its survival. For some years the owners of the farm to the south of the station undertook landscaping to enhance their holiday accommodation.

Today Causeland remains open as a request stop with a basic concrete shelter. When seen in autumn 2008 a flower trough remained but not well tended. There was no seat but two cycle stands stood on the north end of the platform. The suffix 'halt' is currently not in use, though at various times over the years it has been designated as such, particularly between 1953 and 1967. It is thought however that this was never indicated on the nameboard.

CHACEWATER

OPENED: 1st November 1853 (on the Redruth – Truro line originally opened through this site in August 1852) (see text).

CLOSED: Passengers and goods – 5th October 1964 (except for private sidings later closed).

There is some disagreement among railway historians regarding the opening date of Chacewater station. Some sources assume that it came with the commencement of services on the West Cornwall Railway between Penzance and Truro in August 1852. Others, however, backed by evidence from a local paper, state that it opened at the beginning of November the following year. Serving the settlements of Chacewater, about a mile to the south-east, and Blackwater, a similar distance to the north-west, the early station was a basic wooden structure on the down side of the then single track line. The line east to Penwithers Junction (west of Truro) was doubled in July 1913 and west to Scorrier in December 1902. A passing loop and up side platform were added in 1872.

In 1903/1905 the GWR opened a new line to Newquay, branching north from the main line at Blackwater Junction about a half mile west of Chacewater. The first section to St Agnes and

Chacewater. A rather faded overall view east after the 1912 alterations showing the island platform (left) and 1914 replacement hipped roof signal box on the down platform.

Perranporth opened on 6th July 1903 and then on to Newquay from 2nd January 1905. A triangular layout at Blackwater Junction allowed direct workings to Perranporth and Newquay from both east and west. The west curve of the junction was, however, closed from 5th May 1919. From 9th November 1924 the junction at Blackwater was eliminated entirely, the branch line being extended east as a single track parallel to the main line into the up loop at Chacewater station. Twelve years earlier the station had been extensively redeveloped to accommodate the extra traffic generated by the Newquay branch, in particular with the conversion of the up side platform (507 ft) into an island structure with the Newquay branch trains using the

Chacewater. A view east towards St Austell prior to the alterations of 1912 when the up platform (left) was converted into an island platform with the outer face being used by Newquay branch trains. The 1888 signal box stands on the down platform.

Chacewater. The down side building was destroyed by a fire on 2nd February 1947. The replacement building with a wide canopy (right) was erected eight years later and is seen here in a view of September 1956. The footbridge has by now lost its roof.

loop along the outer north side. Thus Chacewater became another classic rural junction station from 1st September 1912.

The principal station facilities were housed within wooden buildings on the down side that evolved from the early West Cornwall Railway era. From west to east in 1913 they contained a porters' room, general waiting room, parcels office, station master's office, booking office, ladies' waiting room, ladies' toilets and gent's toilets. The up side stone building contained, from west to east, toilets, a ladies' waiting room and a general waiting room. This up side building had large canopies on both sides protecting passengers on the up main and branch platforms. In contrast the down side buildings only had a narrow canopy formed by a forward extension of the roofs. These latter wooden buildings were destroyed by fire on 2nd February 1947, a replacement building being erected eight years later in 1955. The platforms were lit by simple oil lamps for many years but these were later replaced by paraffin vapour lamps suspended from tall concrete posts. A typical GWR covered plate metal footbridge linked the platforms at the east end; this lost its roof in later years.

Passenger levels at Chacewater, because of its remote location, were never high, much of the station business being concerned with transfer between main and branch line trains. In 1903 12,090 passenger tickets were issued, the figure increased to 18,494 in 1913 and 22,258 in 1923 but fell to 15,690 in 1933. In 1920 there was a staff of ten based at Chacewater including the station master, two leading porters and five signalmen. By the end of 1924 this had reduced to seven following the elimination of Blackwater Junction and the closure of two associated signal boxes. The station master's house was sited behind the east end of the down platform on the station approach road. It survives today.

Chacewater's goods facilities comprised two short sidings in a small yard on the down side. The sidings, trailing back from the down main line west of the station, served coal wharves, cattle pens and loading docks. The yard contained a 2 ton capacity crane. Although general goods traffic ceased when the station closed in October 1964 the goods yard and site continued in use until 1987, used by Blue Circle as a cement distribution depot, the station building in use as associated offices. The tracks were lifted in September 1992, the site being subsequently occupied by a milk depot. The original 1888 apex roof signal box was replaced in 1914 by a hipped roof 35 lever box at the west end of the down platform. This box remained in use until 12th June 1977, some 13 years after the station closed.

The Chacewater to Newquay line closed for passenger and freight traffic on 4th February 1963. With much of its passenger traffic gone, Chacewater station only remained open for another 18 months, being closed for passengers and freight in early October 1964, the up loop being lifted in 1965. Some evidence of the former down platform remains today but the site of the up island platform is a mound of rubble and grass.

Chilsworthy Halt. A view east towards Gunnislake in 1962. From the platform magnificent views could be enjoyed over the upper valley of the River Tamar (left).

CHILSWORTHY HALT

OPENED: 1st June 1909 (on the Bere Alston – Callington branch originally opened through this site in March 1908).
CLOSED: 7th November 1966.

Serving the village of Chilsworthy, close by to the north-west, the halt, on the up (north) side of the single track line, opened at the beginning of June 1909 some 14 months after passenger services started on the Bere Alston to Callington branch. About a mile beyond Gunnislake station, its siting high on the hillside gave users of the halt magnificent views north over the upper valley of the River Tamar. Immediately to the east of the station was a road overbridge carrying a minor road.

The halt was very basic, the platform being stone faced with stone edging and a surface of compacted chippings. Initially passengers were provided with a small corrugated iron hut with an apex roof but this was later replaced by a wooden shelter with a half open front and a backward sloping roof which extended slightly forward to form a very narrow canopy. Along the rear of the platform was a wooden fence of posts and horizontal narrow planks. In the early days a tall post carried semaphore signals; one source suggests that these were provided 'to enable passengers to stop trains'! Two lamp posts provided illumination at night. Access to the platform was by a sloping footpath linked to the road at the north end of the road bridge. Chilsworthy closed when passenger services were withdrawn on the Gunnislake to Callington section of the branch in early November 1966. Forty years later sections of the platform survive but very overgrown; the base of the platform hut and remains of fence posts can be seen. The road bridge remains in use, as does the original access path to the halt.

COLESLOGGET HALT

OPENED: 17th April 1992 (on the Bodmin & Wenford Railway originally opened through this site in June 1990).

CLOSED: Remains open for passengers to use on the services running in the Bodmin General to Bodmin Parkway direction.

This halt, comprising a concrete platform and wooden hut with a small canopy, opened on the north side of the Bodmin & Wenford Railway in April 1992. At its opening it was intended to serve visitors to Bodmin Farm Park but unfortunately this enterprise subsequently failed. It is however used by visitors wishing to enjoy walks in the adjacent Cardinham Woods. Indeed, the nameboard states 'Alight here for Cardinham Woods'. Trains only stop here travelling down towards Bodmin Parkway. The halt is on a 1 in 40 gradient up towards Bodmin General and restarting the train on this slope could be problematical.

COOMBE JUNCTION HALT

OPENED: 15th May 1901 (with the opening of the link between the main GWR line at Liskeard and the Moorswater – Looe line). (See text for an earlier facility)

CLOSED: Remains open for passenger services on the Liskeard – Looe branch.

Passenger services commenced on the north – south line between Moorswater and Looe in September 1879 (for early history of this line see Looe text). Passengers wishing to transfer to main line services at Liskeard station were faced with a long walk up a steep incline from Moorswater. In 1884 it was suggested that an additional stopping place be provided on the isolated Moorswater – Looe line at the small settlement of Coombe in the valley south-west of Liskeard. Although the gradient between Coombe and Liskeard station was still steep, it was more convenient as passengers walking from Moorswater station to Liskeard station needed to pass through the town itself. Some form of platform was probably provided shortly afterwards. The stop was not advertised but by 1896 it is recorded that trains could be stopped for passengers to alight on giving notice to the guard, that is in today's terms, a request stop. By 1898 when the Liskeard & Looe Extension Railway was under construction (ie the link line), it was proposed to provide a station where it joined the original valley line close to the earlier platform. A loop line of some 650 ft overall with a cross-over half way along its length was also constructed.

Coombe Junction Halt opened with the new link in May 1901 and the former northern terminus of the valley line at Moorswater closed. Erected adjacent to the Duchy Tweed Mills, the original platform was built of old sleepers and was only 90 ft long. By 1923 when the GWR had absorbed the line, the platform had been reconstructed with stone facing and provided with a wooden shelter and oil lamps. The halt has always been unstaffed under the supervision of Liskeard station.

Today Coombe Junction Halt remains open and

Coombe Junction Halt. Looking north in 1962 with the Moorswater Viaduct carrying the main Plymouth to Penzance line in the distance. The building to the right was a tweed mill.

Defiance Platform. A rare, rather indistinct, photograph that shows naval personnel constructing the original wooden platform on the down side of the original single track line in early 1905.

the mill has been replaced by a modern industrial unit. Today most Liskeard – Looe trains omit stopping at the halt and reverse a little to the south at the actual junction. In the spring 2009 timetable only two trains were scheduled to stop in either direction on weekdays at Coombe Junction and none on Sundays. A concrete shelter has replaced the original wooden structure.

COPPERHOUSE/COPPERHOUSE HALT

FIRST STATION

OPENED: 23rd May 1843 (with the commencement of passenger services on the Hayle Railway, Hayle Foundry Square – Redruth).

CLOSED: 16th February 1852.

SECOND STATION

OPENED: 1st July 1905 (on the Redruth – Penzance section of the West Cornwall Railway originally opened through the site in March 1852).

CLOSED: 1st May 1908.

Records indicate that a stopping place, 'Copperhouse' was provided on the Hayle Railway when passenger services started in May 1843. No details of the site, which served the village of Copperhouse, north east of Hayle, are available. Closure came in February 1852 when the West Cornwall Railway, having taken over the Hayle Railway (see Hayle text), realigned the line to the south of the village. This new route opened for passenger traffic in March 1852 but at that time no stop was inserted serving Copperhouse. This was eventually provided over 50 years later with 'Copperhouse Halt' opening on the down side of the then single line in July 1905. However, the halt only lasted just under three years, closing at the beginning of May 1908. No details are known of this very short lived halt.

DEFIANCE PLATFORM

OPENED: 1st March 1905 (on the Plymouth – Truro line originally opened through this site in May 1859).

CLOSED: 27th October 1930.

The original facility that opened in March 1905, on the down side of the single track line, was called Defiance Wearde. This reflected the name of the nearby naval torpedo training school and the adjacent Wearde Quay. The name changed to Defiance Platform as from 1st May 1906. The small (150 ft x 6 ft) platform, built by the navy primarily for the use of its officers and ratings, was accessed by two paths, one for use by the general public connected to a public road and the other for naval use only, linked to the quay.

Re-siting became necessary with the construction and opening of the St Germans deviation line, built to replace an original single track section of the Cornwall Railway, which included five timber viaducts. The new line followed a more inland alignment with easier gradients, reduced track curvature, three viaducts and the Shillingham tunnel. The replacement platform on the new double track line was built in 1907 and came into use from 1st June 1908 when passenger services commenced on

Defiance Platform. An early view of the replacement re-sited platforms which came into use in May 1908 on the now double track line. Note the three pagoda style shelters on the up platform (right) for use by passengers travelling towards Plymouth.

Delabole. Looking north-east over 50 years later in 1963. Note the open front stone waiting shelter and tall signal box on the up side. The station building survives today within a new housing area, 'The Sidings'.

the new route. It comprised two platforms, about 350 ft long, 7 ft wide and 3 ft above rail level. Initially each had one shelter with lamps and a nameboard. Widening and lengthening of the platforms was later carried out, the up to 404 ft and the down to 433 ft. On the up platform three shelters were now installed, reflecting the greatest use being by passengers travelling towards Plymouth. Only one shelter was ever provided on the down side. Inter-platform movements were via long flights of steps to the adjacent road bridge south of the platforms. Defiance Platform formally closed in late October 1930. During the strawberry picking season up until 1954 occasional use was made of the platforms by local trains from Plymouth extended from Saltash. When viewed in early 2009 no trace of the platforms could be seen.

DELABOLE

OPENED: 18th October 1893 (with the opening of the Camelford – Delabole section of the North Cornwall Railway).

CLOSED: Passengers – 3rd October 1966.
Goods – 7th September 1964 (except for private sidings later closed).

A short distance to the east of the village of Delabole, and north of Pengelly, the fortunes of this station were closely related to those of the huge slate quarry immediately to the east. Over the years this generated both employment and large volumes of freight traffic. At one stage the quarry had some 350 employees. The potential for the transport of slate products was clearly a key factor in the routeing of the North Cornwall Railway close to the quarry and records

Delabole. A view in about 1910 of the station with the main building on the down side (towards Wadebridge). Staff pose on the platform as a train from Launceston enters hauled by an Adams A12 'Jubilee' class 0-4-2.

indicate that the slate company was so pleased with the coming of the railway that some three-quarters of a mile of trackbed was provided to the Railway free of charge! After the line opened, the output of slate and slate stone increased greatly; hitherto much had been exported via beached ships at Port Gaverne, some four miles to the south-west.

Delabole opened in mid October 1893 as a temporary terminus following the completion of the fourth section of the North Cornwall Railway from Camelford. The next section on to Wadebridge opened on 1st June 1895. The station was sited immediately to the north of a bridge which carried a road south-east from the B3314 through Pengelly to the quarry. It was a passing place on the otherwise single line, with up and down stone built platforms aligned approximately north – south. The two loop tracks through the station were lengthened in 1911 at the south end from 18th June and at the north end from 25th June. This gave a capacity for 12 carriage passenger trains (seven alongside the platform) or a freight train of 32 wagons, an engine and guard's van. There were rail level board crossings between the platforms at both ends.

Unusually for the North Cornwall Railway, the main station building was on the down side. It was of a standard North Cornwall Railway design comprising a two storey station master's house at the north end and a single storey wing to the south. Constructed of local stone, the upper storey of the house was later clad with local slate. The station facilities of the booking hall and office, station master's office, parcels office and porters' room were within the single storey wing but the ladies' waiting room and cloakroom were in the ground floor of the house. The gent's toilet was in a small structure at the north end of the house. As with other stations on the line, the station master's accommodation was fairly extensive but with no bathroom and with the W C in the backyard. To the north of the building on the down platform was a corrugated iron oil and lamp store, a common structure at North Cornwall Railway stations. Also on the down platform, at the south end, was a water column, the only such facility on the line between Launceston and Wadebridge. After 1935 at the other (north) end was a wooden shed sheltering two local permanent way motor trolleys. An open front stone waiting shelter protected passengers at the centre of the up platform. In 1928 5,900 passenger tickets were issued together with 24 season tickets; in 1936 the comparative figures were 3,339 and 23.

In 1927 the post of station master was abolished, the station coming under the control of Camelford. In the 1930s there were two booking clerks, two signalmen and two porters at Delabole. Staff houses were provided at Pengelly. Staffing, though much reduced over the years, continued until 6th December 1965. The station closed to passengers with withdrawal of services on the line at the beginning of October 1966.

The extensive freight facilities for the handling of both local goods and quarry related traffic were concentrated on a large site behind the down platform at the north end of which was an end loading dock. Facing and trailing points led from the down loop north of the station into the siding complex. A headshunt ran north parallel to the down track. A long inner siding, accommodating some 35 wagons, ran south behind the platform running alongside a small stone goods shed with a canopy on the rail side; it also served cattle pens, stables and stores operated by local merchants. A Southern Railway store was provided in 1930 for leasing out to local traders. A shorter outer yard siding initially ran through a one road 1895 iron frame engine shed terminating at a 50 ft turntable. The shed lasted until 1st July 1912, its use had ceased in 1900, being superseded by the shed at Wadebridge. It was sold to the Delabole Co-operative Society for £20 in 1905 and became their corn store. The turntable was removed. The goods yard was used both for the import of goods for use by local residents and agricultural businesses (eg feeds and fertilisers) but also for the export of local products including, as at many stations in north Cornwall, rabbits. A local cattle market also generated traffic. Goods facilities at the yard ceased as from early September 1964 but the sidings remained in situ until 1965.

Beyond the goods yard to the south and east further sidings were provided for use by the operators of Delabole quarry. In the early years these were used primarily for the export of slate for roof tiles but, as the use of these declined with the advent of clay tiles, further markets were exploited for slate dust used, for instance, in the production of gramophone records. The rail facilities reflected the evolving product type. At first only a short stub siding was provided but in 1895 a wide loading bank was erected to which three 2 ft gauge sidings ran from the quarry. In 1896 another siding was laid for the Earl of Wharncliffe's slate from his Trebarwith quarries. By 1899 the original short siding had been lengthened to 400 yards with a gate at the goods yard end. The slates were packed in straw in 10 ton open wagons, trains being despatched until 1914. With the decline in the export of slate the loading bank became disused and, together with the narrow gauge sidings, it was removed before 1920. However, the quarry continued to be rail linked up to the 1960s with despatch of some slate and also slate dust in sacks.

Rail movements at the station and in the yard were controlled from the 1880s style box constructed of stone and wood with multi-pane windows and a slate roof. Sited at the north end of the up platform, it had 22 levers (4 spare).

For some years the station house was derelict and boarded up but was then renovated as a family home. From 1992 the remainder of the station site was developed for housing, known as 'The Sidings'. The former station house 'The Waiting Room' stands today within this new residential area.

Doublebois. An overall study looking east from a road bridge in 1962. On the up platform (left) is the stone goods shed with a sliding door, the main station building and the 1894 signal box. To the right behind the down platform is a headshunt for a fan of four sidings laid out east of the station in 1943.

DOLCOATH HALT

OPENED: 28th August 1905 (on the Camborne – Redruth line originally opened through this site for passenger services in May 1843).
CLOSED: 1st May 1908.

Dolcoath was a short lived halt on the east side of Camborne adjacent to the famous copper and tin mine. The up and down platforms between Camborne and Carn Brea stations opened in late August 1905 and closed less than three years later at the beginning of May 1908. No details of the buildings are known. An up side siding, originally serving the mine, was subsequently used for coal and then milk traffic. It was taken out of use in December 1983. No trace of the halt survives but the approximate location is identified by today's Dolcoath Avenue, north of the railway in Camborne.

DOUBLEBOIS

OPENED: 1st June 1860 (on the Plymouth – Truro line originally opened through this site in May 1859).
CLOSED: Passengers – 5th October 1964
Goods – 7th December 1964.

Opening in June 1860, Doublebois station served an adjacent hamlet of the same name and the larger settlement of Dobwalls, a mile to the east. The main stone building with a slate apex roof and one chimney stood on the up (towards Plymouth) platform, whilst a stone waiting shelter served passengers on the down side. The station was initially on a passing loop before the line was doubled in 1893/4.

To the rear of the up platform, at the west end, was a small stone goods shed with a sliding door opening on to the platform. The principal goods facilities were located in a yard west of the station on the down side beyond a road over bridge. The yard included a small goods shed, a 2 ton capacity crane, cattle pens and two long sidings. Also on the down side, but east of the station, was a refuge siding; from this a fan of four sidings was built in 1943 to serve an army ammunition depot. The headshunt for these sidings ran behind the down platform. These sidings

Doublebois. A splendid early view of the station looking west towards St Austell. Staff and passengers on both platforms pose for the photograph.

were used by a permanent way depot after the Second World War. Movements at Doublebois were controlled from a signal box on the up platform west of the building. This operated from 1894 to 11th January 1968. Seven to eight men were based at Doublebois in the 1920s and 1930s.

The station itself closed in October 1964 followed two months later by the goods yard. All connections to the sidings were taken out of use in 1968 and the station buildings were demolished. In March 2009 no trace could be seen of the once extensive facilities.

DUNMERE HALT

OPENED: 1st June 1906/2nd July 1906 (on the Boscarne Junction – Bodmin North line originally opened through this site in November 1895).
CLOSED: 30th January 1967.

Sources vary slightly regarding the opening date of this halt on the re-aligned spur line from Boscarne Junction to Bodmin. Most state that it was 2nd July 1906 but a report in the West Briton newspaper indicated that it opened a month earlier on 1st June. This latter date coincided with the introduction, by the London & South Western Railway, of steam rail motors between Wadebridge and Bodmin. The single slightly curved platform on the north side of the line was sited just to the east of Dunmere Junction from which the freight only line ran north to Wenford Bridge. It was also just to the west of a road overbridge carrying the A389 from Wadebridge to Bodmin. An access path lined with concrete posts ran down from the north end of the bridge. Passengers were served by a GWR style pagoda shelter; this was unusual in that GWR trains did not use the halt. It seems likely however, that this style of shelter was erected at that time because the halt's opening coincided with that of the nearby Nanstallon Halt on the main route between Bodmin and Wadebridge along which some GWR trains ran from 1888, following the opening of the Bodmin General to Boscarne Junction loop. A feature of the halt was two decorative lamp posts. The halt closed in late January 1967 with the withdrawal of services on the line. Today the concrete platform remains alongside the Camel Trail which follows the former trackbed of the Bodmin North to Wadebridge line. A fine running in board in green and white Southern style has been erected on the platform. Above the platform is a car park serving users of the Camel Trail located behind the Borough Arms public house car park.

Dunmere Halt. Looking east in 1962 on the single track line to Bodmin North. The GWR pagoda style shelter is unusual as no GWR trains used the halt (see text). Note the decorative lamp post.

EGLOSKERRY

OPENED: 1st October 1892 (on the Launceston – Tresmeer – Wadebridge line originally opened through this site in July 1892).
CLOSED: Passengers – 3rd October 1966.
Goods – 9th May 1960.

Sited about a quarter of a mile south-west of the village of Egloskerry the station, on an east – west alignment, opened at the beginning of October 1892 some two months after passenger services commenced on the second section of the North Cornwall Railway between Launceston and Tresmeer. At its opening the buildings were not quite complete. Egloskerry was on a passing loop on the otherwise single track line; the loop was relatively short, being able to accommodate 22 wagons and a brake van or a seven carriage train and engine. Both the up (towards Launceston) and down platforms were constructed of local stone.

The main building, on the up platform, was of a pattern found at most North Cornwall Railway stations, here at Egloskerry comprising a two storey station master's house at the west end and a single storey wing to the east. Unlike the majority of North Cornwall Railway buildings, which were constructed of local stone, Egloskerry was built of red brick, there apparently being a shortage of suitable stone available in the immediate area. Tresmeer, the next

Egloskerry. An overall view looking east in 1963. On the up platform (left) is the large main brick building, incorporating the slate hung station master's house, and a corrugated iron oil and lamp store. The 1892 signal box is at the far end. A brick waiting shelter stands on the down platform.

station to the west was also built of brick. The upper storey of the station master's house at Egloskerry was slate hung, giving extra protection from the driving rain often experienced in this exposed locality. The station facilities of the booking hall and office, station master's office, parcels office and porters' room were within the single storey wing but the ladies' cloakroom and waiting room were on the ground floor of the house. The gent's toilet was in a single storey structure on the west end of the house. The station master's accommodation was fairly extensive but with no bathroom; the W C was in the back yard. To the east of the main building on the up platform was a small corrugated iron oil and lamp store.

Passengers on the down platform were served by a brick built open front waiting shelter with small windows at either end. Pedestrian movements between the platforms were via a rail level board crossing at the east end of the platforms. Passenger levels at Egloskerry were low. In 1928 4,786 passenger tickets were issued; by 1936 the figure had fallen to 1,714. Between these two years the number of tickets collected fell from 5,286 to 2,863.

The goods facilities at Egloskerry comprised a small goods yard behind, and to the north-east of, the up platform. One long siding trailing from the up line terminated close to cattle pens in the yard. A short spur served an end loading dock at the east end of the platform. There was no goods shed or crane but in the 1930s the Southern Railway provided one of its standard stores in the goods yard which was leased by Troods of Launceston for the storage of agricultural feeds and fertilisers.

Control of the station loop and access to the goods yard was from an 1892 signal box sited on the east end of the up platform. It had a stone base with multi-pane windows and a slate roof. From 25th September 1930 economy measures saw the single line tablet machine, telephone and telegraph instrument resited in the booking office and operated by porters/signalmen. The box retained 14 levers (5 spare). Unusually for the North Cornwall Railway line there was a level crossing at Egloskerry at the west end of the station. It was hand operated and signalmen had to walk the length of the platform to move the gates and operate the locking lever sited in front of the station master's house. In later years these duties were shared by a porter. These gates remained until the closure of the line in 1966.

To the north of the goods yard was a row of six semi-detached railway cottages. In 1924 two signalmen and four permanent way staff were accommodated there. There was no piped water at the cottages or at the station itself, drinking water being delivered in churns from Launceston. During the economies of the 1920s the post of station master was lost at Egloskerry with control transferring to Otterham. There was staffing however at the station until its final closure in early October 1966 in order to control the passing loop and the level crossing gates. Goods facilities had been withdrawn six years earlier in May 1960, the sidings being lifted the following year.

Today the site has been transformed, the station building itself having been renovated and extended into a fine residence, 'The Old Station'. The former trackbed has been partly filled as part of an attractive garden, though the platform edges can be seen. A striking feature is a full sized parcels van on a short section of track between the former platforms south-east of the main building. A number of station signs and sections of railings enhance the scene as a reminder of the railway era over 40 years earlier. Rural workshops were formerly sited in the old goods yard but when viewed in March 2009, development was in progress on a Housing Corporation scheme of seven affordable houses for rent.

Falmouth Docks. A early view of the station showing the south-east road-side elevation and fine overall roof. Horsedrawn omnibuses are serving the passengers.

FALMOUTH DOCKS

OPENED: 24th August 1863 (with the opening of the Truro – Falmouth section of the Cornwall Railway).
CLOSED: Passengers – 7th December 1970 (when the line was cut back to a new terminus closer to the town centre – see text).
Goods – 4th January 1965.
REOPENED: Passengers only 5th May 1975 (for passenger services on the Truro – Falmouth branch).

From the mid seventeenth century Falmouth was a Post Office packet port for international traffic. This role ceased from 1852 by which time Southampton had become a major port, boosted by its rail link to London, which had opened some five years earlier. There was clearly a need for Falmouth to be linked to the growing national rail network. The potential was seen by the Cornwall Railway, whose plans envisaged Falmouth as the western terminus of its line though the spine of Cornwall from Plymouth. The first section of the Cornwall Railway opened from Plymouth to Truro in May 1859 and the extension on to Falmouth four years later in August 1863. The original plan was to site the terminus station close to the town centre but, with the potential of traffic to and from the docks, it was decided to follow an alignment around the west of the town to a terminus close to and above the port complex.

Aligned south-west to north-east, the terminus building (200ft x 90 ft) was a fine Brunel style granite structure with an overall wooden roof (70 ft span), appropriate because the eastern terminus of the Cornwall Railway at Plymouth Millbay also had an overall roof in its early days. The main building, incorporating booking and parcels offices, first, second and ladies' waiting rooms and toilet facilities, was on the south-east side. Under the roof were two tracks alongside platforms and a central track used primarily for carriage storage. Both platforms extended south-west beyond the roof, the down being longer that the up. An umbrella style canopy protected passengers on the downside beyond the roof. Because of its greater capacity, this platform was, from 16th February 1928, signalled both for arrivals and departures. The overall roof was dismantled by the early 1950s and replaced by two standard canopies.

North-west of the station tracks led down to the extensive rail system within Falmouth Docks, a source of much freight traffic for many years. The

Falmouth Docks. An unusual view down on the station in 1958. In the foreground is the surviving main building and above can be seen one of the newly erected standard platform canopies. Top left is one end of the umbrella style canopy that survives today.

Falmouth Docks. Looking under the overall roof in about 1949 shortly before its removal in the early 1950s and replacement by two standard platform canopies.

Falmouth Docks. View towards the buffers in 1962 following the removal of the overall roof and replacement by standard canopies. To the left is the umbrella style canopy on the west end of the down platform.

principal goods facilities at the station itself were sited in the goods yard. South-west of the station on the up side, yard facilities included a large goods shed (100 ft x 61 ft), three end loading docks beyond the shed close to the main building, and a 6 ton capacity crane. Also on the up side, beyond the goods shed, was the 1863 Falmouth stone engine shed and a turntable at its far end. The two road shed was modified in 1887 when a larger turntable was added. The shed closed on 21st September 1925 but continued as a servicing point until demolition in 1932. Also close to the shed was a water tower and engine inspection pit which served for many years after the shed's closure. Train movements at Falmouth were controlled from a 41 lever signal box on the up side between the goods yard and the engine shed. The box closed on 27th February 1966 along with major track reductions in the whole station area. The goods yard had closed just over a year earlier in January 1965; over the period 1962-1965 a camping coach had stood in the yard in one of the end loading dock sidings.

During the late 1960s, in addition to track reduction, most of the station buildings were demolished. The down platform was retained but shortened as from 19th March 1969, a single track now terminating at the north-east end of the umbrella canopy. The station was unstaffed as from 6th May 1968 and then closed from 7th December 1970, branch line trains now terminating at a new station close to the town centre called 'Falmouth'. Following a local campaign and because trains needed to proceed beyond the new facility to the old station to reverse safely, the station reopened on 5th May 1975. At this point 'Falmouth' was renamed 'The Dell'. A further change came from 3rd October 1988 when the original station was renamed 'Falmouth Docks' and the new station became 'Falmouth Town'. Today, as the most southerly station in the British Isles, Falmouth Docks serves passengers on the single platform with the umbrella canopy. In recent years a wall has been added to the north-west of the platform giving extra protection against the elements; this is now partially covered by an attractive mural. To the south-east of the single line are car parks and the Ocean Bowl Leisure Centre. When seen in October 2008 the former station site beyond the buffers was being developed for high rise residential accommodation for students at the University College, Falmouth. To the north, Railway Cottages remain in residential use.

FALMOUTH TOWN

OPENED: 7th December 1970 (on the Truro – Falmouth Docks line originally opened through this site in August 1863).

CLOSED: Remains open for passengers services on the Truro – Falmouth branch.

With the aim of serving the town centre better than the Falmouth Docks station, a new station was opened in December 1970 on an embankment west of the bridge which carries the branch line over Avenue Road. At its opening 'Falmouth', as it was then known, became the terminus for the branch line. The platform concrete components came from Perranporth Beach Halt in north Cornwall, which had closed in February 1963. A wooden shelter was provided at the west end of the platform. A significant problem was, however, that the diesel multiple unit sets working the branch line trains were not allowed

Falmouth Town. Looking west along the concrete platform in 1978. Note that at that time it was called 'The Dell', the name changing from October 1988.

to wait at the station and in particular drivers were not permitted to change ends because the track at this point was on a steep down gradient towards the old Falmouth Docks station, which had closed. Thus all trains in fact continued to run on to the old station for drivers to change ends and then return to the new station before departing for Truro! With the need for this manoeuvre and also with calls for the re-use of the old station close to the docks, the latter reopened on 5th May 1975 with the name of Falmouth. To avoid confusion the new station was renamed 'The Dell'. Yet another change came from 3rd October 1988 when the original station was renamed 'Falmouth Docks' and 'the Dell' became 'Falmouth Town'. Today a modern metal and glass shelter serves passengers on the platform.

FOWEY

OPENED: 20th June 1876 (with the commencement of passenger services on the Cornwall Minerals Railway, Newquay – St Blazey – Fowey).

CLOSED: Passengers – 4th January 1965.
Goods – 1st June 1964 (except for private sidings later closed).

Also temporary closures for passenger traffic during the Second World War: 1st January 1940 – 9th February 1942; 24th August 1942 – 3rd October 1942 and 2nd May 1944 – 2nd October 1944.

With its natural deep water harbour, Fowey came into its own in the 1850s, following the silting up of the River Fowey estuary, restricting use of the old port at Lostwithiel. Initially Fowey was important for the export of timber but traffic increased greatly with the opening to the port of the freight only line from Lostwithiel in 1869 and the Cornwall Minerals Railway line from Newquay and St Blazey on 1st June 1874. This latter was the fulfilment of J T Treffry's dream of linking the north and south Cornish coasts by rail. The line from Lostwithiel, parallel to the River Fowey, laid at the broad gauge, terminated a half mile north of Fowey at Carne Point, where a number of jetties were built. Both lines were constructed with the aim of conveying china clay, china stone and other minerals from inland mines and quarries to the Fowey area for export by sea. In these early days there was no direct connection at Fowey between the two lines.

Two years after its opening to freight traffic, passenger services began, from mid June 1876, on the Cornwall Minerals Railway from Newquay and St Blazey. Having a more direct route to the mines and quarries the opening of the Cornwall Minerals Railway created problems for the earlier freight only Lostwithiel line and it closed from 31st December

Fowey. A typical view at a branch line station with a Lostwithiel train hauled by No 1408 on 21st June 1956.

Fowey. An overall view looking east soon after 1912 when the goods shed (right) was erected. The post 1895 station is to the left, the two platforms connected by a standard GWR covered footbridge. The main building is in the centre of the photo. The overall impression is of a very busy station for both passenger and freight traffic.

1879. Sixteen years later, however, with the assistance of the GWR, this Lostwithiel line was converted to standard gauge and reopened on 16th September 1895, this time for freight and passenger traffic. A link was laid to the Cornwall Minerals Railway line at Fowey station, both lines being operated by the GWR, which had absorbed the Cornwall Minerals Railway. The GWR then invested heavily in the development of the Carne Point jetties.

Fowey station, built on a curved east – west alignment just to the west of Caffamill Pill and to the north-east of the town, opened on 20th June 1876. With its single platform on the south side of the line, it initially acted only as the terminus for passenger trains running on the Cornwall Minerals Railway from St Blazey and Newquay. The booking, waiting and toilet facilities were contained within a wooden building with three chimneys and a wide horizontal platform canopy. The station site had been the terminus for freight traffic since 1874. A large station house was erected south-east of the station building.

With the new link to the Lostwithiel line and the commencement of passenger services on it, the GWR redeveloped Fowey station with the construction of two through platforms, a bay platform at the west end on the south side and the addition of a central track. A standard covered GWR footbridge was added to connect the platforms at the east end. From 23rd August 1936 the central track became a dead end siding with buffer stops at the west end. The siding was lifted on 18th March 1951. The north side platform and the footbridge (now uncovered) were demolished at this time though these had been little used since 1936.

Passenger services to Fowey on the St Blazey line ceased on 8th July 1929, though unadvertised workmen's services continued until December 1934. Fowey station was then served only by passenger trains on the Lostwithiel line. These were suspended for three separate periods during the Second World War in 1942 (twice) and 1944 (once). Passenger numbers were high at Fowey, holiday makers attracted to the town as it developed as a tourist and sailing centre as well as a freight port. In 1903 45,237 passenger tickets were issued; this increased to 51,995 in 1913 and 59,544 in 1923 but fell in 1933 to 33,875.

An early 1874 one road engine shed, east of the station close to the Caffamill Pill, was converted into a goods shed but was demolished prior to the First World War. A new building was erected on the vacated site. A large goods yard was laid out west of the station in 1910 and a goods shed was added in 1912. Yard facilities included a 6 ton crane. In the 1950s a camping coach was based in the yard. The

Fowey. A more detailed photo looking west at the two platforms after the 1890s reconstruction which added the platform to the right and the covered footbridge.

Golant Halt. Looking north at the replacement concrete component platform and hut in 1962.

goods yard finally closed in July 1965, though public goods facilities had been withdrawn a year earlier at the beginning of June 1964. Fowey signal box, at the Lostwithiel end of the main platform, operated from 1895 to 1968.

Passenger services ceased on the Lostwithiel line at the beginning of January 1965. China clay trains continued, however, and these still run today. In October 1968 the line from St Blazey closed entirely, much of the alignment being converted into a road for use by large lorries run by English China Clays. This company also took over much of the station site and former trackbed to Carne Point where all dock facilities were now concentrated. The former station site was taken over by this new road and other buildings, including the library. The large station house survives within the operational area of Impreys china clay business. When viewed in spring 2009 it appeared to be unused and partly derelict. Nearby the author saw 'Chuffers Restaurant' which unfortunately was closed! The site of the former goods yard west of the station is now in use as the 'Old Station Yard Car Park'.

GOLANT HALT

OPENED: 1st July 1896 (on the Lostwithiel – Fowey line opened to passengers through this site in September 1895).

CLOSED: 4th January 1965.

Also temporary closures during the First and Second World Wars: 2nd April 1917 – 1st November 1917; 1st January 1940 – 9th February 1942; 24th August 1942 – 3rd October 1942 and 2nd May 1944 – 2nd October 1944.

A freight only broad gauge line from Lostwithiel to Fowey, following the west bank of the River Fowey estuary, opened for freight traffic in 1869 (see history of line in Fowey text). Closure came from 31st December 1879. Following conversion to standard gauge, the line reopened for both freight and passenger traffic on 16th September 1895. Local newspaper evidence indicates that Golant did not open for another ten months, the date given being 1st July 1896. This riverside halt, to the east of and adjacent to the village of the same name, had one platform on the west side of the single track line. The original wooden platform was later replaced by a concrete component structure on which stood a small hut. There were a number of temporary closures during both the First and Second World Wars (see above). The suffix 'halt' was applied from 19th September 1955. There was no road alongside the river north to Lostwithiel or south to Fowey and the train service was much valued. Closure of the line for passenger services was fought hard but in vain, services ceasing early in January 1965. Resentment was particularly strong because the line remained open for freight (china clay) traffic as far as Carne Point, north of Fowey. This continues today.

GOONBELL HALT

OPENED: 14th August 1905 (on the Chacewater – Newquay line originally opened through this site in July 1903).

CLOSED: 4th February 1963.

The halt was opened to serve the hamlet of Goonbell immediately to the north. Some writers suggest it should have been called 'South East St Agnes' as it was closer to the centre of the town than St Agnes station itself. It opened in mid August 1905 coinciding with the introduction of steam rail motors on the Chacewater to Newquay line. The first section of this line through the site of Goonbell Halt had opened on 6th July 1903 as far as Perranporth. The extension on to Newquay opened at the beginning of January 1905. The brick faced platform, aligned west – east was on the down (north) side of the single line adjoining the village. It is likely that as at Mithian Halt on the same 1903 section of line the original platform was constructed of wood, being rebuilt by the early 1920s. West of the halt a road overbridge carried a minor road leading north into Goonbell. Access to the platform was via a sloping path linked to the road at the north end of the bridge through a metal kissing gate. Passengers were served by a GWR pagoda

Goonbell Halt. A view looking east at the brick faced platform and GWR style pagoda hut in 1962. Access is via the sloping path behind the hut.

style hut. Along the front edge of the platform were paving slabs behind which was a chippings surface. Illumination was by lamps at each end of the platform on decorative posts. Following withdrawal of services on the line and closure of the halt early in February 1963, the cutting in which the halt stood has been infilled and the land combined with an adjoining field. Today a single parapet of the bridge is still in place, as is a section of fencing and the kissing gate.

GOONHAVERN HALT

OPENED: 14th August 1905 (on the Chacewater – Newquay line originally opened through this site in January 1905).
CLOSED: 4th February 1963.

Serving the hamlet of Goonhavern immediately to the west, the halt opened in mid August 1905 coinciding with the introduction of steam rail motors on the Chacewater to Newquay line. The section of the line through Goonhavern Halt from Perranporth to Newquay opened eight months earlier at the beginning of January. The first section from Chacewater to Perranporth had opened in July 1903. On a west – east alignment, the 102 ft long platform on the down (north) side of the line was sited just to the east of a road overbridge carrying the B3285 across the single track line. Photographic evidence shows that in the early days the platform was constructed of wood but by the early 1920s it had been rebuilt with a brick face and a paving slab edge with a chippings surface behind. A pagoda hut stood

Goonhavern Halt. Looking west in the early 1960s. The brick faced platform with paving slab edge and a chippings surface replaced a very early wooden structure. Passengers are served by a typical GWR pagoda style hut.

on the later platform but an early photograph does not show any shelter. Access to the platform was via a sloping path linked to the road at the north end of the road bridge. At the head of the path was a lamp; two further lamps stood on the platform. The halt closed when services were withdrawn on the line at the beginning of February 1963. Today there is no trace of the halt. The road overbridge has also gone but the location where the line crossed the B3285 is fairly clear on the east side, being now an area of scrub and woodland.

GRAMPOUND ROAD

OPENED: 4th May 1859 (with the opening of the Plymouth – Truro section of the Cornwall Railway).
CLOSED: Passengers – 5th October 1964.
Goods – 1st June 1964.

This small station opening in early May 1859, in a predominantly agricultural area, was sited largely in a cutting on the eastern side of a small settlement of the same name that developed around the station. It principally served the village of Grampound, some two miles to the south-east. In its early days it also acted as a rail head for Newquay to which a horse bus provided a link until 1876 when the line from Fowey opened to the resort for passenger traffic.

The station's main wooden building, with a tall chimney and small horizontal canopy, was on the east end of the up platform. Passengers on the down side were provided with a matching waiting shelter, also with a horizontal canopy and tall chimney. There was no footbridge, with inter platform movements being via a rail level board crossing at the north-east end of the platforms. A large stone goods

Grampound Road. Staff pose for the photographer in front of the main building in this view looking south-west in about 1912. A matching wooden waiting shelter serves passengers on the down platform (left).

shed stood on the up side adjacent to and north-east of the station building. A siding ran to the goods shed whilst another swung west away from the line towards the Railway Hotel. Two sidings, again north-east of the station, served another yard on the down side. The signal box (27 levers) controlling movements at the station and in the yards, was south-west of the building on the up platform. It operated from 1898, when the line through the site was doubled, until 2nd June 1972. All sidings and a cross-over had been taken out of use nearly eight years earlier on 19th September 1964, the goods facilities having been withdrawn at the beginning of June. The station itself closed four months later in early October 1964. This closure was a big loss to the local community and resulted in the longest section of the Cornish main line without a station or halt, the 14½ miles from St Austell to Truro, Burngullow and Probus & Ladock Platform having closed earlier. Passenger ticket sales had never been great, a figure of 17,708 during 1913 had fallen to 7,318 in 1933. It is surprising therefore that records show that nine staff were based at Grampound Road in 1903, no doubt many of these were associated with the freight traffic handled at the large goods shed. This shed is the only structure that survived. The platform, the station building and the signal box remained for some time after closure but have now gone.

Grampound Road. Looking north-east in the 1920s. The 1898 signal box and main building stand on the up platform. Behind, and dominating, the building is the large goods shed.

GROGLEY HALT

OPENED: 1st June 1906/2nd July 1906 (on the Bodmin – Wadebridge line originally opened through this site for passenger traffic in October 1834).
CLOSED: 30th January 1967.

Sources vary slightly regarding the opening date of this halt on the line between Bodmin and Wadebridge. Most state that it was 2nd July 1906 but a report in the West Briton newspaper indicated that it opened a month earlier on 1st June, the day when the London & South Western Railway introduced steam rail motors between Wadebridge and Bodmin.

Sited south-east of the small settlement of Brocton in the Camel valley and near the woodlands of Great Grogley Downs, the platform was originally built of wood with passengers protected by a GWR style pagoda hut. Such a shelter was probably provided at the instigation of the GWR which had run services from Bodmin Road to Wadebridge on the generally LSWR line since 1888, following completion of the Bodmin General to Boscarne loop. No GWR trains were however normally scheduled to stop here. In 1957 the platform was replaced by a concrete structure, the original having become unsafe. A flat roofed shelter with a small canopy, replacing the pagoda hut, served passengers until closure in late January 1967. Today the concrete platform remains in situ in good

Grogley Halt. The original facility with a wooden platform and GWR pagoda style hut. Both were replaced in 1957 with a concrete platform and flat roofed structure.

condition beside the Camel Trail, a cycle and pedestrian way using the trackbed of the line from Bodmin to Wadebridge and Padstow. A fine running in board in green and white Southern style has been erected on the platform. A car park has been provided behind the platform for the benefit of the Trail users, accessed by a track using the alignment of the former Ruthern Bridge mineral branch including a two span bridge over the River Camel.

GUNNISLAKE

FIRST STATION

OPENED: 2nd March 1908 (with the opening of the Plymouth, Devonport & South Western Junction Railway branch, Bere Alston – Callington).

CLOSED: Passengers – 31st January 1994
Goods – 28th February 1966

SECOND STATION

OPENED: (Passengers only) 6th June 1994.

CLOSED: Remains open as the terminus of the branch line from Plymouth via Bere Alston (the Tamar Valley line).

Gunnislake opened at the beginning of March 1908 when passenger services began on the Plymouth, Devonport & South Western Junction Railway branch from Bere Alston to Callington. It was on the site of the Drakewalls depot of the earlier (1872) East Cornwall Mineral Railway whose trackbed was taken over by the 1908 line (see Callington text). The depot was named after a settlement just to the south.

The station was built about a mile south-west of the village of Gunnislake, which was some 300 ft below in the valley of the River Tamar. It was just to the north of a low rail bridge over the A390 road between Tavistock and Callington. The 1908 Gunnislake station comprised a single island platform along which ran a main up (towards Bere Alston) line and a down loop. West of the north – south aligned platform was the goods yard which included an inner siding alongside the down loop and two outer sidings, one of which terminated adjacent to a cattle dock. On the up side a long siding trailed back parallel to the platform track terminating at buffers.

Gunnislake. The island platform shortly after its opening in 1908. At the up platform is Hawthorn Leslie 0-6-0T No 3 A S Harris, the third new locomotive purchased for the Plymouth, Devonport & South Western Junction Railway and named after one of its directors. Of particular interest is the PD&SW Railway cart stating 'Furniture removed to all parts'.

Gunnislake. Looking north in 1962 at the main building of wooden construction with corrugated iron cladding. A solitary goods truck stands in the down side goods yard.

Alongside the buffers was a ground frame hut containing ten levers, controlling movements at the station. There were no signal boxes on the Callington branch. The single line tablet instrument was in the office on the platform. Two short outer sidings trailed from the long siding.

The station building on the island platform was of wooden construction with corrugated iron cladding. Wooden backward sloping canopies with saw tooth valances were attached to either side. The main facilities for booking and waiting were within the structure. Photographs indicate that during the 1950s and 1960s a small hut stood on the platform north of the building. Access to the platform was via a short subway under the down loop at the south end of the station. At one time a wooden gate stood at the top of the subway slope with notices of 'Way Out' and 'Please show Tickets'. Passenger numbers in the 1920s and 1930s were high and, unusually for Cornish stations, increased considerably in this period. In 1928 19,183 passenger tickets were issued and 28,520 collected; by 1936 the equivalent figures were 23,397 and 30,719. In the goods yard the principal business was in the handling of local products from the Tamar valley, in particular fruit. In 1935 a new jam factory opened close to the station generating extra freight traffic.

Decline began to set in at Gunnislake from the mid 1960s with the withdrawal of freight services at the end of February 1966. The up siding and two outer goods yard sidings were taken out of use from 2nd August of that year. A significant change came from 7th November 1966 when Gunnislake became a terminus station following the withdrawal of passenger services on to Callington, the tracks along this section being lifted the following year. The survival of the remainder of the branch line to Bere Alston via Calstock was because of the remote nature of the communities and the lack of good road connections to Plymouth. For a short while both sides of the island platform continued to be used but from 5th May 1968 the down loop and adjacent siding were disconnected and subsequently lifted, only the former up line remaining.

During the 1970s the station building was demolished and replaced by a small concrete hut. This too was subsequently replaced by a metal and glass shelter, the former goods yard and site of the down loop becoming a car park with the subway filled in.

A further change came during 1994 when, after some years of debate, the 1908 station north of the A390 bridge was closed at the end of January and replaced by a new structure south of the road on the site of former coal sidings. This re-siting allowed the low bridge to be removed and associated traffic restrictions to be lifted. In constructing the new station the trackbed was lowered by some 60 ft as, at this point, the original track was steeply graded up in the Callington direction and this would have prejudiced the safe use of the new concrete platform on the west side of the single track. Passengers are protected with a metal and glass shelter and behind the platform is a large car park and bus turning circle. It now operates as a park and ride facility for commuters into Plymouth.

The new station opened at the beginning of June 1994. For the four months period after the closure of the first station trains had terminated at Calstock with a bus connection to Gunnislake. Funding for the new station came from Cornwall County Council and the European Regional Development Fund in partnership with the South Wales and West T O U and Railtrack Great Western. Housing, accessed by Sand Hill Park, has been developed on the site of the first station.

Gwinnear Road. Looking west in 1962. The importance of the junction role is seen in the nameboard 'for Helston, The Lizard, Mullion and Porthleven'. A Helston branch train can just be seen behind the nameboard.

GWINEAR ROAD

OPENED: c November 1853 (on the Penzance – Truro line which had opened through this site in March 1852) (see text).
CLOSED: Passengers – 5th October 1964.
Goods – 9th August 1965.

There is no clear agreement among railway historians regarding the opening date of this station. Some accounts on Cornish railways state that a station was sited on the Hayle Railway, which opened for passengers between Hayle and Redruth in May 1843. If there was, it would have been very primitive in the form of a small hut. Another source, however, says there is no evidence in timetables and local press that any facility was provided at this stage. There is no dispute, however, that, with the coming of the West Cornwall Railway, a station was opened with the name of Gwinear Road, though there is again a disagreement over the exact date. Some sources suggest that opening came at the commencement of passenger services on the line in March 1852, while another states that the first reference in the Bradshaw timetable only came in November 1853 and a reference is made in the Penzance Gazette of 2nd November 1853.

Whatever the exact opening date, records do show that this early station was a short single platform with a small hut on the down side of the line, together with a run round loop for goods traffic. There was a group of sidings on the down side. The station was not, it appears, used for passing purposes at this stage. The name Gwinear Road was very appropriate with the station in a remote location serving a number of small rural communities but in particular the village of Gwinear, about one and a half miles to the south-west. The major development of the station

Gwinnear Road. A fine 1888 view west of this classic rural junction station. The standard gauge line to Helston is to the left while mixed gauge track runs through on the two main lines, the third rail having been added in 1866. Conversion to standard gauge came in 1892.

came with the opening of the eight and a half mile branch line south to Helston on 9th May 1887. Gwinear Road became a classic example of a rural junction station.

The Helston branch left the main line east of the station initially in an easterly direction before turning south. When the branch opened, the main line was only single track, the section east to Camborne being doubled in January 1900 and west to Angarrack in June 1915. The rebuilt station had two platforms, that on the north side (578 ft) had a single face serving the up line and that to the south was an island structure, the north face (578 ft) serving the down main line and the south face (540 ft) the branch line. There was no run round loop alongside the branch track and thus engines needed to use the down main line for this manoeuvre.

The main station building, of timber construction with projecting horizontal canopies on both sides, stood on the down side island platform. It incorporated booking, waiting, office and toilet facilities. The up side wooden building, with a sloping projecting canopy formed by an extension of the pitched roof, functioned principally as a waiting shelter. The canopies of both buildings had decorative groove and hole valances. The up side building was later extended at the east end; being of wood construction the buildings were less substantial than those at many stations on the main line. A feature of the station was the large nameboard on the island platform, 'Gwinear Road for Helston, The Lizard, Mullion and Porthleven'. Apart from rail services to Helston, the other places were linked to Helston by road vehicles, in the early days horse drawn and then motorised. Until 1938 the platforms were lit by oil lamps but then electric lighting was introduced. The two platforms were connected by an open plate girder footbridge at the east end, erected shortly before the First World War. This footbridge also crossed the branch line linking to the approach road, which ran south-east from the station. Alongside the road was, at one stage, a refreshment room. Also to the east was the station master's house, close to the branch line junction. Beyond the east end of the platform was a level crossing which, because of its angle, is said to have had the longest gates in Cornwall. A ticket collecting platform relating to the branch line was sited east of the crossing until 1903.

Passenger numbers were not as high as at many stations in Cornwall, not surprising because of its remote location. From a peak in 1913 of 37,963 tickets issued, the number fell to 13,288 in 1938. In 1929 the station employed 14 people, including a station master, some of whom were involved with the extensive freight traffic handled at Gwinear Road.

A complex of sidings east of the station on the down side beyond the Helston branch junction formed a very busy marshalling yard. From 1883 to 1892 there were three sidings and, from 1887, a transfer shed. This shed was required as the Helston branch was standard gauge and the main line broad gauge between 1887 and 1892. Most of the sidings date from about 1915. By 1945 there were eight, these being used by the military. The yard was one of the main storage and marshalling points in Cornwall for trains sending Cornish vegetables to London and the Midlands. The scale of local freight traffic originating at Gwinear Road itself was less than at many Cornish stations; this was usually handled at two dead end sidings at the west side of the station on the up side. One of these sidings was a late addition in 1933. There was no goods shed. The track layout in the Gwinear Road locality also included two long refuge sidings which were used to stable slow moving goods trains that could hold up faster passenger trains. In 1901 a cattle dock was erected, served by a short siding east of the level crossing, alongside the branch junction.

Two signal boxes controlled movements at the station complex. An early 1887 Gwinear Road West Box stood at the east end of the up platform. This closed on 30th November 1916 with the opening of a new West Box (49 levers) at the east end of the down island platform. A wheel in this box operated the long level crossing gates. Gwinear Road East Box was sited at the far end of the siding complex east of the station. With 15 levers, this opened on 5th December 1900. Both of the later boxes were of the hipped roof type with five pane windows.

The Helston branch closed on 5th November 1962. This deprived Gwinear Road of much of its passenger traffic and, only just under two years later, the station closed to passengers in early October 1964. At the same time the goods services on the branch ceased and the track was soon lifted. Goods facilities continued at Gwinear Road for a short while but ceased in early August 1965, when all remaining sidings were taken out of use and lifted. Both signal boxes also closed in 1965, the West Box on 31st October when automatic half barriers replace the old level crossing gates. The East Box had closed four months earlier on 20th June. Today remains of the down island platform can still be seen but all of the remaining structures have gone.

Hayle. A view looking east in about 1910 showing the West Cornwall Railway era main building on the down (towards Penzance) platform. Unlike many stations in Cornwall, these early buildings were not replaced in the GWR era. The large goods shed behind the platform dominates the scene.

HAYLE

FIRST STATION

OPENED: 23rd May 1843 (with the commencement of passenger services on the Hayle Railway, Hayle Foundry Square – Redruth).

CLOSED: 16th February 1852 (with the withdrawal of services on the Hayle Railway, pending its takeover by the West Cornwall Railway).

SECOND STATION

OPENED: 11th March 1852 (with the opening of the Penzance – Redruth section of the West Cornwall Railway).

CLOSED: Passengers – remains open for services on the Plymouth – Penzance line.
Goods – 8th June 1964 (except for private sidings later closed).

Hayle played a key role in Cornwall's early railway history, with mineral ores being carried to the quays for export to smelters and coal and timber imports brought from the quays. Freight services began on the Hayle Railway between Hayle and Redruth in June 1838 and it is believed that some passengers were unofficially carried on these trains. When passenger services started officially on the railway in May 1843, it is not certain that a specific station building was used at Hayle, with trains recorded as starting and terminating at Crotch's Hotel, close to Foundry Square at the head of Penpole Quay. A Mr W M Crotch, a local innkeeper, operated the railway in the early days. Records indicate that a station building came into use in Foundry Square from 27th May 1844. From this point the Hayle Railway ran north along the creek before turning east alongside Copperhouse Creek towards Angarrack. The route included a number of inclines where ascent and descent were rope assisted. The most famous of these inclines was that at Angarrack. Early records also suggest there was a further 'station' called Hayle Riviere close to Hayle Bridge (now North Quay), which also came into use on 23rd May 1843 but closed on 16th February 1852 or earlier.

In 1852 the West Cornwall Railway, by an Act of 1846, incorporated the Hayle Railway in order to improve it and extend the line east to Truro and west to Penzance. A number of variations were made to the alignment of the old Hayle Railway line including the elimination of the rope assisted inclines. Another major feature of the new line was the construction of a 277 yard long 34 ft high viaduct across the head of Penpole Creek and above the first Hayle station in

Hayle. The original Hayle Railway station which closed in February 1852. A photo of 1938 indicates that at that time it was used by the Hayle Women's Unionist Association. The building was demolished in December 1948. In the background is the viaduct carrying the main Plymouth to Penzance line on the post March 1852 alignment.

Hayle. This photo of about 1960, also looking east, shows the waiting room and signal box on the up platform. This 1912 box was unusual in that, because of the narrow platform, there was a narrow lower storey locking room with the upper storey on brackets jutting out over the platform. Closing in July 1982 it was subsequently demolished.

Foundry Square. Originally constructed of timber, the viaduct was reconstructed in stone in 1886.

A new station site was thus required and this was constructed at the east end of the new viaduct at the west end of the town. Hayle's second station, opening in March 1852, was developed on a passing loop on the otherwise single track standard gauge line. Broad gauge tracks were added to give mixed gauge through the station in November 1866, with broad gauge passenger trains to Penzance starting on 1st March 1867. The tracks at Hayle were reverted back to standard gauge from May 1892. The track was doubled west to St Erth in September 1899 and east as far as Angarrack in December 1909. At the station a goods loop ran behind the up platform whilst on the down side a dead end siding ran behind the platform into a typical Brunel style large goods shed. The buildings on the up and down platforms (both 440 ft long) were simple timber framed structures clad in horizontal wood boards with low pitched gable roofs. The main down side building, which incorporated the station's main facilities, also had a small horizontal canopy. The up side structure, with no canopy, functioned as a waiting room. The platforms were linked by an open metal bridge at the west end. Passenger traffic at Hayle was relatively high for many years with about 52,000 tickets being issued per year, together with about 300 season tickets. In 1903 56,862 tickets were issued. In 1938 the figures were nearly the same at 55,006 and 367 seasons, in contrast to many other Cornish stations where the numbers fell greatly over the 35 year span. In about 1930 approximately 15 staff were based at Hayle under a class 3 station master; twenty years earlier the total had been 18.

Unlike at most other stations on the Cornish main line from Plymouth to Penzance, Hayle retained the original West Cornwall Railway buildings during the GWR era. They were, however, replaced in the 1960s by prefabricated structures which were themselves replaced by small concrete huts, which continue to shelter passengers today., The footbridge has gone, passengers now crossing the track by a board crossing at the west end, controlled by coloured lights.

The principal goods yard, including a large goods shed, was on the down side behind the platform. The one siding ran into the shed, which had a goods office at its western end. Also in the yard in 1938 was a 15 ton capacity crane. From just west of the station, on the up side, a line curved north from the west end of the goods loop leading to two long sidings and linking into the Hayle Wharves branch, which descended at 1 in 30. A short siding from the goods loop served an 1879 one road engine shed which ceased to be used in 1896 and was officially closed in 1906. It was still standing in 1950s. Beside the shed was a water tank on a tall masonry base. Most of the sidings and connections to the main line were closed and removed between 1964 and 1967, general goods facilities at the station being withdrawn in June 1964. The up goods loop was however in use until 3rd May 1967. The connection to the Hayle Wharves survived however, the Wharves branch remaining in use until July 1982, fuel oil and chemicals being the main form of traffic after general traffic ceased on 1st May 1967. This industrial branch was lifted in 1983 and most remnants of the industrial era have gone, housing having been constructed along some of its length, including Harbour Way. The former goods yard on the down side is now used for car parking.

When the GWR re-signalled Hayle in the mid 1890s, two signal boxes were installed: Hayle East and Hayle West. These boxes had a short life, both being replaced in 1909 by an entirely new box at the west end of the up platform. In most features it was a typical GWR hipped roofed box with five pane windows, but because of the shallow nature of the platform, it had a narrow lower brick locking room, the glass and timber upper storey jutting out over the platform on supporting brackets. With its 35 lever frame, it remained in use until 7th July 1982. It was subsequently demolished.

Helston. A wonderful assembly of early road vehicles outside the station in about 1910. They include a horse drawn hotel carriage (right) and a GWR motor bus providing a link to The Lizard.

HELSTON

OPENED: 9th May 1887 (with the opening of the Helston Railway, Gwinear Road – Helston).
CLOSED: Passengers – 5th November 1962
Goods – 5th October 1964.

Great celebrations took place on the northern edge of Helston on 22nd March 1882, when the first sod of the Helston Railway was turned at Tile House Field. Contemporary accounts state that flags were hung, triumphal arches erected and street trees planted. Most shops were closed and the local school had a holiday. An early idea was that the event was so significant that the Prince of Wales (who had laid the foundation stone of Truro Cathedral) should be invited to turn the sod, but the idea was dropped, the honour falling to the Mayor of Helston, Mr R S Martyn.

Some five years later the flags and bunting came out again on a public holiday to celebrate the opening of the line in early May 1887. The engine of the first train, the 9.40 a.m. to Gwinear Road on the Truro to Penzance main line, was adorned with flags and evergreens. The Helston Railway directors rode on the 12.50 hrs train from Gwinear Road, which was greeted by the Helston Volunteer Band's rendering of 'See the Conquering Hero comes' (a tune often used at the opening of new lines!). The Mayor and Corporation joined the directors on a trip to Gwinear Road returning at 3.10 p.m. for a lunch at the Angel Hotel at which there were loyal toasts and toasts for the success of the railway. In responding to a toast to the landowners, a local church minister praised the good behaviour of the navvies involved in the line's construction!

During the five years of the construction there were frequent delays and, in particular, debates regarding the actual site of Helston station, the latter as late as 1886. Eventually the location of the original sod turning at Tile House Field was selected. This was on

Helston. Another wonderful collection of road vehicles outside the station, photographed in May 1936.

Helston. A general view looking south in about 1958. Note the gent's toilet at the north end with its entrance behind a wooden screen, a common practice at many stations. To the left is the large goods shed, which survives today within a housing development.

the side of a hill sloping towards the south, with the northern end of the station complex within an excavated area and the southern end on an embankment. Helston was laid out, not as a terminus, but as a through station, an early plan being to extend the line on to the Lizard. A single stone platform (271 ft long) was erected on the west side of the line which terminated at a carriage shed some 200 yards beyond the platform. An engine release loop ran alongside the platform track.

The main stone built station building (100 ft x 25

Helston. The former goods shed on 13th March 2009, now beautifully renovated as a social centre in the Henshorn Court housing development.

ft), aligned north-west to south-east and Britain's most southerly station, had a hipped slate roof topped by four chimney stacks. There was a full length horizontal platform canopy and also a small canopy over the rear road side entrance. The window and door openings were slightly arched. From south to north the building housed a refreshment room (privately operated), a parcels office and store, the station master's office, the booking office, general and ladies' waiting rooms, and, at the extreme north end, further stores and the gent's toilets. At the north end of the platform were two further buildings, one a wooden store (20 ft x 7 ft) and the other a brick built staff mess room (13½ ft x 9 ft). The main building was very similar to that at St Ives. The rear of the station was approached by a sloping access road along which were a number of tradesmen's sheds.

Passenger numbers at the station varied over the years: in 1903 36,006 passenger tickets were issued, the figure more than doubled to 73,606 in 1913 but fell again to 30,383 in 1923 and 15,189 in 1933. A ticket platform was in use beyond the north end until 1903. Eleven staff were based at Helston in 1903, the number rose to 22 in the 1930s.

The proposed extension of the railway to the Lizard was never implemented and the GWR inaugurated a bus service to there from 17th August 1903, the first of several such bus links introduced by the Company. Four vehicles ran the service which was also used by the Royal Mail. A further GWR bus service began from Helston to Porthleven on 2nd October 1909. Towards the end of its life, Helston station was used from April 1947 by personnel based at the Fleet Air Arm station at RAF Culdrose, one mile south of Helston. A particular attraction that, through the years, brought much business to Helston station was the annual May-tide Furry and Flora day, including the famous dance.

Helston's goods facilities, concentrated east of the station, included a solid stone goods shed (50 ft x 50 ft) lit through five arched windows, three on the west wall and two on the east road side, all openings surrounded by yellow and white bricks. A loop siding ran through the shed entering and leaving via large doorways; a further opening in the east wall gave access for road vehicles to a spacious loading platform on which there was a 2 ton capacity crane. At the south end of the shed was a lean-to office. Other facilities in the goods yard included a loading platform for both end and side loading, cattle pens, a 6 ton capacity crane, coal wharves and stores.

Adjacent to the east side of the yard was an abattoir. Goods handled in the yard included farm feeds, flowers and general merchandise. In the 1950s serpentine stone was also sent out by rail loaded from a chute on the down side. Also of interest in the yard was a large corrugated iron building south of the goods shed called on plans 'the Motor Shed'. This reflected its original use as a shelter for GWR motor-buses used on the routes to the Lizard and Porthleven. It was later used by both Western National buses that took over the routes and also, after 1933, by GWR delivery vehicles.

At the south end of the station site on an embankment a carriage shed had the capacity for two carriages. Built of semi-prefabricated timber components, it measured some 100 ft by 15 ft, the walls being clad in vertical match boarding. The low pitched roof was topped by a low clerestory giving the building the outward appearance of a wooden engine shed. The actual engine shed (1887) was north of the station to the west side, served by a trailing siding. A single road facility of standard GWR design (43 ft x 21 ft), it was built of local stone and had arched windows and door openings. A raised clerestory section aided smoke emission. Adjacent to the shed was an office and mess room, two coaling stages and a standard GWR mushroom style water tower with a flexible hose.

Helston signal box, sited at the north end of the platform, was an unusual form of the GWR box having vertical boarding as its upper structure instead of horizontal characteristic of the 1880s. A porch protected the box entrance at the north end. The original 14 lever frame was replaced by a 21 lever version in 1958, operating signals and points.

From the late 1950s decline set in, the first building to go being the carriage shed in 1957. Closure of the engine shed came in December 1963. Passenger services ceased at the beginning of November 1962 and goods facilities were withdrawn with the closure of the Helston branch in early October 1964, the first Cornish branch to close. The track was lifted in the following year. Today much of the station site is covered by housing for elderly people (Henshorn Court), the only surviving building being the goods shed now splendidly converted for use as the social centre within the residential complex. A section of the southern end of the platform edge is still in situ close to the south-west wall of the former goods shed. Station Road survives but on a slightly changed alignment.

HUNT'S CROSSING

A request stop on the Launceston Steam Railway [*see Launceston (Steam Railway) text*].

LATCHLEY

OPENED: 2nd March 1908 (with the opening of the Plymouth, Devonport & South Western Junction Railway branch, Bere Alston – Callington).
CLOSED: Passengers – 7th November 1966.
Goods – c November 1949.

Latchley opened at the beginning of March 1908 when passenger services began on the Plymouth, Devonport & South Western Railway branch from Bere Alston to Callington. It was at the site of the Cox's Park Depot of the earlier (1872) East Cornwall Mineral Railway, whose trackbed was largely taken over by the new line (see Callington text).

It was one and a half miles south of the village of Latchley some 500 ft below in the valley of the River Tamar. The single track ran alongside a north facing stone built platform on the down (towards Callington) side of the line. On the platform passengers were provided with a very small corrugated iron hut with a backward sloping roof and small windows on either side. Opposite the platform was the earlier station master's house and goods shed of the East Cornwall Mineral Railway. In front of the house and shed was a loading platform behind which at its east end ran a short siding. Photographs show that this siding was level whereas the running line towards

Latchley. Looking east towards Callington in 1962. Passengers were provided with a very small corrugated iron shelter on the down side platform. Opposite the platform (left) was the earlier station house, goods shed and loading platform of the East Cornwall Mineral Railway. This house and the down platform remain today.

Callington rose slightly to cross an ungated minor road west of the station which ran north to the village.

The exact date of the withdrawal of the very limited goods services at Latchley is not recorded but it is thought to have been about November 1949 after which the goods siding was removed. The station (latterly sometimes known as a halt) closed entirely with the withdrawal of passenger services on the Gunnislake to Callington section of the line in early November 1966. Staffing had ceased some thirty years earlier in 1936.

Today the old East Cornwall Mineral Railway house survives as a residence, a garage now standing on the former trackbed. The down side platform remains in situ.

Launceston North. Looking west towards the buffers in 1939. The main station building with the wood canopy faces south. A truck stands at a loading platform (centre) that was probably never used by passenger trains. To the left is the signal box which, from the end of 1916, operated signals and points at both stations.

LAUNCESTON

The status and role of Launceston, an ancient market town at the centre of a large agricultural area in East Cornwall, declined during the first half of the nineteenth century a trend that partly reflected the late arrival of the railway compared with other Cornish towns. Change for the better came in the second half of the century with the development of two adjacent stations on a site in the valley of the River Kensey below and north of the town centre and the famous castle. The first in 1865 was the terminus of the broad gauge Launceston and South Devon Railway (later GWR) running from Tavistock in west Devon and the second was a station on the first section of the North Cornwall Railway (later LSWR), which eventually ran from Halwill Junction (Devon) to Wadebridge and Padstow. Following the opening of this second station they were

Launceston. A general view looking north over the two stations. In the foreground is the London & South Western Railway station with its road side frontage (including a canopy) and waiting shelter (extreme right). Behind is the south facing building of the GWR station with, to its right, the large goods shed.

Launceston North. The forecourt in the summer of 1960 when the building was only in use for goods traffic, the passenger trains from Tavistock having been diverted to the South station from June 1952.

known as the 'Great Western' and 'South Western'. From 10th August 1915 most of the traffic movements at the two stations were rationalised and amalgamated, the pair thereafter being known as 'LSW & GW Joint'. From 1922 it changed to 'SR & GW Joint'. Finally, as from 18th June 1951, the suffix 'North' was added to the former GWR station and 'South' to the other.

LAUNCESTON NORTH

OPENED: Passengers – 1st July 1865 (with the opening of the Launceston & South Devon Railway, Tavistock (Devon) – Launceston).
Goods 21st August 1865.

CLOSED: Passengers – 30th June 1952 (trains being diverted to the 'South' station).
Goods – 28th February 1966.

Launceston North station, sited on the northern side of the joint station site, opened for passenger traffic at the beginning of July 1865 and goods services commenced two months later at the end of August. The line from Tavistock had been formally opened on 1st June. As the introductory Launceston text notes, this first station was, after the second station opened in 1886, known as Launceston 'Great Western'. Subsequent names were 'LSW & GW Joint' (August 1915 – 1922), 'SR & GW Joint' (1922 – 18th June 1951) and 'North' (from 18th June 1951).

The platform layout was basically U shaped, the northern arm (350 ft long), aligned west – east, being the up/down passenger platform alongside which ran a track terminating in buffers at the west end. Photographs indicate that at some stage the platform was extended at the east end. The southern arm (270 ft), backing on to the South Western station, was primarily used for the loading of goods and livestock, the latter using adjacent cattle pens. The track alongside this southern platform, terminating at buffers, was probably never used by passenger trains. A third central track formed part of a run round loop for passenger trains at the northern platform; a spur from the loop also terminated in buffers at the west end. The two platforms had stone faces backfilled with hard core. The surfaces were generally of chippings except close to the station building on the northern platform where there were stone paving slabs. The platform edges were formed of large rounded slabs and a single brick course.

The main station building, surviving throughout its life from the Launceston & South Devon era, was at the west end of the northern platform. It was constructed of Cornish stone with granite blockwork forming the corners. Windows and door apertures had semi-circular Italianate style arches. On the north road side there were eight windows and three doors and on the platform side there were six doors and seven windows. At the west end there were two windows and one door and at the east end of the building two doors. All doors were of solid panelled hardwood; the windows were eight paned with two quadrant fanlights at the apex. The platform was covered by a long horizontal wooden canopy attached to the front of the building and supported by seven centrally placed 12 inch square wooden pillars on cast iron supports. The canopy valance was of a saw tooth pattern. The central road-side doorway on the north side was protected by a small square horizontal canopy. The building's apex style roof was covered by Delabole slates and topped by three ornate cement rendered chimneys. An unusual feature of the building was that the front platform wall extended above the gutter level; this higher blank wall section was originally intended to form one side of an overall train shed similar to that at Tavistock South, a feature that was never implemented at Launceston. The main building incorporated the usual accommodation provided at a west country terminus station: booking office, ladies' and general waiting rooms, gent's toilets, a parcels office and other offices. A small stone building also stood to the east of this main building. Throughout its life the station was gas lit.

A staff of ten was based at the station in 1903. From 1915, following the rationalisation of workings at the two stations, the station master was always a LSWR/SR appointment but the staff were employed by the separate companies. Passenger numbers at Launceston GW were very constant between 1903 and 1923, 18,215 passenger tickets being issued in the former and 18,036 in the latter. By 1933 the total had dropped greatly to 6,512.

The station was also important for goods traffic, extensive mineral and agricultural traffic being handled. Livestock was particularly important on Tuesdays, the day of the local cattle market when special cattle trains often ran. The main goods yard, north of the station buildings, had two long sidings, one of which passed through a goods shed. The other long siding ran through the northern part of the yard. A third short siding, deviating from the goods shed siding, served a loading platform and an end loading dock at the rear of the northern passenger platform. Adjacent to this short siding was a 7½ ton capacity crane. As noted above, goods were also handled on the station's southern platform. In the centre of the main yard was a typical broad gauge style goods shed, its stone construction with a slate roof matching that of the station building. At each end of the shed were tall arched openings for the rail wagons, protected by large sliding doors. Inside the shed, on the north side, was a 75 ft long loading platform with a 2 ton capacity crane that aided the transfer of goods from road to rail. On the south side were three arched windows again matching those on the station.

The original single track engine shed opened with the line in 1865 and was extended by the GWR in 1899. Sited south-east of the main station building, it was accessed by a trailing siding from the southern platform track. A Cornish stone building of some 100 ft x 22 ft at ground level, it was lit by arched windows along each side. On its south side was a lean-to small office/mess room (35 ft x 15 ft). The shed was officially closed on 31st December 1962 when the goods depot was reduced to siding status under the supervision of S R staff. It closed at the end of February 1966. Adjacent to the west end of the shed was a large GWR metal water tank mounted on a girder frame work supported by six tubular legs. The structure included a water crane with a rotating boom. A short spur parallel to the engine shed siding accessed a 45 ft turntable sited south-west of the water tower. In 1952 a large storage shed for agricultural feeds was erected in the yard north-west of the engine shed and east of the goods yard. Some 150 ft long, the asbestos structure stood on brick legs. In the latter years the activities in the two adjacent goods yards was largely integrated, the former Great Western yard being designated 'North' and the former Southern yard 'South' as from 18th June 1951, the same date this designation applied to the stations themselves. Today the Newport Industrial Estate has been developed over the majority of the former sites of the two goods yards and the stations themselves. The estate includes a large supermarket. Also surviving are some of the stone buildings associated with the former goods activities of local traders.

A small original signal box standing on the up platform east of the main building controlled movements at the Great Western station. However, following the rationalisation and amalgamation of movements in August 1915, control passed to a northern extension of the South Western box as from 31st December 1916. There were separate GWR and LSWR/SR frames but under the overall control of LSWR/SR staff.

By then known as Launceston North, the station closed to passenger traffic at the end of June 1952 from which date passenger services on the line from Tavistock and Plymouth were re-routed to Launceston South using a link line east of the two stations which had opened on 6th April 1943 and was used for war-time traffic from 22nd September 1943. These diverted services ran until 31st December 1962 when the line closed to passenger services, the last trains being severely affected by the snow storms of Christmas/New Year. The Launceston North station building was used for freight traffic until the yard closed at the end of February 1966. The middle track had been removed in 1964.

Launceston South. Looking west in 1962. The main building with its impressive apex style canopy stands on the down platform. The separate small building at its east end contains the station master's office. On the up platform stands the extended signal box and the open front stone shelter.

LAUNCESTON SOUTH

OPENED: 21st July 1886 (with the opening of the Halwill Junction (Devon) – Launceston section of the North Cornwall Railway).
CLOSED: Passengers – 3rd October 1966.
Goods – 28th February 1966.

Sited some 300 ft below, and to the north of, the town centre and castle, the station opened in July 1886 as the terminus of the first section of the North Cornwall Railway from Halwill Junction in west Devon. This terminal status lasted six years until the second section opened from Launceston to Tresmeer on 28th July 1892. As the introductory Launceston text notes, this second station to be opened in the town was initially known as Launceston 'South Western' (the earlier Launceston 'Great Western' had opened to passengers in July 1865). Subsequent names were LSW and GW Joint (August 1915 – 1922), SR & GW Joint (1922 – 18th June 1951) and 'South' (from 18th June 1951).

South of, and adjacent to, the 1865 Great Western station, the South Western station was a two platform facility acting as a passing place on the North Cornwall Railway (later the London & South Western Railway) from Halwill Junction through to Wadebridge and Padstow.

Two curved tracks ran through the station alongside the stone built up (north) and down platforms. A long headshunt extended east from the down side track and from this, from west to east, trailed three sidings: firstly a short siding leading to cattle pens, secondly one that ran through the engine shed terminating at a turntable and thirdly a siding that led to two tracks, one running through the goods shed and another parallel to the shed serving adjacent buildings occupied by local traders.

The main station building, constructed of local stone with Portland stone quoins, stood on the down platform. Its design has been described as 'hall and cross wings' with a central section parallel to the platforms and tracks and two wings at right angles. The single storey structure, similar to that at Wadebridge but unlike most other North Cornwall Railway buildings, did not incorporate accommodation for the station master. This was provided in a separate house close to and south-west of the station. Launceston's building housed booking and parcels

Launceston South. The road side elevation of the main building from the approach road. Note that the canopy between the wings shown in the earlier general view of the two stations has gone in this view of 1963.

Launceston South. Looking east in 1962. The main building on the down platform (right) did not include accommodation for the station master. This was in a separate house off the picture to the right. Note the 1916 extended signal box on the up platform controlling movements at both stations. The water tank in the distance stands in front of the Launceston North engine shed.

offices, a staff room, waiting rooms and toilets. The station master's office was in a separate small stone building beside the east end of the building. The steeply pitched roof was covered with Delabole quarry slates and was topped by two tall chimneys. A wide apex style canopy supported by four pillars protected passengers on the platform. Early photographs indicate that in its early days a canopy covered the main road-side entrance between the projecting wings but this was later removed. The station was lit by gas up to the 1960s; in its last years the booking office and signal box had electric light. A large open fronted stone shelter with a slate roof served passengers on the up platform. Pedestrian movements between the platforms were via a round arch footbridge beyond the west end of the platform ramps; this bridge was the subject of some criticism regarding the steepness of the steps.

Launceston South was the scene of much passenger activity, in particular as the arrival and departure point for excursion trains. During the Second World War a number of trains carrying evacuees from the London area arrived at the station. In 1928 16,530 passenger tickets were issued but by 1936 the number had nearly halved to 8,889 though, to compensate, the number of season tickets issued had increased fifty fold from 2 to 100! Between the two years the number of tickets collected fell from 34,117 to 19,697.

The station's goods facilities were concentrated in a large goods yard behind, and to the south-east of, the down platform. One of the sidings ran through the goods shed. The stone building had a slate roof with a tall chimney at the north-west corner and a 2 ton crane within. Sliding wooden doors ran across the two rail entrances and two further doors were in the northern wall for use by road vehicles. Alongside the southern wall of the shed a further siding served buildings occupied by local traders, including Bartletts. A large saw mill stood near the southern edge of the yard. The yard handled considerable volumes of foodstuffs, general merchandise, agricultural products and livestock. The last was particularly important on Tuesdays, the day of the local cattle market. In the latter years there was considerable integration of the activities of the two goods yards at Launceston, given the designations of 'North' and 'South', similar to the stations themselves, as from 18th June 1951. Goods facilities were withdrawn at Launceston South at the end of February 1966.

The engine shed, close to and north-east of the goods shed, opened with the station in 1886. The iron framed and corrugated iron clad building was active up until the 1960s, though little used in its last years. In 1913 a small 48 ft turntable was provided beyond the west end of the shed. This was used until 1963. Water columns stood at the departure ends of the two platforms; these were fed from a large metal water tank sited on the up side at the west end of the station just beyond the footbridge. An 1880s signal box stood behind the up platform west of the waiting shelter. From 31st December 1916 the box was extended at the rear to accommodate the operation of signals and points at the Great Western station and yard. This reflected the time when many of the operations at the two stations were rationalised and amalgamated, partly because of the manpower shortage due to the First World War.

From the end of June 1952 until 31st December 1962 Launceston South, as it was by then known, also became the terminus for services on the former GWR branch from Plymouth and Tavistock. This followed the closure of the North station to passengers, trains using the 1943 link between the parallel lines east of Launceston. Launceston South itself closed to passenger traffic at the beginning of October 1966, some seven months after closure of the goods yard. Today the Newport Industrial Estate has been developed over much of the former sites of the two goods yards and stations. The estate includes a large supermarket. Also surviving are some of the stone buildings associated with the former goods activities of local traders. The establishment of the Launceston Steam Railway in the early 1980s led to the purchase of the western section of the South station site for a car park to serve the new station which was sited west of the station beyond the St Thomas Road bridge. A pedestrian link was established under the bridge. A former GWR starting signal stands in the corner of the car park. One stone abutment of the round arch footbridge at the west end of the station site is the only remnant of the South station structures. A modern housing block 'Station Court' has been developed on the site of the demolished station house at the east end of Station Road. Nearby on St Thomas Road, north of the railway bridge, is the Railway Inn.

LAUNCESTON (STEAM RAILWAY)

OPENED: 26th December 1983
CLOSED: Remains open for services on the Launceston Steam Railway

The Launceston Steam Railway opened on Boxing Day 1983 running on a half mile of the former trackbed of the North Cornwall Railway to Wadebridge. The 1 ft 11½ gauge line now runs west for some 2½ miles from its eastern terminus at the site of former gas works and siding which ceased to be used in 1965. On the main building is an impressive canopy erected in 1986/87 which originally protected passengers at Tavistock North station. Facilities at the station include a café, booking office, gift/book shop and museum. Tours of the workshop are also available. The café and bookshop were originally built in 1919 for the first Ideal Home Exhibition and were erected as a bungalow in Surrey. The museum and workshop were originally used by the Launceston Gas Company. The current western terminus of the Steam Railway is at Newmills station (opened 1995) with an intermediate request stop at Hunt's Crossing. At Newmills there is a riverside farm park. At the time of its 25th anniversary in early 2008, the possibility of extending the line beyond Newmills to Egloskerry was being considered, to be built in connection with a cycleway linking the Tarka and Camel cycle and pedestrian Trails.

LELANT

OPENED: 1st June 1877 (with the opening of the St Erth – St Ives branch).
CLOSED: Passengers – remains open as a request stop for services on the St Erth – St Ives branch.
Goods – May 1956 (see text).

Lelant station, on a south – north alignment, was built on a single track section of the branch line very close to the western shoreline of the River Hayle estuary. On the eastern edge of the village of Lelant, it opened when services commenced from St Erth at the beginning of June 1877, on the last Cornish branch to be laid at the broad gauge. To the north of the station a siding originally led down to Lelant Quay. Mixed gauge, (i.e. the addition of a rail at standard gauge) was introduced through the station to the Quay in October 1888. The whole branch to St Ives and the siding were converted to standard gauge in 1892; the quay siding closed early in the twentieth century.

On the down (west) side of the single track a wooden building, with an apex slate roof and two chimneys, originally incorporated three waiting rooms, one for the then three passenger classes. The timber construction was very unusual in Cornwall but was probably because of the difficulty in creating adequate foundations for a heavier stone structure close to the shore. The stone platform was lengthened at the north end in 1894. This coincided with the replacement of the original 1877 signal box by a ground frame. The box had controlled access to the Quay siding.

To the south of the building was a spacious forecourt. The only goods handled at Lelant were those carried on the passenger trains and this ceased in May 1956. A staff of two were based at Lelant until

Lelant. The station master stands in front of the wooden building in this view north in about 1910. Wood was probably used because of its siting close to the shore of the River Hayle estuary and the difficulty of providing good foundations for a heavier stone building.

1930 after which there was only one. Staffing ceased totally from 29th September 1958. The suffix 'halt' was then used until 5th May 1969.

Today the wooden station building survives; with an extension at the southern end, it is in residential use. A small open glass shelter serves passengers at what is now a request stop.

LELANT SALTINGS

OPENED: 29th May 1978 (on the St Erth – St Ives branch originally opened through this site in June 1877).

CLOSED: Remains open for passengers only on the St Ives branch.

For many years the popular resort of St Ives has suffered badly from traffic congestion aggravated by the lack of car parking. To relieve this situation, a park and ride facility was opened at the Spring Bank Holiday weekend in 1978 at Lelant Saltings, about a quarter of a mile south of Lelant station. A concrete platform was erected on the down (west) side of the line close to the western shoreline of the River Hayle estuary. Behind the platform a large car park was laid out at which visitors could park their vehicles and travel into St Ives by train.

This park and ride station immediately proved to be a success and by September 1978 some 136,000 passengers had use it. In May 1979 the platform was doubled in length to accommodate four carriage trains. Today Lelant Saltings continues to be a success story. A waiting shelter is provided at the foot of the ramp down from the platform to the car park, the limited width of the platform precluding siting there. Today most trains after 0900 hrs to and from St Ives stop at Lelant Saltings, which is not a request stop, unlike Lelant station itself. At times, during the summer, it is the busiest station in Cornwall!

Lelant Saltings. A 1979 view north of the extended concrete component platform erected for the St Ives park and ride. Today a short ramp links the platform to a large car park and a waiting shelter stands at the foot of this ramp.

LISKEARD

OPENED: Passengers – 4th May 1859 (with the opening of the Plymouth – Truro section of the Cornwall Railway).
Goods – 10th October 1859.

CLOSED: Passengers – remains open for services both on the Plymouth – Penzance line and the Liskeard – Looe branch.
Goods – 16th December 1963.

Liskeard. Thirteen GWR staff pose in front of the long low building on the down platform. Note the large number of metal advertisements in this photograph taken early in the twentieth century. They are very valuable collectors' items today!

The development of Liskeard station came in two phases. The original structure opened in 1859, serving passengers on the Plymouth to Truro section of the Cornwall Railway and this was followed in 1901 by the addition of a separate platform at right angles to the 1859 station for passengers on the new connection to the hitherto isolated line to Looe.

Sited in a cutting on the southern edge of the town, the station was originally on a passing loop on the otherwise generally single track line. The line to the west of Liskeard as far as Doublebois was doubled in February 1894 and the line to the east to Trevido viaduct was doubled two years

Liskeard. Looking north-west in about 1907. The station building (top right), high above the platform, is in its original form with a line side canopy. The 1892 signal box is on the up platform between the distant road bridge and the station footbridge. A 4-4-0 Bulldog class is arriving with an up train towards Plymouth.

later in August 1896. This doubling of the line either side of Liskeard came after the removal of the broad gauge track in 1892.

At the west end of the station a high stone bridge spans the main line, carrying the Liskeard to Looe road. The main station building, accommodating the principal facilities, developed high above the up (towards Plymouth) platform on top of the cutting with its main entrance facing north towards the town, the road access being off the north – south Looe road.

In a style used by Brunel at many Cornish stations, this stone building, which survives today, has low gable ends, an overhanging roof and tall chimneys. It originally incorporated the station master's office, booking office, booking hall, ladies' room, general waiting room, parcels office, urinal and stores. Over the years the original building has been extended and altered a number of times. In the 1940s a brick extension was added on the south side, the line side canopy being removed. In 2004/2005 a major redevelopment of the building was undertaken at a cost of some £835,000, the brick extension being replaced by a large metal and glass structure incorporating a seating area overlooking the platforms in the cutting. The ticket office, café and toilet facilities were also upgraded. On its northern side a new full length canopy was installed replacing a

Liskeard. Looking north-east in 1962 along the Looe branch platform opened in 1901. The wooden structure remains largely intact today. To the right is a metal store whilst the wooden hut to the left contained an 'Electruk' platform barrow and battery charging equipment. At the far end of the curved platform is a water tank and beyond that a signal box which was closed in 1964.

Liskeard. An overall view looking south-east from the road bridge in 1962. At the far end of the down platform (right) the 1915 signal box can be seen over the top of the building. The site of the original box is seen in the bottom left of the photo with a large billboard at the rear. The open metal footbridge links to the sloping path (left) up to the main building. Top left is the former GWR sleeping car body used as a Staff Association clubroom.

shorter version that had been removed some years before. Modifications were made to the main entrance and a new paved area was laid out. On its south side a ramp was constructed from the new structure linking to the original ramps that lead to the platform and the high metal footbridge that connects the platforms. Much of this extensive redevelopment was financed from the European Regional Development Fund.

There are also a number of buildings on the platforms, the main structure being on the down platform because of its distance from the main station building. The original down side stone structure was a long low building with a plain horizontal canopy. From west to east it incorporated stores, urinals, a ladies' waiting room, an open fronted shelter and a general waiting room. In 1894 a water tank and column were erected at the west end of the platform fed by a water pipe from the top of the cutting. In 1907 the platform was extended at the west (Penzance) end by some 200 ft and in 1947 a small brick waiting shelter, lit and heated by gas, was added on this platform, west of the road bridge. The main down side building was demolished some years ago, replaced initially by a concrete waiting shelter which, in turn, has now been replaced by a modern metal and glass structure.

In contrast, the structures on the up platform have generally been more modest, being closer to the high level main building. An original Brunel era stone shelter was provided at the foot of the ramp and remains today in use as a waiting room, the interior walls covered with coloured murals. At the east end of the platform a long timber shelter with wooden seats and a canopy over the platform was a later addition which also continues to serve passengers.

In 1901, with the opening of the connecting line to the Moorswater – Looe line in the valley below, a new north – south single face curved platform was completed at right angles to the main station up platform at its east end. Passenger services commenced on 15th May 1901. The largely wooden building with a canopy over the platform incorporated from south to north, the booking hall, booking office, parcels office, general waiting room, ladies' waiting room, open fronted shelter and urinal. This structure generally survives intact with, when visited in autumn 2008, one of the rooms in use as a small booking office with souvenirs of the Looe line on sale. Gas lighting of the building was retained until the early 1960s. There was a small metal store at the south end of the platform. In 1923 this branch platform was extended from its original 195 ft to 420 ft coming into use in April 1924. It was again lengthened in 1936 to 640 ft, use commencing on 3rd January 1937. At the north end

Liskeard. The station frontage on 3rd July 1963. In 2004/2005 the major redevelopment of the building included the installation of an almost full length canopy along this wall. The shorter canopy seen in this photo had been removed some years before.

of the platform a water tower was also installed. A loop opposite the platform for engines running around branch trains was taken out of use on 8th March 1964.

One other structure of note at Liskeard was a grounded GWR sleeping car sited east of the main station building and above the branch building. It was used as a Staff Association Club for many years but has now gone, the site being used as a short term car park.

Liskeard was also an important focus for freight traffic, the principal goods yard being west of the station on the up side. Sidings served a loading bank (1 track), cattle pens and a typical Brunel style timber goods shed through which ran two tracks. Remodelling of the yard took place in 1925. Reductions came in the 1960s and general goods services at Liskeard ceased in December 1963. The main yard remained open however until June 1981. Subsequent lifting of the tracks allowed westward extensions of the up platform in 1984 and 2006. In 2000 a footpath was laid from the west end of the up platform to a new car park on the old goods yard site.

To the east of the station on the down side was originally a single road stone engine shed (38 ft x 10 ft 6 inches) with a coal store opened in May 1869. There was also another siding to which access was gained by a small turntable. The shed ceased to have a locomotive allocation from 10th October 1912 but was not officially closed until 1st April 1918. It was subsequently demolished. The turntable had been removed in 1909. Also at the east end of the station, this time on the up side, was a siding trailing from the down line which gave access in the early days via a wagon turntable to what was known an Isaac's siding. Both of these areas at the east end of the station were later converted into more conventional sidings, that on the down side principally for refuge purposes. Further sidings were also sited to the east and north-east of the branch platform. Most of these were abandoned and lifted by the early 1970s and today the site is used for car parking, in particular as park and ride for the Looe branch, which started in 1986. Two large stone buildings remain however opposite the branch platform.

An 1892 signal box (20 ft 9 inches x 12 ft) stood at the rear of the up platform between the station footbridge and the high road bridge. Because of its restricted site the operating floor, containing 21 levers, overhung the lower locking room at the front of the structure. From 3rd June 1915 this was replaced by a new box with a frame of 36 levers at the east end of the down platform. Constructed entirely of timber with a hipped slate roof it was of a GWR style standard at that time. By mid 1988 only 17 levers were in use. This box remains operational today, manned for 24 hours, operating the points and semaphore signals still in use in the Liskeard area. Operations on the Looe line were controlled for many years from a small 18 lever box at the north end of the platform. The box closed on 15th March 1964 and was demolished. With the diverse operations at Liskeard station it is not surprising that 17 staff were based there in 1903, a figure that rose to 30 in 1923.

LOOE

OPENED: 11th September 1879 (with the commencement of passenger services on the Moorswater – Looe line).

CLOSED: Passengers – remains open for services on the Liskeard – Looe branch.
Goods – 4th November 1963.

Looe comprises two communities either side of the River Looe, linked by a 19th century seven arch road bridge. Originally it developed as a fishing port but subsequently became an important sea outlet for the mines and quarries of the Caradon area of east Cornwall. It also served as a port for the import of lime, sand and seaweed for local agriculture. Initially these products were conveyed to and from the port by the Liskeard and Looe Union Canal opened in 1827.

In 1844 the Liskeard & Caradon Railway opened from the mining area firstly to a temporary terminus on the canal at Tremabe and then on to Moorswater in March 1846. The Liskeard & Looe Railway Act of 1858 authorised the construction of a line south from Moorswater down the valley to Looe parallel to the earlier canal. Mineral traffic commenced on 27th December 1860, the line being worked by the Liskeard & Caradon Railway from March 1862. Coinciding with a fall in mineral traffic, pressure mounted for the introduction of a passenger service on the line. These services finally started from Moorswater to Looe on 11th September 1879. Traffic was however limited to local movements on this isolated line, which lacked a link to the main Cornwall Railway which had opened between Plymouth and Truro in May 1859, crossing the north-south valley line over the famous Moorswater viaduct west of Liskeard. It was not until 8th May 1901 that the curved and steeply graded link from Liskeard station to the valley line opened, the tracks joining at Coombe Junction. At this point Moorswater station, north of the junction, closed, being replaced by Coombe Junction Halt. Mineral traffic on the valley line largely ceased by the middle of the First World War and the tracks above Moorswater were lifted in 1917 contributing to the war effort to accumulate scrap metal. From the early 1920s the Liskeard – Looe branch became primarily a tourist/holiday line though fish imports continued to be carried. By this time the canal had closed.

This account of the evolution of the rail traffic in the Liskeard/Looe area forms the context for the description of the valley railway stations and halts. At Looe the terminus was built on the east bank of the Looe river in an area known as Shutta, directly opposite the confluence of the East and West Looe rivers. The single platform was on the east side of the line and, at the end of the 19th century, the small wooden station building, with a corrugated iron roof, incorporated a booking office and a waiting room with a toilet. A small wooden goods shed stood close to the north end of the building and a cast iron gent's urinal was probably provided on the platform at the south end. To provide for the increased traffic generated by the opening of the Liskeard link line in 1901, a canopy was introduced over the platform, a ladies' waiting room was added, and the gent's urinal was incorporated into a lean-to extension at the south end of the building. A plan dated about 1912 indicates that at that time the facilities from south to north were toilets, a ladies' waiting room, the booking hall, the booking office and a goods lock up. Beyond the building was a further small goods shed and office.

Looe. A general view from the north-west in the early 1900s. The platform canopy on the main building and the platform extension indicate that the photo post dates work undertaken to develop the station after the opening of the Liskeard link line in 1901. A number of structures on and behind the platform north of the building are for the handling of goods. Note the large water tank on the masonry tower and the moveable jib to deliver the water. A train pulls away from the sidings to the south of the station.

Although there were small alterations and extensions over the years, this basic station building then served Looe until its demolition in 1968. The platform was extended in 1901 from 75 ft to 200 ft to accommodate the longer trains now operating from Liskeard. In 1928 it was extended north by a further 96 ft. Photographs indicate that both these extensions were constructed with a timber front wall reinforced with old Barlow rail filled behind and surfaced with ashes. The original platform had a masonry front wall, the surface around the station building being paved with flagstones.

In the 1930s a number of fairly ambitious schemes were proposed for the station area but were not implemented as, at that time, proposals were under consideration for a new more direct rail line to Looe from St Germans on the main line via Hessenford and Downderry. This was planned to terminate at a new Looe station east of, and high above, the town. The new line was not progressed and, in the late 1930s, more limited improvements were undertaken at the station; additional goods and parcels facilities were provided by extending the building at the north end. The platform canopy was extended along the full length of the building which now incorporated, from north to south, the goods shed, parcels office, booking office, booking hall, ladies' room and gent's toilets. These improvements came into use for the 1939 holiday season but the outbreak of the Second World War brought a sudden halt to tourist traffic. Back in 1913 44,484 passenger tickets were issued at Looe. This figure rose to 51,446 in 1923 but fell to 24,287 in 1933. Both in 1910 and 1924 ten staff were recorded as being based at Looe.

A number of other features of the station building and platform must also be noted. An elevated tank at the Liskeard end of the platform provided water for the engines and non drinking water at the station itself. A masonry tower supported the metal tank (capacity 1661 gallons); a bag on a movable jib delivered water to the engine tanks. When the platform was extended north in 1928 the tank had to be moved back and the jib extended. Beyond the tank to the north was a loading bank facing onto the line. This was primarily used to load cattle brought from the adjacent cattle market. The bank was, at one time, equipped with a weighbridge and a water standpipe, the latter used for watering the animals and washing the bank itself. Another feature in the early years was a small signal room with a bay window sited within the station building between the passenger and goods accommodation; this operated four signals. In about 1920 a miniature signal box (5 ft x 4 ft 6 inches) with

Looe. The forecourt side of the building on 30th August 1951. By this time entry to the booking office was via the rear door rather than a side gate alongside the building and a platform door. Exiting passengers continued to be directed via the gate to avoid congestion in the booking office. Note the board indicating the bus stop for Polperro.

a 7 lever frame was erected on the south end of the platform to replace the earlier facility.

Beyond the south end of the station a number of freight and servicing facilities were in use through the years. The main running line beside the platform led into three loops. That on the east side ran through an engine shed (30 ft long) and a curved carriage shed (100 ft long), both constructed of corrugated iron. The former shed was provided in November 1901 when the new services from the main station at Liskeard required an engine to be stabled overnight at Looe. Two further goods sidings were also laid, one terminating at an end loading dock and the other at Looe road bridge, both served by a 3 ton capacity crane.

A further track ran south through a gate, across a

Looe. The 1238 hrs to Liskeard (and N Wales!) stands beside the new station building on 29th August 2008. At that time the booking office/information point was open with advertising boards on the platform.

public highway, past the east end of the road bridge and south to serve Buller Quay and the general quayside, including the fish market. The Looe engine shed closed on 2nd April 1917, the redundant building being sold for £20 in 1920. In the late 1920s the carriage shed was removed. By this time traffic using the quay line was largely confined to fish, the mineral traffic having virtually ceased.

After the Second World War the holiday traffic resumed in earnest. In contrast, by the early 1950s, the quayside line was disused. Today there is no trace. In a similar way the goods sidings south of the station became redundant and more and more of the yard was used for car parking. Few additions were made to the station building in the post war period. Electric lighting was introduced in the booking and parcels offices in 1950 but elsewhere gas continued to be used. In 1956 the platform was largely reconstructed, with the timber faced northern extensions being demolished and rebuilt with concrete blocks. Concrete slabs were laid along the whole length of the platform edge and around the building. From the early days entry and exit to and from the station building was only from the platform, to which access was through a small gate at the south end of the building. However by 1951 the arrangements were altered with entry to the building now being through the rear wall directly into the booking hall. Exiting passengers were directed via the platform and the small gate.

In 1961 diesel multiple units replaced steam hauled trains on the Looe branch and these no longer needed to use track beyond the platform. A buffer stop was introduced some 20 yards beyond the south end of the ramp. In July 1966 the platform was shortened further by 15 yards thus allowing more land to be taken for car parking.

The final major changes came from 28th April 1968 when half of the platform and associated track was removed. The old building was demolished and replaced initially be a bus stop type shelter and a hut which served as a staff mess room and ticket office. This, in turn, was replaced in the early 1990s by the current stone building with an open shelter section at the north end and an office/mess room. Staffing ceased on 30th September 1968. The goods yard had closed in early November 1963 and all sidings were lifted in 1964. The small platform signal box ceased to operate from 15th March 1964.

When visited in August 2008, the latest building had eight individual metal seats in the open shelter section. At the southern end was a combined booking office/ information point/souvenir shop, though this was not open throughout the day. At the south end of the platform was a general tourist information hut, though this was not open at all during the visit. At the north end of the platform the entrance from the small car park behind the building had two old rails as gate posts. Close by were an old GWR seat and two cycle stands on the platform. Between the building and the tourist hut were two seats, one of GWR vintage and the other a modern metal structure. South of the station Looe police station occupies the site of the former southern section of the station and part of the goods yard whilst further south again a petrol filling station and car parking cover the remainder of the former goods yard.

Lostwithiel. The up side wooden building, though listed, deteriorated over the years and its rather poor condition is shown in this 1977 photo. Four years later it was dismantled for possible re-erection but this did not happen. The down side island building was dismantled earlier in 1976.

LOSTWITHIEL

OPENED: 4th May 1859 (with the opening of the Plymouth – Truro section of the Cornwall Railway).
CLOSED: Passengers – remains open for services on the Plymouth – Penzance line.
Goods – 1st June 1964 (except for private sidings later closed).

The station opened in 1859 close to the centre of the town on the River Fowey, which had, for many years, been the commercial and administrative centre for an area of mid Cornwall. The coming of the Cornwall Railway without doubt boosted Lostwithiel's economy, particularly because the Company decided to base its workshops in the town. For some years these workshops became the town's principal employer. In the 1930s fourteen employees were, in addition, based at the station itself.

When opened, Lostwithiel only served trains on the broad gauge main Plymouth to Truro line. Ten years later however, on 1st June 1869, the Lostwithiel & Fowey Railway opened a broad gauge track line south from Lostwithiel to Carne Point just north of Fowey. The line was for freight traffic only, principally china clay trains. As such it functioned for nearly eleven years but from 1st June 1874 it had faced serious competition for the china clay traffic from the newly opened southern section of the Cornwall Minerals Railway from St Blazey to Fowey. The Lostwithiel branch was forced to close on 31st December 1879. Fifteen years later on 16th September 1895 it was reopened as a standard gauge line, this time for both freight and passenger traffic. There was now an end on connection with the St Blazey line at Fowey. The Lostwithiel to Fowey passenger services lasted until January 1965.

Lostwithiel. The much changed view on 28th September 1994 showing the new brick buildings on both platforms which continue to serve passengers today. The 1893 signal box was still in situ in early 2009.

Lostwithiel station, on a generally north-south section of the line, developed facilities to serve the expanding functions. The principal wooden building, with a horizontal canopy, and accommodating the main facilities, stood on the up single sided platform. At the south end of this platform was a dock siding. The east side down platform became an island when a bay platform with an adjoining track, terminating at buffers at the north end, came into use for Fowey branch line passenger trains in 1895. A wooden building with an all round horizontal canopy served both main line and branch passengers. A covered footbridge was also added at this time at the north end of the platforms, though later this metal structure lost its roof. The bridge was demolished in the early 1960s.

The two main buildings were unfortunately allowed to deteriorate over the years. The down side building lasted until 1976 when it was dismantled for later erection at Marsh Mills on the Plym Valley Railway. The up side building, although listed, was also dismantled five years later for possible re-erection at St Agnes, but this never happened. New buildings were erected on both platforms, the principal brick structure on the up side was officially opened by the Mayor of Lostwithiel on 18th November 1982. A small shelter serves passengers on the down side.

Lostwithiel's freight facilities were principally focussed to the south of the station on both the up

Lostwithiel. Looking north in 1962. The main wooden building stands on the up platform (left) with a camping coach in the former dock siding. A DMU to Fowey stands on the outside of the down island platform; this service was to last until early 1965. The footbridge has lost its roof. Trucks with china clay loads are to the right.

Luckett. Looking east in early 1909. The photo, reproduced from an old postcard, is of interest in that it refers to 'Stoke Climsland' station, a name that only applied from its opening in March 1908 until the beginning of November 1909. To the left is the earlier house, goods shed and loading platform of the East Cornwall Mineral Railway.

and down sides. The wooden goods shed, through which ran one siding, was sited on the up side close to the end of the platform. General goods services ceased at the beginning of June 1964. The surviving goods shed was dismantled in 1982 with the aim of preservation but again this did not materialise. South of the goods shed on the up side were the large buildings of the original Cornwall Railway workshops. These lasted for many years after the Cornwall Railway era but were later used for industrial units. From 2004 they were converted into housing. Much of the goods yard on the up side has also been taken over for housing and also some car parking.

On the down side both south of the station and east behind the platform were extensive sidings principally used by china clay trains passing through Lostwithiel en route for Fowey. For many years the station was the busiest centre for shunting and marshalling such trains in Cornwall. Sidings adjacent to the station with buffers at the Bodmin Parkway (north) end are still in use. A milk depot on the up side north of the station was provided with a siding in 1932; this facility lasted until about 1980.

Lostwithiel's main 1893 signal box stands at the north end of the down platform; this operated the adjacent level crossing gates, which were replaced by lifting barriers on 1st June 1969. In 2001 only 39 of its 63 levers were in use. It survives today. A further box beyond the south end of the station, on the down side opposite the goods shed, controlled the many sidings east of the station and access to the Fowey branch. Known as the Lostwithiel Branch Box, it was in use from 1895 to 1923. Today the replacement station buildings continue to serve both main line and local trains, though many of the former do not stop here. The palm trees on the platform are a reminder that travellers are now in the mild climate of Cornwall!

LUCKETT

OPENED: 2nd March 1908 (with the opening of the Plymouth, Devonport & South Western Junction Railway branch, Bere Alston – Callington).
CLOSED: Passengers – 7th November 1966.
Goods – 10th September 1962.

Luckett opened at the beginning of March 1908 when passenger services began on the Plymouth, Devonport & South Western Junction Railway branch from Bere Alston to Callington. It was at the site of the Monks Corner depot of the earlier (1872) East Cornwall Mineral Railway whose trackbed was taken over by the 1908 line (see Callington text).

It was sited to the north-east of Kit Hill, immediately south-east of a road overbridge carrying a minor road to Luckett, a village in the valley bottom one and a half miles to the north. Despite the proximity of this village, the station, at its opening, was called Stoke Climsland, a village over two and a half miles to the north-west. Following complaints over the misleading name, it was called Luckett from 1st November 1909. At the station the main running line ran alongside the single north facing stone platform opposite which was a goods loop. Alongside the loop

Luckett. A view west over 50 years later in 1962, showing details of the corrugated iron clad wooden building and the former buildings of the East Cornwall Mineral Railway (right). These latter survive today in a fine residence. Note the small ground frame hut beside the road bridge and the very small platform flower beds enclosed by white stones.

was a loading platform, a survivor from the earlier depot days. Behind the loading platform was the East Cornwall Mineral Railway stone built station house and goods shed.

The PDSWJR station building, a wooden structure with corrugated iron cladding, stood at the middle of the platform. Along its front was a backward sloping canopy with a saw tooth valance. Support for the canopy came from wooden pillars. At one time there was a small open metal hut on the platform east of the building. In the early days there was a siding on the south side of the line east of the platform, which at one time served a carriage shed built in 1910 and used for hay drying in the First World War. West of the station on the north side of the line adjacent to the road bridge was a small hut containing the ground frame that operated the loop points. There was no signal box on the whole branch.

The station, in addition to use by local residents, was also patronised by walkers climbing to the 1091 ft Kit Hill summit. In 1928 3,695 passenger tickets were issued at Luckett and 3,368 collected; the equivalent figures for 1936 were 3,573 and 1,882. Locally grown produce was sent from Luckett, this included Tamar Valley strawberries often loaded onto passenger trains. The relatively limited goods services were withdrawn at Luckett in mid September 1962. The station closed entirely with the withdrawal of passenger services on the Gunnislake to Callington section of the line in early November 1966. Staffing had ceased earlier in the year on 7th March.

Today the East Cornwall Mineral Railway house survives with extensions as a fine residence, 'Old Luckett Station House'. The former loading platform is a feature in the garden. The station platform also survives, though covered in grass, but the original building has gone. In its place is a recent structure incorporating swimming and sauna facilities modelled on the style of the original building, including a canopy. The road bridge remains in situ.

LUXULYAN

OPENED: 20th June 1876 (with the commencement of passenger services on the Cornwall Minerals Railway, Newquay – Fowey).

CLOSED: Passengers – remains open as a request stop for services on the Par – Newquay branch.
Goods – 1st June 1964 (except for private sidings, later closed).

With the name of 'Bridges for Luxulyan', the station opened with the start of passenger services on the Cornwall Minerals Railway in mid June 1876. Sited at the top of a long bank (1 in 37/40), which climbed up through the Luxulyan Valley from Par, its name changed to Luxulyan from 1st May 1905, reflecting the name of the nearby village, east of the line. The name refers to the Cell or Holy Place of St Sulyan.

When opened by the Cornwall Minerals Railway, on a north-west to south-east alignment, there was a main line and a short passing loop beside which there were up and down single face platforms. A small wooden station building was provided, set back behind the south east end of the up platform. An 1890 local guide book stated that 'simple refreshments may be had at the station master's cottage', which was close to the station building. A small Cornwall Minerals Railway signal box stood beyond the south-east of the station on the up (towards Fowey) side.

In 1910 there were major changes to the station layout when an island platform was constructed between the main running line and a lengthened passing loop. A GWR pagoda style shelter was provided on the island. The Cornwall Minerals Railway station building was retained. A new GWR signal box (27 levers) on the up side, this time opposite the middle of the platform, replaced the earlier Cornwall Minerals Railway box from 30th March 1911. A water tank on a masonry tower stood on the down side; an adjacent tall wind pump assisted the supply of water to the locomotives.

Luxulyan goods yard was on the up side behind

Luxulyan. Looking north-west in June 1958 at the post 1910 station layout. Note the island platform, the original Cornwall Minerals Railway station building (to the right of the camping coach), the 1911 GWR signal box and the water tank on the masonry tower. Note the pagoda style shelter on the island platform.

the signal box. A northern extension to the yard contained a loading wharf, to which ran a narrow gauge line from the Treskilling clay works. Horses, and later a capstan, were used to move small clay wagons on to the loading wharf. This line operated from 1916 to 1975. The station passing loop was lengthened in May 1936 to accommodate the long holiday trains en route to and from Newquay. The goods yard was also the location of camping coaches for the periods 1936 to 1939 and 1952 to 1963. The level of passenger numbers was never high at Luxulyan: in 1903 4,845 passenger tickets were issued, the numbers rose to 5,772 in 1913 and 7,465 in 1923 but fell to 4,187 in 1933. Three or four men were based here between 1903 and 1938 but the station became unstaffed on 12th July 1964.

This depletion of staff was but one example of the decline that set in from the 1960s. Goods facilities were withdrawn from the station at the beginning of June 1964 and on 27th September the goods yard closed. Also in 1964 the passing loop was removed leaving only the former down side face of the platform in use. The station building was demolished. The signal box closed in September 1964 when all the trackbed was lifted, leaving only the main running line and the siding to the clay loading wharf which survived until 1975. The late 1960s also saw the removal of the water tower and wind pump.

Early in the 1980s, the GWR pagoda shelter was replaced by a simple concrete hut which remains today on the surviving platform. Some of the former goods yard is now being used for storage and when seen in November 2008 some development was in progress in the south-east of the former yard.

MARAZION

OPENED: 11th March 1852 (with the opening of the Penzance – Redruth section of the West Cornwall Railway)

CLOSED: Passengers – 5th October 1964.
Goods – 6th December 1965.

Marazion station was sited at the point where the line west from Hayle reached the marshy area immediately behind the shore of Mounts Bay. The village of Marazion was about a mile to the south-east and passengers at the station had a spectacular view of St Michael's Mount. The site, however, did have drawbacks with a number of storms interrupting services between Marazion and Penzance during the 1850s and 1860s. Particularly vulnerable were the timber viaducts in this section; in July 1921 an embankment was completed carrying a new double track line all the way to Penzance. The line west from Marazion had been doubled to Penzance viaduct in August 1893 but the line east to Hayle remained single track until June 1929.

When opened by the West Cornwall Railway in March 1852, Marazion was a small station with a typical Brunel style wooden building and platform on the south side of the line. Similar to other early small West Cornwall Railway buildings, it had a low-pitched roof and small projecting canopy. The station was known as Marazion Road until 24th June 1896.

Marazion. A detailed view looking east in the late 1920s. The road bridge which replaced an earlier level crossing is seen through the dominating covered footbridge. The main station building can be seen beyond the signal box. A small matching stone shelter stands on the up platform (left).

In the 1880s Marazion station was reconstructed and further work took place in 1893 at the time of track doubling to the west. As a result of this work all the original West Cornwall Railway structures were swept away. At the new station both platforms were some 500 ft long backed by wooden fencing. The down side platform was later extended at the east end. The main building stood on the down platform with a matching waiting shelter on the up side. Both buildings were constructed of dressed granite blocks and had slate hipped roofs, that on the main building was topped with two chimneys and the up shelter had one. Also on the down side platform east of the main building was a goods lock up store and an open shelter with a canopy used for storage purposes. A covered plate girder footbridge connected the two platforms from west of the main building on the down side to east of the shelter on the up. By the 1960s this was replaced by a concrete component structure. Until the 1920s the road from Marazion to Penzance crossed the line east of the station at a level crossing with four gates. When the line was doubled between Hayle and Marazion the level crossing was replaced by a skew girder road over bridge.

Marazion's goods facilities were extensive. The principal yard was on the up side west of the station. A goods platform was added in 1861 and two sidings in 1862 and 1864. These were followed, one each in 1881 and 1892 until a total of six were provided three of which had loading platforms alongside, mainly used for vegetables, especially broccoli. Access to these six sidings was via a goods loop that left the down main line via a trailing connection and then crossed the up line on the level before running behind the up platform and rejoining the running lines east of the station. Sidings were also laid behind the down platform, one in 1901 and one in 1907. Two more sidings were added east of the station when that section of the line was doubled in 1929. A further two were added in this location in 1936. Like many other stations in West Cornwall, these extensive sidings were used for the loading of local agricultural produce. They were also used at times for the storage of the large number of carriages on holiday trains terminating at Penzance in the summer months. A GWR 1880s standard signal box with a gable slate roof, a brick and timber structure and a tall brick chimney stood on the down platform west of the main building and footbridge and opposite the up side waiting shelter. A particular feature of the box was an enclosed porch at the west end at the top of the steps. At its maximum operation it had 38 levers.

Marazion. Looking east in this overall view of 1963, platforms are now linked by a concrete component bridge. Through this the main building and the open storage shelter with a canopy can be seen on the down platform (right). The up side waiting shelter has lost its canopy seen in the late 1920s photograph. Note the camping coach to the right of the signal box, one of many based at the station.

Menheniot. A view from the south east end of the up platform on 11th June 1966 provides good detail of the Brunel style down side building. Dominating the scene behind the buildings are structures associated with Clicker Tor Quarry which was rail connected until 1969.

Passenger numbers were high at Marazion early in the twentieth century. In 1903 30,277 passenger tickets were issued and this was exceeded in 1913 with 35,282. In the following twenty years there was a major fall to 9,906 in 1933 and 6,734 in 1938, though by that time season ticket sales had reached 111. Staff numbers also varied from year to year but also seasonally with extra staff being employed to cope with all the vegetables and flower traffic. In 1903 there was a basic staff of 14; this reduced to 12 by the 1920s and to 11 in the 1930s. The station was controlled by a class three station master.

From the late 1930s Marazion station became associated with camping coaches, the first being installed in 1937. However, in the early 1960s they became a major feature. In the 1963 summer season six ex Southern Region Pullman carriages were sent to the Western Region for use as camping coaches, four at Marazion and two at Fowey. In 1964 however British Railways decided that there was no place for such coaches but the four at Marazion plus the two from Fowey were retained for use by the British Railways Staff Association, all now sited at Marazion behind the down platform. Their use continued until the mid 1980s though their condition deteriorated on this exposed site. At this point they were sold to a private owner who hoped to maintain them as holiday accommodation but this was unsuccessful. Subsequently two were transferred to Petworth station in Sussex where they form bedrooms at a holiday establishment. The remaining coaches suffered further damage both from storms and vandals and when the site was viewed in autumn 2008 no coaches remained.

The camping coaches did however survive longer than virtually all of the other facilities at Marazion. The station itself closed in October 1964 and goods facilities were withdrawn in December 1965. The extensive up side sidings were lifted in September 1966, the signal box closing on 18th September. The remaining sidings east of the station went in the following year. Today the only survivor is the former down side station building. In 2002 it was a cycle hire centre but in autumn 2008 it was in use as a public house, 'Station House' with picnic tables outside.

MENHENIOT

OPENED: 4th May 1859 (with the opening of the Plymouth – Truro section of the Cornwall Railway).
CLOSED: Passengers – remains open as a request stop for local services on the Plymouth – Penzance line. Goods – 9th September 1963.

Opening in May 1859 with the commencement of passenger services on the Plymouth to Truro section of the Cornwall Railway, the station principally served the village of Menheniot, about one mile to the north. In some timetables it was described in the early days as 'Menheniot for Looe'; this was before the station opened at Looe in 1879. Initially the station was on a passing loop on the otherwise generally single track line; track doubling took place in the area in the late 1890s. The principal stone building, a Brunel style Italianate chalet type, stood on the down (towards Liskeard) platform. The shallow hipped roof overhanging on all sides provided

Menheniot. The surviving up platform stone shelter on 29th August 2008.

shelter to the platform. A stone open fronted shelter served passengers on the up side. In the early 1920s six staff were based at the station but it became unstaffed from 26th April 1965.

An open metal plate footbridge connected the platforms west of the main building and east of the shelter. By the mid 1980s this bridge had been replaced with an open lattice structure, this time at the west end of the platforms. This bridge remains today. The original Menheniot signal box stood on the down platform just beyond the building and the first footbridge. A replacement box also on the down platform was sited just to the east of the second bridge. This box closed on 30th September 1973 but survived for many years as a staff mess room. It has now been demolished and an area of white concrete marks its former site.

A small goods yard was sited behind the main building. From 7th May 1931 a siding served the adjacent Clicker Tor Quarry which provided ballast for the railway. The goods yard closed in September 1963 but the quarry siding remained in use until the end of 1969. The siding and a goods loop were removed in 1973.

Menheniot was one of many small stations on the Plymouth to Penzance line which British Railways proposed for closure in 1964 and was the only one to be reprieved. Today it is served only by local trains and from May 2009 became a request stop. The main building on the down platform has been demolished following a fire and no shelter is now provided. In autumn 2008 two bicycle stands were the only provision on the platform. The original up platform stone shelter survives.

MITCHELL & NEWLYN HALT

OPENED: 14th August 1905 (on the Chacewater – Newquay line originally opened through this site in January 1905).

CLOSED: 4th February 1963.

About one and a half miles west of the village of Mitchell and three quarters of a mile south-east of St Newlyn East, Mitchell & Newlyn Halt opened in mid August 1905, coinciding with the introduction of steam rail motors on the Chacewater to Newquay line. The section of the line through this halt from Perranporth to Newquay opened eight months earlier at the beginning of January (see Shepherds text). Services on the first section from Chacewater to Perranporth had started in July 1903. When opened, Mitchell & Newlyn had a wooden platform on an embankment east of a rail bridge over the road linking the two settlements it served. It was accessed by three short flights of wooden steps on the side of the embankment. Behind the platform was a GWR style pagoda shelter supported by a number of wooden posts. By the early 1920s this rather precarious structure had been replaced on the down (north) side of the line by a more mundane concrete component platform (100 ft) to the west of the rail overbridge, again on an embankment. The pagoda hut was replaced by a small open corrugated iron shelter within which was a seat. Also on the platform was a further seat and one lamp post. The halt closed

Mitchell & Newlyn Halt. A rare photograph of the initial wooden structure sited on an embankment. The GWR pagoda style hut is supported by wooden posts; access to the platform is via three flights of wooden steps.

Mitchell & Newlyn Halt. The replacement concrete component platform with the corrugated iron open shelter on the down (north) side of the line in 1962.

at the beginning of February 1963 when services were withdrawn on the line. Forty years later the concrete platform and shelter could still be seen albeit covered in much vegetation. When the author visited the location in March 2009 he was not able to view the site of the halt on the embankment, though the access path, lined by railway style fence posts, from a point adjacent to the surviving abutments of the railway overbridge was clear. A notice beside the path stated 'Private property, no public access'.

MITHIAN HALT

OPENED: 14th August 1905 (on the Chacewater – Newquay line originally opened through this site in 1903).
CLOSED: 4th February 1963.

Serving the hamlet of Mithian, a quarter of a mile to the south-west, the halt opened in mid August 1905 coinciding with the introduction of steam rail motors on the Chacewater to Newquay line. The first section of the line as far as Perranporth had opened through the site of Mithian Halt on 6th July 1903. Services on the extension to Newquay started at the beginning of January 1905. The 102 ft long platform, in a cutting, was aligned approximately north – south on the down (west) side of the single track line between two road overbridges carrying minor roads. It was originally constructed of wood but by the early 1920s this had been replaced by a brick faced structure with a paving slab edge and a chippings surface behind. A GWR pagoda style shelter stood

Mithian Halt. Looking south west in 1962 at the 1920s structure which had replaced the earlier wooden platform. The GWR pagoda style hut had survived from the halt's opening in 1905.

on both the wooden and brick structures. Illumination was provided by lamps on posts at either end of the platform and a seat was provided in front of the station nameboard towards the north end of the platform. Access to the halt was via steps linked to the road at the west end of the bridge south of the platform. Following the withdrawal of services on the line and the closure of the halt early in February 1963, the cutting was filled in. One parapet of the bridge north of the halt survives.

MOORSWATER

OPENED: 11th September 1879 (with the commencement of passenger services on the Moorswater – Looe line).
CLOSED: Passengers – 15th May 1901.
Goods – 16th December 1963 (except for private sidings later closed).

Moorswater opened when passenger services were introduced in September 1879 on the hitherto mineral only line south to Looe (for early history of this line see Looe station text). Sited slightly to the north and within the shadow of the massive Moorswater viaduct carrying the main Plymouth to Truro line across the valley, the granite block platform (84 ft long, ramps 10 ft) with a sleeper border and granite chipping surface, stood on the east side of the line. The station building (30 ft x 15 ft), a white painted wooden structure with a galvanised iron roof, was divided into two spaces, one used as a booking office and the other as a waiting room. At the southern end was a toilet and at the other end, a small goods shed. A short distance away was a primitive shelter constructed of zinc under which goods could be

Moorswater. Staff pose in about 1890 at this short lived station which opened when passenger services were introduced on the hitherto mineral only line south to Looe in September 1879. It closed 22 years later when the Looe line was connected to the main Plymouth to Penzance line at Liskeard.

transferred from carts to rail wagons. Two or three sidings were available with movements being controlled from a small signal box with a stone built locking room, a timber upper operating room and slate hipped roof.

In May 1901, with the opening of the link between the valley line and Liskeard, a new halt opened at Coombe Junction and the section north under the viaduct was closed for passenger traffic including Moorswater station. Following closure, the track in front of the redundant platform was removed; the building survived however, being converted to private living accommodation for railway employees who worked on the continuing freight operations. In 1944 it was recorded that the raised platform could still be traced and 'a bungalow type residence forming part of the old station building is used by the man who carries out night duties at the engine shed'. The building was still standing in 1949 but was demolished in April/May 1951. The former platform was still visible in the mid 1990s. General goods facilities had continued at Moorswater until December 1963.

MOUNT HAWKE HALT

OPENED: 14th August 1905 (on the Chacewater – Newquay line originally opened through this site in 1903).

CLOSED: 4th February 1963.

Sited about a mile east of the village of Mount Hawke, the halt opened in mid August 1905 coinciding with the introduction of steam rail motors on the Chacewater to Newquay line. The first section

Mount Hawke Halt. Looking south in 1962. The brick faced platform with a paving slab edge and chipping surface probably replaced an earlier wooden structure. The pagoda style hut stood on both structures.

Nancegollan. A fine overall view in 1954/5 of the station as remodelled 17 years earlier. The brick constructed main building is on the down (towards Helston) platform. Adjacent to it is a red brick store with a slate roof. A small wooden shelter stands on the up platform.

of the line as far as Perranporth had opened through the site of Mount Hawke Halt on 6th July 1903. Services on the extension to Newquay started at the beginning of January 1905. The brick faced 100 ft long platform aligned north – south, was on the up (east) side of the single line just to the north of a road overbridge carrying a minor road. It is likely that, as at Mithian Halt on the same 1903 section of the line, the original platform was constructed of wood, this being replaced by about 1920. Access to the platform was via steps linked to the road at the east end of the bridge. Passengers were served by a GWR pagoda style corrugated iron hut. Along the edge of the platform were paving slabs behind which there was a chippings surface. Illumination was by lamps at each end of the platform on decorative posts. Following withdrawal of services on the line early in February 1963 and closure of the halt, the cutting in which it stood was infilled. Today a tarmac track runs north over the filled cutting; entrance to the track is through two gates on each of which is a red metal template in the shape of a steam engine. Former railway style concrete posts align the track. The road overbridge has gone.

NANCEGOLLAN

OPENED: 9th May 1887 (with the opening of the Helston Railway, Gwinear Road – Helston).
CLOSED: Passengers – 5th November 1962.
Goods – 5th October 1964.

The development of Nancegollan station was undertaken in two distinct phases, pre and post 1937. In the centre of the small settlement of the same name, it opened in May 1887 with the commencement of services on the Helston branch. The original station comprised one 220 ft long platform on the up (towards Gwinear Road) side, a passing loop running alongside a loading platform/dock and a short bay siding behind the south end of the platform. The stone building, with an apex slate roof, at the north end of the platform was an almost identical structure to that which always stood at Praze, the next station to the north. This building incorporated from south to north: store and lamp rooms, the station master's office, the booking office, a general waiting room and, at the far north end, the gent's urinal. Passenger numbers were not high at this first station; in 1903 9,239 passenger tickets were issued. This rose to 10,819 in 1913 but fell to 9,272 in 1923 and 5,272 in 1933. Five staff were based at Nancegollan in the early 1930s.

In 1937 the station was completely remodelled, now including a down running line, an up side passenger loop, up and down platforms, a goods loop behind the up platform and a large goods yard. An extra metal girder arch had to be added to the

Nancegollan. A general view from the station approach road also in 1954/5. Behind the up side shelter is the fan of four sidings laid out in the 1940s. On the far right is a glimpse of the 1937 signal box at the north end of the up platform.

west end of the original stone road overbridge north of the station to span the goods loop. The main brick built station building, now on the down platform, had a large horizontal platform canopy and an apex slate roof. Adjacent to it at the south end was a red brick store with an apex roof at right angles to the platform. Passengers on the up platform were provided with an open front wooden shelter with a small canopy. The new station came into use on 19th September 1937, now a crossing point – the only one on the Helston branch.

The post 1937 freight facilities, sited behind the up platform, were linked to the main running line via the long goods loop. Three dead end sidings were laid in the late 1930s, parallel to the loop. In the early 1940s the outermost of the sidings was removed to permit the layout of four sidings curving west at right angles, these being needed to assist in the construction of nearby airfields. Between the goods loop and the innermost of the original three sidings was a long loading platform (187 ft). Also provided in the yard was a large prefabricated building for the storage of large quantities of agricultural produce exported from Nancegollan. Old coach and wagon bodies also gave extra storage in the yard. During the summers from 1958 to 1962 a camping coach was based at the station, holiday makers using the station's washing and toilet facilities.

From September 1937 traffic movements were controlled from a GWR style signal box (30 levers) beyond the north end of the up platform adjacent to the road overbridge. Its lower storey was red brick, its upper storey wood with a slate apex roof. Steps led down to the end of the platform. In the pre 1937 era only a ground frame south of the first building controlled the points and signals.

Passenger services ended at the beginning of November 1962, goods facilities ceased with the closure of the branch in early October 1964, the first Cornish branch to close. Today only the two sections of the stone and girder bridge survive and industrial units cover the former station site and the goods yard. A solitary rusting lamp post stands in the cutting north of the bridge.

NANSTALLON HALT

OPENED: Goods – c 1888.
Passengers – 1st June 1906/2nd July 1906 (on the Bodmin – Wadebridge line originally opened through this site in 1834).
CLOSED: Passengers – 30th January 1967.
Goods – 2nd May 1960.

Sources vary slightly regarding the opening date of this facility on the line between Bodmin and Wadebridge. Most state that it was 2nd July 1906 but a report in the *West Briton* newspaper indicated that it opened a month earlier on 1st June, the day

Nanstallon Halt. The longer concrete replacement platform in the early 1960s. The GWR pagoda hut had been retained after its introduction on the earlier wooden platform, an unusual feature on this predominantly LSWR line (see text).

Nanstallon Halt. An early picture looking west at the original short wooden platform without even a shelter. Although the platform dated from mid 1906, the signal box and level crossing gates had probably operated from 1888. A GWR pagoda style shelter was subsequently added.

when the London & South Western Railway introduced steam rail-motors between Wadebridge and Bodmin.

Sited midway between the settlements of Nanstallon a half mile to the south-east and Boscarne a quarter mile to the north, it stood immediately east of a gated level crossing that carried the road connecting the two. West of this crossing was a short siding on the south side of the single track line that once terminated by a small goods shed. This siding and a squat LSWR style signal box on the north side of the line probably dated from 1888, the box controlling the level crossing gates.

The platform, on the north side of the line, was originally a very short timber structure without a shelter. One was soon erected, surprisingly a GWR pagoda style structure. This was probably provided at the instigation of the GWR which had run trains on the generally LSWR line since 1888 running between Bodmin Road and Wadebridge. These were introduced with the completion of the Bodmin to Boscarne loop in that year. The platform was later replaced by a concrete structure but the pagoda hut was retained.

The goods siding closed at the beginning of May 1960 and it seems likely that the suffix halt came at this point after goods facilities ceased. The halt remained open until 30th January 1967 when passenger services between Bodmin Road and Wadebridge were withdrawn. The signal box lasted a further eleven months as freight traffic continued on the line; it closed on 17th December 1967. Today the concrete platform survives beside the Camel Trail. With the exception of the front edge, it is fenced off and a garage for a nearby property stands at the centre. Above its doors is a notice 'Nanstallon Halt'. A fine running in board in green and white Southern style has been erected on the platform itself. The Bodmin & Wenford Railway is aiming to extend its line from Boscarne as far as Nanstallon as the first phase of its long term ambition to reach Wadebridge, the track being laid alongside the Camel Trail. At Nanstallon a two carriage long platform would be constructed close to the original halt.

NEWMILLS

OPENED: 1995
CLOSED: Remains open for services on the Launceston Steam Railway.

The western terminus of the Launceston Steam Railway (see Launceston (Steam Railway) text).

NEWQUAY

OPENED: Goods – 1st June 1874 (with the commencement of freight services on the Cornwall Minerals Railway, Newquay – Fowey).
Passengers – 20th June 1876 (with the commencement of passenger services on the Cornwall Minerals Railway, Newquay – Fowey).
CLOSED: Passengers – remains open for services on the Par – Newquay branch.
Goods – 7th September 1964.

The coming of the railway to Newquay was related initially to the transport of minerals and clay from Cornwall's inland mines and quarries to the harbour. The first tramway, constructed by the local landowner,

J T Treffry, carried loaded wagons on 29th January 1849. The Cornwall Minerals Railway was formed in 1872 with the aim of linking the north and south coasts of Cornwall by taking over and extending already existing tramways leading to Newquay and to Fowey. Freight movements between these two towns began at the beginning of June 1874. By that time, however, iron mining was in decline and china clay extraction was in a slump. To generate extra income a passenger service began on the north – south line in June 1876 using small four wheeled coaches.

The arrival of passenger trains in Newquay without doubt marked a turning point in the history of the town. Trade at the harbour had always suffered in competition with that at the south coast ports, which enjoyed the advantage of being on the English Channel. From this time however, Newquay began to exploit its major asset of attractive sandy beaches. The metamorphosis from a fishing and trading port to a holiday resort had begun. The significance of this was reflected in the enthusiastic welcome for the inaugural passenger service. A local holiday was declared and it is recorded that the crowded station was gaily decorated with flags. The arrival of the first train was greeted with the playing of the national anthem. In his welcoming speech the chairman of the local Board said, 'We feel sure that the extension of the railway system to Newquay will attract thousands of visitors to our beautiful beaches and magnificent cliffs and materially contribute to the prosperity of the neighbourhood'. The following events, often taking place when new railway lines were operated, included a lunch at Prout's Hotel (now the Red Lion Inn), triumphal arches, a procession, teas for 200 children and finally a bonfire and fireworks. There was clearly much optimism and there is no doubt that, after a slow start, the railway played a major role in the growth of Newquay and the development of a large tourist industry, particularly between the late Victorian era and the end of the 1950s.

The station, sited a little inland from the cliff top overlooking Newquay Bay and Great Western Beach, evolved over many years reflecting the increase and decrease in passenger numbers. On an approximate north – south alignment, the original structure, built by John Ennor, comprised a single west facing platform behind which was a granite building containing the main facilities. A small Cornwall Minerals Railway signal box stood beyond the south end of the platform on the up (east) side and a small one road stone engine shed, opened on 1st June

Newquay. A large crowd of excursionists arrive at Newquay in the summer of 1903. The photo provides a rare view of the station prior to the major expansion which came into use from June 1905. These changes involved the removal of the turntable in front of the engine.

1874, was on the down side opposite the end of the platform. This shed was accessed via a trailing siding from a loop line linked to a small turntable at the buffers end of the line beyond the north end of the station. To the west of the station itself were two goods sidings and beyond this again a link line that ran north via a level crossing over Station Road (now Cliff Road) to the Harbour branch. With a passenger service of only three or four trains per day on the line to Par and little goods traffic these limited station facilities were adequate until the early 1900s, though a W H Smith bookstall was provided in 1896.

As from 2nd January 1905 services into Newquay

Newquay. In 1962 two DMUs stand in the station - that to the left by the original platform, that to the right by the east face of the island platform. To the left of the photograph is the north end of the granite built main station building.

Newquay. A 'Metro' 2-4-0 T stands with a train to Par at the original single face platform in about 1910. The main building is on the right of this picture. The two face island platform (left) came into use on 7th June 1905.

began on a new GWR branch from Chacewater via St Agnes and Perranporth. To accommodate the increased traffic both from this line and from a growing volume of holidaymakers both on day trips and for longer holidays major expansion of the station took place in 1904/5, coming into use from 7th June 1905. The work included an extension of the original single Cornwall Minerals Railway platform, which became platform 1, and the construction of an island platform, platforms 2 and 3. The old Cornwall Minerals Railway signal box was demolished to accommodate the single face platform extension and replaced in 1905 by a GWR box on the down side, south of the station in front of a new (1st May 1905) two road stone engine shed, north of which was a large turntable. This latter replaced the earlier turntable beyond the north end of the station from June 1905. The old engine shed had been demolished in 1904. An enlarged goods yard contained a larger goods shed with one through siding and a canopy on the east road side and an office at the north end. Also in the yard was a 5 ton capacity crane and cattle pens. A diagram dated 1912 indicates that the main station building contained from north to south: a cloakroom, an office, the station master's office, a waiting room, ladies' toilets and gent's urinals. A stone building with a small canopy across the north end of the station beyond the buffers was used for mail and parcels traffic. Parcels traffic was also handled in a separate pagoda style hut on the platform south of the main building; beyond this was a metal oil store. Canopies protected passengers on both platforms; an additional canopy ran between the platforms behind the buffers.

The harbour line closed in 1926 and was removed in 1928. This was followed by the closure of the engine shed and turntable on 22nd September 1930 to allow extension of the sidings. The shed itself was demolished in August 1936. The volume of holiday traffic was increasing and in order to accommodate the longer trains the original single face platform was extended by a wooden section in April 1928 and lengthened again in concrete components from 9th July 1934. The island platform was extended on a slight curve in spring 1938. Water columns were erected on the south ends of the platforms. A number of sidings for carriage storage were laid in 1936 beyond the far west side of the goods yard. Double track on the Tremance viaduct south of the station came into use from 20th March 1946. The platforms were again lengthened at this time and the 1905

Newquay. View on 30th August 1951 of the building at the north of the station behind the buffers, then used for mail and parcels. A van is being loaded underneath the canopy.

Newquay. A view north from the remaining section of the island platform (originally no.2) on 31st October 2008, the single track terminates at buffers alongside the photographer. The surviving canopies surround an open concourse with seats. The main station building overlooking Station Road (right) had been demolished in 1992.

signal cabin was replaced by a 45 lever frame box. The number of passenger tickets issued varied greatly over the 1903 – 1933 period. In the former 22,530 were issued; the figure rose to 85,649 in 1913 and to 102,758 in 1923. There was then a fall to 46,891 in 1933. The number of staff employed at Newquay rose from 18 in 1903 to 27 in 1938.

Following a post-war peak in the mid 1950s when up to 20,000 passengers arrived at Newquay on a summer Saturday, decline began from the early 1960s. This started with the closure of the line from Chacewater in February 1963. Newquay's goods facilities were withdrawn in September 1964; the goods yard sidings were lifted and goods shed demolished soon after. The outer line alongside the island platform was shortened in 1966. Two of the carriage sidings were lifted in 1968 and a further two a year later. This latter severely restricted the number of trains that could be stored at Newquay. Further decline came when the extensions to platform 1 were declared unsafe and use was restricted to the original section. The long island platform canopies were cut back on 9th June 1964; at the same time the water columns were demolished. Further sidings were removed in the mid 1980s.

In late 1987 the last scheduled locomotive hauled train ran into Newquay and soon after the engine run round between the platforms was removed. From 11th October 1987 all remaining track was lifted except a single line running alongside the outer side (platform 3) of the island platform. The signal box also closed on that date and subsequently was destroyed in a fire. From 18th January 1988 the single track was diverted to the inner side of the island platform (platform 2), this still being the case today. Use of the track alongside platform 1 had by then ceased.

Today the trains terminate at buffers alongside the old platform 2, some way south of the remaining canopies which surround an open concourse area with seats. On the west side of the concourse is a small building, acting from 2001 as a travel centre, open only in the summer months. Overlooking the concourse is a café. The fine stone building on the east side was demolished in 1992, a small section of the building at the north end remains and a row of modern shop units has been developed in front of it overlooking Cliff Road. Entrance to the station is now gained through an arch at the west end of the shop units. Passengers on the one platform now in use are served by a small modern brick shelter, its canopy supported by three stanchions. This shelter replaces an earlier bus stop type shelter. Also on the platform is a small ticket office only open in the summer.

Today Newquay is served by branch line trains from Par. In the 2009 spring timetable seven trains ran per weekday in each direction but no service on Sundays. This was a significant improvement over that provided in recent years. In the summer 2008 timetable the local services were supplemented by through trains to and from London, Manchester and Newcastle, all using the single remaining platform.

OTTERHAM

OPENED: 14th August 1893 (with the opening of the Tresmeer – Camelford section of the North Cornwall Railway).
CLOSED: Passengers – 3rd October 1966.
Goods – 7th September 1964.

At a height of 800 ft above sea level, less than one mile east of the summit of the North Cornwall Railway to Wadebridge, Otterham was the most exposed station on the line. It opened in mid August 1893 when services commenced on the third section of the North Cornwall Railway from Tresmeer to Camelford. In a thinly populated area, it primarily served the village of Otterham some two miles by road, and one mile by footpath, to the north-east. It was also the rail head for a number of small rural villages and hamlets and coastal settlements from Crackington Haven to the north and Boscastle to the west. The coming of the railway was a key factor in the development of tourism along this section of the north Cornwall coast. Otterham station had good road links, being sited at the junction of the A39 and B3262 and a number of road services brought passengers and goods to the station from a wide area.

On an east – west alignment, Otterham was a passing place on the generally single track line, with up (towards Launceston) and down stone built wide platforms, immediately to the east of the overbridge carrying the A39 from Bude to Camelford. Inter platform movements were via a rail level board crossing at the east end of the platforms. The main station building, towards the west end of the up platform, was of a standard North Cornwall Railway design comprising a two storey station master's house at the west end and a single storey wing to the east. It was constructed of local stone with Portland stone quoins and decoration. The west side of the upper storey of the station master's house was slate hung, giving extra protection against the weather. The station facilities of the booking hall and office, station master's office, parcels office and porters' room were within the single storey wing but the ladies' waiting room and cloakroom were in the ground floor of the house. The gent's toilet was in a single storey structure on the west end of the house. The station master's accommodation was fairly extensive but with no bathroom and the W C in the back yard. To the west of this main building on the up platform, and adjacent to the road bridge, was a small stone open front shelter. A larger open front stone shelter stood opposite the main building on the down platform. Lighting was by oil throughout the life of the station.

Passenger numbers were never high at Otterham. In 1928 3,831 passenger tickets were issued; the figure fell to 2,136 in 1936. Over the same period the number of tickets collected fell from 4,512 to 3,208. During the Second World War, on 1st October 1942, a large airfield opened at Davidstow Moor, some two miles to the south. At 970 ft it was the highest airfield in the United Kingdom. It remained operational for only two years and closed in 1945. The RAF and USAF station had generated considerable passenger and goods traffic at the station.

The goods facilities were concentrated in a yard behind the up platform. Two sidings were accessed by a link track that trailed back from the up line east of the station. Both of these sidings accommodated approximately 20 goods wagons. Alongside the sidings were a number of stores used by local merchants and in the 1930s the Southern Railway erected a fertiliser and seed store house for leasing. There was no specific goods shed in the yard but a corrugated iron goods shed stood on the east end of the up platform. Alongside were a cattle pen and a 2½ ton capacity crane. The yard handled large

Otterham. A general view east in 1963, the main station building on the up platform includes the two storey station master's house. Beyond the building is a corrugated iron goods shed at the east end of the platform adjacent to the signal box. An open front stone shelter serves passengers on the down platform (right).

Padstow. Crowds greet the first train to arrive at the station on 27th March 1899. The mixed carriage train is hauled by an Adams 4-4-0. The 1899 signal box is to the left.

amounts of goods related to the surrounding countryside. This included foodstuffs and fertilisers and also, like a number of stations on the line, the export of rabbits. The cattle market at Hallworthy was a particular source of traffic. From the end of the Second World War a Cow & Gate dairy factory, developed on the former airfield site at Davidstow, exported some of its products through Otterham station. Camping coaches stood in the yard in 1935. Goods facilities were withdrawn in early September 1964.

Otterham signal box, a stone and brick structure with multi-pane wooden windows and a slate roof, was beyond the east end of the up platform. Unlike some of the other stations on the line, the economics of the 1930s did not require the transfer of the single line tablet, telephone and telegraph equipment to the booking office. The box closed, together with the down side loop through the station, on 7th February 1965, the loop and sidings being removed in the following October. Until its final closure in October 1966 the few trains used the up platform.

The station master's post was retained during the 1930s, taking control also of the stations at Tresmeer and Egloskerry. North of the goods yard a terrace of six houses was provided by the railway for its staff. Built in 1894 they cost £1,312. Otterham station became an unstaffed halt as from 20th September 1965.

Today the station building survives as a house, though when viewed in March 2009, it was in a rather poor condition with a caravan on the former trackbed and a 'For Sale' notice on the fence. The platforms are grassed over with some of the edging still visible. To the north of the house a caravan park was originally on part of the site but this has now been replaced by an estate of chalet type housing 'Otterham Park' with the date of 1996 on the sign. The area is now known as Otterham Station, shown as such on the modern Ordnance Survey map. The A39 road bridge was demolished as a part of a road widening scheme. The railway cottages north of the station site survive in residential use.

PADSTOW

OPENED: 27th March 1899 (with the opening of the Wadebridge – Padstow section of the North Cornwall Railway).
CLOSED: Passengers – 30th January 1967.
Goods – 7th September 1964.

On the west bank of the River Camel close to the estuary, Padstow, with its sheltered harbour on the north coast of Cornwall, was an important port from the sixteenth century, trading with Ireland and other ports on the Bristol Channel. Shipbuilding also developed and dominated in the early nineteenth century. By the end of the 1880s the industry was in decline, the last ship being launched in 1889. From the late 1840s the traders and residents had become increasingly concerned that Padstow was isolated from the evolving Cornish railway system. This was aggravated by the fact that the Bodmin & Wadebridge Railway, opened in 1834, was so close. There were

Padstow. A view looking north in the early 1900s including an LSWR train at the station, the rail served fish auction shed and the then South Western Hotel. The turntable in the foreground is in its original position before the construction of the Railway Jetty and its sidings.

therefore great hopes for a revival in Padstow's fortunes with the arrival of the railway in late March 1899, following the completion of the last link of the North Cornwall Railway from Wadebridge. Direct trains could now run over the North Cornwall Railway to Exeter via Launceston and also to Bodmin Road on the Cornwall Railway between Plymouth and Penzance. It was anticipated that the railway would boost the prospects for the fishing industry and tourism. In the latter case this would be in the form of day trippers and long stay visitors. For these visitors the South Western Hotel (from 1915 The Metropole) was opened in May 1901 at a cost of £12,000 on a site overlooking the harbour. The date of 1900 is prominent on the front wall. Road transport was laid on to other local beauty spots.

Padstow. A view north towards the buffers in 1962. Note the large station master's house and the gent's toilet in a lean-to structure on its south end. To the right are carriage sidings and, above the canopy, the now Metropole Hotel dominates the scene.

Developed largely on reclaimed land and the site of an earlier shipyard, the station was on an approximate north – south alignment. At its opening it comprised a single one face platform some 100 yards long; by 1912 it had been lengthened by 120 ft at the north end. The layout included a platform track and a run-round loop together with sidings running north towards the South Quay at the harbour entrance. Alongside these sidings was a fish auction shed (160 ft x 50 ft) built by the North Cornwall Railway. In 1912 this was extended by 100 ft. A small goods yard was also laid out from the outset on the down side behind the south end of the platform. Subsequent track developments included the provision of a carriage storage siding parallel to the run-round loop (1905), extension of the fish shed sidings and the laying of two long sidings on a new Railway Jetty that created an outer basin. This new layout generally came into operation from about August 1914. This major extension of the sidings resulted in the fish traffic dominating activities at Padstow for some years. The tonnage of fish carried was over 3,000 in 1911. The importance of fish generated traffic was emphasised in about 1930 when the Southern Railway built an enlarged fish shed. Some 1,000 wagons of fish left Padstow per year at that time.

The station building, a stone structure of a standard North Cornwall Railway design, comprised a two storey station master's house at the south end with a single storey wing to the north. The slate roof had overhanging eaves and three tall chimneys. A wooden canopy with a saw tooth valance protected passengers on the platform. There was a small canopy over the road side entrance to the booking hall; this was removed in later years. The station's main facilities of the booking hall and office, parcels office and porters' room were within the single storey wing but the ladies' waiting room and cloakroom were in the ground floor of the house. The gent's toilet was in a lean-to structure on the south end of the house. The station master's accommodation was fairly extensive but with no bathroom and the W C in the backyard. At the south end of the platform was a metal lamp store. Passenger numbers were generally high at Padstow: in 1928 17,492 passenger tickets were issued and 34,512 collected; in 1936 the equivalent figures were 11,901 and 27,918. The staff numbers were also relatively high, the post of station master being retained until the station's closure.

The goods yard, to the rear of the south end of the platform, included one main siding leading from the down line. This ran alongside a small stone goods shed terminating adjacent to a cattle dock and pen at the back of the platform. The shed had small horizontal canopies over the road and rail side doors. Another shorter siding was removed in 1933. The volume of freight traffic handled in the yard was modest compared with Wadebridge; this included imports such as coal, fertiliser, building materials and timber in addition to household goods. Exports included cattle and, as at many Cornish stations, rabbits. The large volumes of fish exports were handled at the fish shed and sidings on the up side; these sidings, at their maximum, were some 1½ miles long. By the late 1940s, the volume of fish exports was declining much then being transported by road.

Rail movements at Padstow were controlled from an 18 lever square stone and brick box with wooden windows and an apex slate roof and porch. Opened on 12th December 1899, it stood at the south end of the platform. There was no engine shed at Padstow but in 1900 a servicing point and a 55 ft turntable were installed south-east of the station on the river side. This had to be moved in 1914 when the Railway Jetty sidings were laid. The turntable was replaced in April 1947 by a 70 ft turntable needed to accommodate the Bulleid Pacific locomotives hauling the long distance holiday trains to the resort. It ceased to be used in the early 1960s.

Padstow. Looking south on 12th March 2009 along the former platform towards the station building. To the left is the large modern building which, since 2001, has replaced the old fish auction shed.

Transfer of rail operations at Padstow to the BR Western Region in 1963 was said to herald the run down of facilities, the withdrawal of goods facilities coming in early September 1964. The carriage siding, dock side tracks and those on the Railway Jetty were removed over the period January to March 1965. The down side yard and the signal box were closed from 9th January 1966 but the run around loop was retained until passenger services ceased, any change of points still required being operated by a two lever ground frame. From early 1965 long distance through passenger services ceased with rail cars linking Padstow and Wadebridge to Bude line trains at Halwill Junction in west Devon. This basic service ceased on 1st October 1966. Limited passenger services continued to Bodmin Road until these too ceased on 30th January 1967 and Padstow station closed.

Today the station building, minus the canopy, survives as Station House, occupied by offices of Padstow Town Council. Sections of railings and platform remain. The 1930s fish shed survived for many years, a section housing the Padstow Shipwreck Museum. This shed has now been replaced by a large modern structure that is Phase 1 of Padstow Town Council's Waterfront Development; it was formally opened in 2001 by the town mayor. Funded by the Town Council, North Cornwall District Council, the European Regional Development Fund and the South West Regional Development Agency, the building was the 2000 winner of the CPRE/RIBA Cornwall

Architecture Award. When viewed in March 2009 occupiers included Rick Stein's Fish and Chip Shop and Deli, Padstow Fisheries, Padstow Seafood School and Rig Marine Chandlery. Some of the station site is used for car parking at the northern end of the Camel Trail, a cycle and pedestrian way, using the former trackbed from Bodmin and Wadebridge. Fifteen cycle stands are available at the front of the building and nearby is 'Padstow Cycle Hire'. The Hotel Metropole still stands overlooking the harbour and former railway site.

Par. The east road side elevation recorded on 7th July 1963. Note the small canopy protecting the entrance to the booking office. This canopy and the remainder of the building, apart from the two tall chimneys, survive today in excellent condition. St Austell speedway is well advertised!

PAR

OPENED: 4th May 1859 (with the opening of the Plymouth – Truro section of the Cornwall Railway).

CLOSED: Passengers – remains open for services on the Plymouth – Penzance main line and the Par – Newquay branch.
Goods – 1st June 1964.

Par opened in May 1859 on a passing loop of the broad gauge main Cornwall Railway line between Plymouth and Truro. The line west to St Austell was doubled as from 15th October 1893 and east to Lostwithiel from 19th December 1894, both after the abolition of the broad gauge. The station, on a generally north-south alignment, became a junction from 1st January 1879 with the opening of a standard gauge link line west to St Blazey on the north-south Newquay to Fowey line of the Cornwall Minerals Railway, which had opened to goods traffic in 1874 and for passenger trains in 1876. Between 1876 and 1878 passengers were conveyed by horse drawn coaches between the St Blazey and Par stations. There was no direct running between the main and link lines until 1892 when the broad gauge was abolished on the former. From this time Par station served trains on the Plymouth to Penzance main line and also trains running to Fowey and Newquay via St Blazey. In this latter case a train often left Par and was split at St Blazey, one half taking twelve minutes on the journey south to Fowey and the other half taking fifty five minutes to reach Newquay on the north coast. Passenger trains to Fowey ceased in July

Par. The station complex in a photograph dated as about 1898, some 14 years after a major re-build. The main building on the down platform is to the left. On the island platform (centre) is a large wooden structure serving passengers for the Newquay branch on the outer face and main line passengers on the inner. A goods train stands at the up main platform.

Par. An up main line train (centre) and branch train from St Blazey stand either side of the island platform during the 1903 floods. The fence on the island platform beside the branch train locomotive was removed when the platform was widened and lengthened in 1924. The large goods shed dominates the scene to the right.

1929, services to the port concentrating on the Lostwithiel to Fowey branch.

Station facilities developed over the period 1859 to 1892 including a major rebuild in 1884 to serve the new junction status. The result was a one face down platform and an island platform with the east face used by main line trains and the west by the Fowey/Newquay trains. The main stone built building with a large canopy, apex roof and two chimneys, was developed on the down platform; from south to north the building incorporated the ladies' cloakroom and toilet, the booking hall, the booking office, a parcels office, a store and the gent's toilet. A small wooden canopy protected the roadside entrance. The building was enlarged in 1908. On the island platform towards the north end was a wooden building also with a canopy and apex roof which from south to north incorporated the ladies' cloakroom and toilet, the ladies' waiting room, a general waiting room, a refreshment room and kitchen and a gent's toilet. At the south end of the island was a wooden canopy under which were seats protected by wooden screens. The main line platforms were lengthened in 1913 and the branch platform was also extended in 1924. A footbridge connected the down and island platforms, sited south of the main down side building and between the building and canopy on the island. Originally covered, it had lost its roof by the early 1960s.

Par's goods facilities were concentrated in a yard on the up side west of the island platform. It included a coal store, cattle pens, a 2 ton capacity crane and a weighbridge in addition to a large wooden goods shed through which ran two sidings. The shed was originally used for transhipment prior to 1892 with tracks of both broad and standard gauges running through. The yard closed in October 1964, general goods services had been withdrawn at the beginning of June. The goods shed was used for carriage storage until 1965 after which it was demolished. The sidings were altered in 1968 to accommodate a freightliner depot but this facility was short lived and the sidings were mostly lifted with one being retained for use by engineers.

An 1890 signal box, which replaced on earlier 1879 box, was originally off the south end of the island platform but the platform was subsequently extended beyond it. A 57 lever frame was installed from 1913 and a further panel in 1965. In 1985, following the closure of both the St Austell and Burngullow boxes, an electronic signal control panel was installed at Par, although levers continued to operate semaphore signals and points at Par itself. Beyond the box a large water tank supplied water columns at each end of the platforms. Some 24 staff were based at Par in 1924.

Par. A general view looking south in 1962. The extended and widened island platform is in the foreground. The footbridge has lost its roof.

Penmere Platform. A view north in the 1950s showing the single face platform, the booking office/waiting room and the metal goods shed.

In 1974 there were major changes, the entire layout being rationalised and simplified. The main island building was demolished. Today the station remains basically the same as after these 1974 changes. The down side building is generally closed to the public except for toilets at the north end. A booking office window faces the platform in front of which is a small metal and glass shelter. Under the surviving canopy on the island platform a wooden/ glass shelter serves passengers, erected to replace the demolished building; it supplements the earlier sheltered seats. The surviving signal box that continues to operate today is now the oldest in Cornwall. Main line trains all call at Par; the spring 2009 timetable scheduled seven weekday trains each way between Newquay and Par, a significant improvement in the service run in recent years. In the summer 2008 timetable two through London Paddington to Newquay trains were scheduled to call at Par, whilst one each to and from Newcastle and Manchester passed through the station.

PAR BRIDGE HALT

OPENED: July 1897 (on the St Blazey – Fowey line opened for passenger services through this site in June 1876).
CLOSED: 1908.

This was a non timetabled halt for visitors to Par Sands to the south of the Fowey line east of Par. Records suggest that only special excursions stopped here. One source suggests that it was also used by normal services on alternate Wednesdays in the summer. Whatever the truth, it is clear that Par Bridge Halt has the honour of being the least used of all stations and halts in Cornwall! No details of the halt are known.

PENMERE PLATFORM

OPENED: 1st July 1925 (on the Truro – Falmouth line originally opened through this site in August 1863).
CLOSED: Remains open for passenger services on the Truro – Falmouth branch.

At an estimated cost of £854 for the facilities and the work, Penmere Halt, as it was first called, was authorised on 9th October 1924 ‘ to serve a large housing estate in course of development’ on the west side of Falmouth. It opened at the beginning of July 1925. The term ‘platform’, which usually denotes a staffed halt, was soon applied to Penmere, a single platform (300 ft long) on the east side of the single line with a booking office/waiting shelter and metal goods shed. On 26th January 1928 an additional ladies’ waiting room and toilets for gentlemen and ladies, adjacent to the existing buildings, were authorised at a cost of £300, but the author has seen no evidence that these were constructed.

In 1940 a loop was installed leading to a fan of four sidings to the south of the platform on the up (towards Truro) side. These were in a Ministry of Defence oil depot which closed in March 1967. A photo of 1958 shows that the main building and goods shed were still in place but by 1993 only a small stone hut served passengers. After some years of neglect a group of local residents formed the ‘Friends of Penmere Station’. With the group’s encouragement a brick shelter with a wooden canopy supported by three stanchions was erected in 1999 similar to that now installed at a number of other

surviving small stations and halts in Cornwall. The work resulted in the receipt of a national award in September 2000. Two GWR era and two modern metal seats stand alongside the shelter and, when visited in late October 2008, Penmere was by some way the busiest of the stations on the Falmouth branch line.

PENRYN

OPENED: Passengers – 24th August 1863 (with the opening of the Truro – Falmouth section of the Cornwall Railway).
Goods – 5th October 1863.
CLOSED: Passengers – remains open for services on the Truro – Falmouth branch.
Goods – 8th November 1971 (except for private sidings later closed).

Built in the west of, and high above, the small town of Penryn, the station opened in August 1863 as a crossing point on the otherwise single track broad gauge line from Truro to Falmouth. For a period prior to 9th May 1887, it was named 'Penryn for Helston'; the suffix was then dropped as, on that date, the Helston branch opened. The main stone built building of Italianate design, with a narrow horizontal canopy and two tall chimneys, stood on the down (towards Falmouth) platform. From south to north the building incorporated the station master's office, booking offices, general waiting room, ladies' toilet, 1st class waiting room, cloakroom, parcels office and, finally, a gent's urinal. On the up platform was a matching stone waiting shelter, though without a platform canopy. Inter-platform movements were via a wooden board crossing at the north end.

Penryn's sizeable goods yard, serving a range of local industries and agriculture, was on the down side, with a large stone goods shed (67 ft x 45 ft) sited behind the south end of the platform. Access was from a trailing connection south of the station. One siding ran into the shed and two others served the yard, one between the platform and the shed and the other beyond the shed running alongside a loading dock. Movements at Penryn were originally controlled from an 1894 box beside and north of the main building on the down platform.

Major changes came at Penryn in 1923 when replacement of the life expired timber Penryn viaduct,

Penryn. An interesting photograph looking north showing the changed layout at the station shortly after it came into use on 24th June 1923. A raised path has been constructed across the old lines (centre right). The new platforms (left) are complete but unlit. A new signal box stands at the south end of the new down platform.

Penryn. A classic view in about 1910 looking north as a train to Falmouth hauled by a class 4-4-0 No 3521 approaches the platform and the waiting passengers. The layout is that which operated up until major changes in 1923.

Penryn. Looking south in 1963 along the 1923 down platform. The original station building and the goods shed are still in place seen behind the station running in board. These buildings have now been demolished and a new brick shelter stands on the down platform.

north of the station, involved realignment of the branch line. Track curvature through the station area was reduced, the crossing loop was lengthened and two new platforms were constructed, a little to the west of the originals. These were straighter than the previous structures and closer together because of the now standard gauge of the tracks. A replacement hip roof shelter was erected on the new up platform. On the down side the original main building was retained and initially was connected to the realigned new down platform by a raised path across the former running lines. These new arrangements came into use on 24th June 1923.

Also in 1923 two more sidings were laid out at the south end of the station together with a cattle dock. A further two sidings were also added at the north end; the main goods yard and shed remained in their original locations in the yard. The yard crane had a capacity of 6 tons. A 32 lever signal box was erected at the south end of the new down platform. Camping coaches were based in Penryn over the period 1934–38.

Facilities at Penryn were much reduced in the early 1970s. The goods yard closed in early November 1971; on the same date the signal box ceased to operate and the up side loop and all sidings at the Falmouth end of the station were taken out of use. The two sidings at the Truro end, broadly on the alignment of the original passing loop, remained for engineers' use until 1979 but were then lifted.

The goods shed was subsequently demolished though the original down side building remained, in later years in poor condition. In the mid 1990s this was also demolished, with much of the station site and goods yard then taken over for car parking. In recent years a new brick shelter with a canopy supported on three stanchions has been erected on the former down platform. It is of a style found at a number of small stations and halts that survive in Cornwall.

During late 2008/early 2009 a new 400 metre passing loop was laid at a cost of £7.8 million in a scheme led by Cornwall County Council, the principal aim being to allow a much enhanced service on the Falmouth branch. The loop and the revamped station were formally opened on 18th May 2009 by Kevin Lavery, the Chief Executive of the new unitary Cornwall Council. The old down platform has been lengthened and sub-divided, the southern end beyond the new loop (platform 2) is for Truro bound trains. Facilities at the new station include new platform surfaces, waiting shelters, ramp access and a new car park. Sections of the old up platform remain alongside the new loop.

PENZANCE

OPENED: 11th March 1852 (with the opening of the Redruth – Penzance section of the West Cornwall Railway).

CLOSED: Passengers – remains open for services on the Plymouth – Penzance line.
Goods – see text.

Sited close to the sea and on the east side of the town, Penzance station opened in March 1852 with the start of passenger services on the Redruth to Penzance section of the standard gauge West Cornwall Railway.

Penzance. This view dates between 1867 when the broad gauge arrived and 1876 when the large wooden goods shed (left) was largely destroyed by fire. To its right is the original West Cornwall Railway engine shed. To the right of the picture is the 1852 station building with its single face platform served by mixed gauge track.

Penzance. This view in about 1910 looking west from Chyandour Cliff road shows the changed station layout from 1879/80 with an enlarged roof, two side platforms and two central sidings for carriage storage. A Cornish Riviera express train stands at platform 1 (right).

There were no special celebrations at this time, these being delayed until the opening of the line east on to Truro on 25th August 1852. A public holiday was then declared in the town, special events included a lunch for the 'labouring men' and a celebratory lunch at the Ball's Hotel attended by the mayor and 120 guests. The many speeches referred to the momentous nature of the event with the completion of the link to Britain's rail network. This was seen to be a turning point in the history of Penzance. Mothers and children were given a special tea and in the evening there were a number of dinners, a firework display and dancing at the Prince's Hall until the small hours. There were also celebrations some 15 years later with the arrival of the first broad gauge passenger train on 1st March 1867, an event that marked the start of through trains to and from many parts of southern England. Broad gauge freight trains to the town had commenced in the previous November. These train movements became possible after a third rail at broad gauge was added to the original standard gauge line in 1866.

When opened in 1852, Penzance station had limited facilities very similar to those at a number of branch line terminals in the West Country, that is one platform used by both arrivals and departures, covered by a wooden train shed. Once open to longer distance broad gauge trains, there were many calls for the cramped facilities to be improved. This was achieved in 1879/80 with completion of an expanded station comprising, under an enlarged roof (250 ft x 80 ft), two side platforms and tracks between which were two sidings for carriage storage. The station site was aligned north-east to south-west and a key factor in its layout was that the original site sloped north-west to south-east thus requiring excavation on the north-west side to create level conditions. Reflecting this, the principal stone building across the south-west end of the station behind the buffers was partly at two levels. A number of further improvements and changes were made when the mixed gauge tracks at the station were changed back to standard in 1892.

The basic form of the buildings and track layout remained the same until the 1930s. In 1937, along with other major changes at the station, the platform format and track layout were altered to provide extra accommodation for holiday traffic. Permission had been granted for a major expansion of the station site. As a result there were now four longer platforms. An island structure to the north-west (platforms 1 and 2) and a one face platform to the south-east (platform 3) were under the original 1879/80 roof. A fourth platform face (no. 4) was added alongside the outside of the south-east wall. Platforms 3 and 4 combined beyond the roof to form a second island. The booking facilities and other offices were at street level in the main building at the south-west end behind the buffers, access to the platforms being via

Penzance. This view looking west in 1958 illustrates the final major layout change dating from 1937. This included an island platform and a side platform terminating at buffers under the roof and a further platform terminating alongside the outside of the south-east wall. These latter two platforms combined beyond the roof to form a second island. This layout remains today. The goods sidings to the left of the station have now been replaced by a bus station, information centre and car parking.

a balcony and flight of stairs. The main entrance was on the west corner of the building under a lantern roof. Waiting rooms, a parcels office and toilets were around the concourse behind the buffers and alongside the side down platform. Refreshment rooms were provided on the southern corner of the L shaped buildings. The main passenger exit was alongside the refreshment room in the south-east wall. In 1913 140,000 tickets were issued; by 1931 the figure had reduced to 82,224 with 1,130 season tickets and in 1937 the figures were 75,218 and 2,622. In 1903 52 were employed at the station; by the early 1930s the number had risen to 60 and by 1938 to 78.

Today the basic structure of the station remains the same though a significant action was the replacement of the roof in 1990 at a cost of £200,000. Passenger trains principally use platforms 1 to 3 with platform 4 in reserve or for storage. The use of the actual buildings has undergone major changes. The rooms behind the buffers at a higher level are no longer in public use, the travel centre/booking office and café now provided in pre-fabricated structures sited in the old concourse and toilets located alongside platform 3. The south-east interior wall is decorated with murals 'celebrating Cornwall and its vibrant creative scene'. The main entrance and exit are in this wall.

The history of the freight facilities and locomotive depots at Penzance is also one of change. In the early West Cornwall Railway era, goods traffic was concentrated on a cramped site between the station and Albert Quay. The yard contained a Brunel style wooden goods shed with two covered sidings, one of which extended beyond the shed to serve a loading platform and Albert Quay. The original 1852 West Cornwall Railway engine shed was between the goods station and the station building. In 1876 there was a serious fire at the goods shed and, when

Penzance. The booking office entrance at the west corner of the building beneath the lantern roof in about 1970.

Penzance. A view down from the booking office steps on 17th July 1960. A main line train stands at platform 1.

reconstructed, it was combined with the engine shed to form a larger shed with three covered sidings. Two further sidings terminated in loading docks, the longest of which was 270 ft. The goods shed incorporated a 140 ft long loading platform. Additional goods sidings were provided at Ponsandane, east of the station on the up side. During the late 1930s these were expanded to become the town's principal goods yard. The yard included a large goods shed coming into use from 1st December 1937. The yard has now closed, the site being occupied by a supermarket. The original goods yard beside the station was redeveloped, the shed being demolished. A number of loading bays with canopies were constructed for parcels and perishable goods, the latter being particularly important for local farmers. Land was also reclaimed from the sea to create a larger area for development. The use of these loading bays ceased in 1987 and today the area is unrecognisable with uses including the town bus station (forming a good public transport interchange with the railway), a new information centre and extensive car parking.

Similar changes have arisen with the locomotive facilities. As noted earlier, the original 1852 West Cornwall Railway shed was sited between the goods shed and the station. From 1876 to 1914 it was replaced by a two road shed beyond the north-east of the station. This was on the site of an earlier 1866 shed which had supplemented the original 1852 facility. At the 1876 shed was a workshop, coal stage and turntable. The constrained nature of the 1876 site precluded any further development and thus in 1914 the facilities moved again, a four road brick built motive power depot (210 ft x 66 ft) opening at Long Rock, a mile north-east of Penzance station on the up side. There was an additional bay on its north side for repair work. Long Rock was adapted for use as a diesel depot in 1958 and closed to steam on 10th September 1962. It continued to service diesels until 1976. It was then demolished and replaced by a new depot in October 1977 for use by High Speed Trains, costing some £1.5 million.

Train movements over the years have been controlled by signal boxes at the north-east end of the station on the up side. The original box, which was fitted with a new frame in 1892/3, lasted until 1912. A second box operated until 1938 when this too was replaced from 24th April by a hipped roof brick and timber structure with a 75 lever frame. This continued to operate after semaphore signals were replaced at Penzance as from 20th December 1981 and remains in use today.

PERRANPORTH

OPENED: 6th July 1903 (with the opening of the Chacewater – Perranporth section of the GWR Chacewater – Newquay branch).
CLOSED: Passengers and Goods – 4th February 1963.

During the nineteenth century the coastal village of Perranporth and the surrounding area were important

Perranporth. Looking south-east in about 1910 at the island platform, the two platform buildings with a wide all round canopy and the large brick goods shed. The steps down to the subway from the platform are below the 'way out' notice at the north end of the platform (left). In the foreground is a horse drawn portable steam engine, probably used for agricultural purposes.

for fishing and tin mining but there was clearly potential for tourism with the excellent large sandy beaches. A link to Cornwall's rail network was seen as a key factor in the realisation of this potential. The residents and traders of Perranporth were very concerned that other south west coastal towns and villages which had earlier rail links had a great advantage.

The station opened as a terminus in early July 1903 with the start of services on the Chacewater to Perranporth section of the GWR branch to Newquay. The extension on to Newquay opened on 2nd January 1905. To the east of the village centre and the beaches, the station was located a short distance south-east from a point where the line, in passing through the village, abruptly changed direction from south-west to north-east to north-west to south-east. A siting of the station closer to the centre and beaches was problematical as the line there was in a deep rock cutting. The problem was addressed some 28 years later when Perranporth Beach Halt was opened about a mile to the west.

The scale of the station buildings, on a north-west to south-east alignment was a clear indication of the hope there was for a great influx of visitors. From its opening Perranporth had a substantial wide stone island platform alongside which ran two tracks, this being a passing place on the Chacewater to Newquay line, a role also played by the stations at St Agnes and Shepherds. The station facilities at Perranporth were housed within two adjacent brick buildings linked by a wide all round wooden canopy. There were also three tall chimneys. The northern larger building contained a cloakroom and the booking facilities and the southern the ladies' waiting room and the gent's toilet. Access to the long platform was via a subway towards the northern end that linked to the station approach road to the west.

Perranporth. A view south along the island platform in the early 1960s shortly before the station closed. The scale of the all round canopy is impressive. Beyond the buildings is a glimpse of the 23 lever signal box. To the right is the goods shed with an office at the north end.

Perranporth Beach Halt. Looking north-east in 1962 along this 1931 concrete component platform with corrugated iron building designed to serve passengers travelling to and from the beach.

The top of the subway steps was surrounded by metal railings. In later years there was a small metal hut at the north end of the platform beyond the subway.

In the six months following its opening in July 1903 6,287 passenger tickets were issued. In 1913 the full year figure was 16,612; this rose to 23,907 in 1923 but then more than halved to 10,249 in 1933. In the early years many services on the line were by steam rail cars introduced in 1905. The fall in the 1933 figure can be attributed to the opening of Perranporth Beach Halt in 1931, closer to the beach. There was a major increase in rail passengers to Perranporth after the Second World War. In the 1950s through carriages ran to and from Paddington on summer Saturdays, the journey taking nearly eight hours! Trains had sections to Penzance and Perranporth which divided at Chacewater. When opened there was a staff of seven based at the station but this was down to five in 1938.

Perranporth's goods facilities were to the west and south of the station buildings on the up (towards Chacewater) side of the line. A long siding trailed from the up side station loop beside the north end of the island platform. It ran south-east through a brick built goods shed which had a goods office attached to the north end, a small horizontal canopy over the road side entrance and a small chimney at the north end of the slate roof. From the north end of this siding a short spur siding trailed back beside cattle pens, which were apparently not used to any great extent. Rail operations at the station were controlled from a 23 lever wooden signal box on the south end of the platform which was open throughout the life of the line. The provision of water for the locomotives was important on the steeply graded line and north of the station, beyond a rail overbridge, was a metal water tank on tall legs and also a pumping house. These supplied water columns, one at the south end of the platform and the other between the main building and the subway.

Passenger and goods facilities ceased at Perranporth early in February 1963 with withdrawal of services on the Chacewater to Newquay line and the buildings were demolished. The station site has been redeveloped as an industrial estate, Old Station Business Park. Station Road is another reminder of the earlier era at Perranporth.

PERRANPORTH BEACH HALT

OPENED: 20th July 1931 (on the Chacewater – Newquay line originally opened through this site in July 1903).

CLOSED: 4th February 1963.

As noted in the text relating to Perranporth, that station was not conveniently sited in relation to the fine sandy beaches. Thus, with the ever growing tourist trade, the GWR decided to erect a halt on the line west of the existing station and about a quarter of a mile from the main beach. Opening in July 1931 Perranporth Beach Halt on the up (east) side of the single track line, had a long concrete component platform at the centre of which was a corrugated iron structure. Facilities at the halt included a waiting room, booking office, three seats, electric lighting and an approach path. The total cost was £720. In December 1948 approval was given for the renewal of the building and for the provision of toilet accommodation but the author has seen no evidence that these changes were implemented. The halt was only staffed in the summer months; in some records, being staffed, it was called 'Perranporth Beach Platform'.

The line and the halt closed in early February 1963 and seven years later a section of the concrete platform was removed and re-erected at a new facility at Falmouth, which opened early in December 1970 (see Falmouth Town text). Today the site of the halt has been redeveloped for housing, 'Taverners Halt'. An abutment of the bridge to the south-west over St Michael's Road and the railway embankment south-west from the bridge remain, the latter in use as a footpath.

Perranwell. A general view north in about 1960 looking at the down side platform and the low granite building with two tall chimneys. To the left the front of the up side shelter can just be seen.

PERRANWELL

OPENED: 24th August 1863 (with the opening of the Truro – Falmouth section of the Cornwall Railway).
CLOSED: Passengers – remains open as a request stop for services on the Truro – Falmouth branch.
Goods – 4th January 1965.

The station opened in August 1863 as simply Perran. From 19th February 1864 it was renamed Perranwell after a village half a mile to the south west. It was built on a spur of high ground between two typical Cornish valleys across which the line ran on high viaducts, the Carnon to the north and the Perran to the south. The actual site is in a cutting at the Falmouth end and on an embankment at the other.

Perranwell. The outstanding feature of the station was the 1894 elevated signal box under which ran a siding into the goods yard. Behind the box, in this view of about 1960, is the large stone goods shed with the office at its south end.

On a curve in the line, Perranwell had a passing loop on the original broad gauge line. The principal low granite building, with a wide horizontal canopy and two tall chimneys, was on the down side. It contained booking and parcels offices, ladies' and general waiting rooms and toilets. A matching waiting shelter without a canopy stood on the up platform. Movements between the platforms were via a rail level board crossing at the north-east end. Staffing ceased on 6th May 1968.

Perranwell goods yard (46 ft x 35 ft), with a large stone goods shed, was behind the down (towards Falmouth) platform. Three short sidings, which trailed back from the down line, ran through the goods yard, one into the goods shed which had an office at the south-west end. A camping coach stood in the yard in the summers of 1936-1939 and 1952-1964. The yard closed for general traffic in early January 1965, although occasional sugar beet and flower traffic continued for a further two years. A cattle dock and pens were erected in 1907 on the up side south of the station and an extra siding was added beyond the pens in 1920.

A particular feature of Perranwell was the 1894 elevated 21 lever signal box which straddled the siding that ran into the goods yard immediately behind the south-west end of the down platform. Its high position was required because of the curved nature of the line at this point which restricted visibility. The box closed on 18th April 1966, when the passing loop, up platform and up siding were taken out of use.

Today the signal box and station building have gone. A modern brick shelter serves passengers on the former down platform. The derelict redundant up platform can still be seen. The goods yard and shed are occupied by a scaffolding firm.

PORT ISAAC ROAD

OPENED: 1st June 1895 (with the opening of the Delabole – Wadebridge section of the North Cornwall Railway).
CLOSED: Passengers – 3rd October 1966.
Goods – 7th September 1964.

Just south of a country road between St Teath and Pendoggett, the station opened at the beginning of June 1895 with the start of services on the fifth section of the North Cornwall Railway from Delabole to Wadebridge. The name Port Isaac Road was very apt as the small coastal port was some three miles to the north-west. The village of St Teath was about two miles to the north. The potential for the transport of fish landed at Port Isaac and for the growth of tourism along the nearby north Cornwall coast was the impetus for the establishment of this isolated station.

On an approximate north-west to south-east alignment resulting from the very winding nature of the line in this area, Port Isaac Road was a passing place on a curve on the otherwise single track line. The up (towards Delabole) and down stone platforms alongside the two loops had Delabole slate copings. A rail level board crossing at the north-west end provided for inter-platform movements, there being no footbridge. As at the majority of stations on the North Cornwall line, the main station building was on the up platform. It was of the standard North Cornwall Railway design with, in this case, the two storey station master's house at the north-west end and a single storey wing to the south-east. The building was constructed of local stone with a slate roof; unlike a number of stations, the station master's house was not clad with protecting slates. As at St Kew Highway and Padstow there were overhanging eaves. The main station facilities of the booking hall and office, station master's office, parcels office and porters' room were in the single storey wing but the ladies' waiting room and cloakroom were in the ground floor of the house. The gent's toilet was in a small structure with a lean-to roof on the north-west end of the house. The accommodation for the station master was fairly extensive but with no bathroom

Port Isaac Road. Looking south-east towards Wadebridge in 1963. The main building, incorporating the station master's house, and the signal box are on the up platform (right). In the centre of the down platform is an open front stone shelter.

and with the W C in the backyard. An open front stone shelter served passengers in the centre of the down platform. In 1928 4,446 passenger tickets were issued at Port Isaac Road and 6,128 collected. The comparable figures for 1936 showed significant falls to 1,855 and 3,218. Some of the passenger traffic at the station was generated by the development of tourist accommodation in the Port Isaac area, one feature that originally prompted the development of the station.

Port Isaac Road. A view looking north-west at the up side main building. Unlike some other stations on the North Cornwall Railway line the house section is not slate clad. In the foreground is the 17 lever signal box.

The potential for goods traffic was, as also noted above, a key factor in the siting of Port Isaac Road, where appropriate facilities were constructed on the up side behind the platform. From just south of the up platform a long headshunt, extended in 1902, trailed back from the up side loop parallel to the line south to St Kew Highway. It was on a shelf site to keep it level with the station tracks, the line to St Kew Highway dropping sharply away. From this headshunt a long siding trailed back north-west into the goods yard, running alongside cattle pens, a small goods shed and a number of buildings operated by local traders for the storage of feeds, corn and fertilisers. The stone goods shed, matching the station building, had a large canopy on two legs over the rail side aperture and a small canopy over the road side door. Within the shed was a 2 ton capacity crane to deal with heavy loads. From this siding ran a short spur, extended also in 1902, that led to a loading dock at the south-east end of the up platform. On some plans it was called the 'Fish Dock'. It is recorded that in October 1897 some 150 tons of fish were despatched from Port Isaac Road to Exeter, Birmingham and London. Over the years a fair quantity of flowers and fruit was also despatched and also after 1918, like other stations in north Cornwall, Port Isaac Road handled exports of crates of rabbits. Goods facilities were withdrawn at the station in September 1964 and the yard was finally taken out of use in December 1965. Some fish continued to be exported on passenger trains until this too ceased with the withdrawal of services at the beginning of October 1966.

Port Isaac Road signal box, a square stone structure with multi-pane windows and a 17 lever frame stood on the up platform south-east of the main building. Unlike some other stations on the line the single line tablet equipment was not moved to the booking office during the economies of the early 1930s. Although the post of station master at the station was abolished in 1927, with the overall control passing to Camelford, a reasonable level of staffing continued at Port Isaac Road. Two signalmen also acted as porters, operating the station track loops until closure of the line

Following closure, the station building was used as an office for a nearby fertiliser firm. Subsequently it was renovated for residential use with the goods shed and other buildings adapted for business uses. Because of the relatively few changes, the building itself is one of the best preserved of the original structures on the former North Cornwall Railway.

PRAZE

OPENED: 9th May 1887 (with the opening of the Helston Railway, Gwinear Road – Helston).
CLOSED: Passengers – 5th November 1962.
Goods – 5th October 1964.

Close to the attractive Clowance woods and midway between the villages of Praze-an-Beeble and Crowan, the station was on an embankment south-east of a bridge carrying the line over the B3303 Camborne to Helston road. It opened with the start of services on the Helston branch in early May 1887. The track layout comprised a main running line on the up side and a goods loop on the down. On the single 223 ft long stone platform on the up side was the main building (60½ ft x 16½ ft) with a low slate roof topped by two brick chimneys. There was no platform canopy. Constructed of local stone with brick door and window surrounds, it contained the station's booking, waiting and toilet facilities. There was no rear entrance, access to the platform being via a small gate beside the north end of the building. A mushroom style water tower stood off the north end of the platform and beyond this was a platelayer's hut. There was no signal box at Praze, the single track layout being controlled from a ground frame contained within a wooden hut with a slate roof beside the north end of the main building. A small canopy covered the space between the building and the ground frame hut and also protected passengers entering the station via the gate. A red brick shed

Praze. A view in the 1960s, looking south-east showing details of the building doors and windows and the ground frame hut (right). Note the small canopy on the right between the building and the hut under which passengers accessed the platform

Praze. GWR 0-4-4 T No 34 stands with a branch train to Helston in about 1910. Crew and passengers pose for the camera in front of the stone building.

behind the ground frame hut provided extra storage space.

Passenger numbers at Praze varied considerably over the years. In 1903 8,551 passenger tickets were issued, the number rose to 10,306 in 1913, fell to 8,073 in 1923 and dropped again to 4,821 in 1933. Two men were employed here until 1930 but only one thereafter. At one time, in the early days, there was a station master. After the Second World War Praze was unstaffed.

Over the years there were few changes at Praze though in about 1950 the goods loop was changed to a siding, the connection to the running line at the south end being taken out. The siding and small adjacent yard with a weigh-house were used principally for truck loads of coal and agricultural produce. They remained in use until closure of the line to goods traffic in October 1964. Passenger services had ceased just under two years earlier at the beginning of November 1962. Today there is no trace of the station and a large dwelling 'Woodland Lodge' stands on the site with access from the B3303 south of the two surviving parapets of the rail overbridge.

PROBUS & LADOCK PLATFORM

OPENED: 1st February 1908 (on the Plymouth – Truro line originally opened through this site in 1859).
CLOSED: 2nd December 1957.

Opening at the beginning of 1908 it was sited between the stations at Grampound Road and Truro and served a largely agricultural area in particular the settlements of Probus, a mile to the south-east, and Ladock, two miles to the north. The two platforms serving the up and down tracks, were largely of wooden construction but at the east end evidence suggests that there were later brick

Probus & Ladock Platform. Looking south-west soon after its opening in 1908. Permanent way staff are clearly not expecting the imminent arrival of a train!

Quintrell Downs. Looking west in the early 1920s at the original pagoda style shelter in the centre of the platform. To the left is the then ground frame hut.

extensions. Both platforms had GWR style corrugated iron pagoda shelters which were elongated in the late 1920s. Photographic evidence indicates they were also repositioned at the west end. The term 'Platform' was the GWR term for a staffed halt and this was the case here with, at one time, three staff provided including a station master, the latter very unusual for a 'Platform' facility. Both passengers and parcels traffic were handled but not large goods traffic. In 1913 9,063 passenger tickets were issued and 3,032 parcels were handled, a total revenue of £827 compared with the direct staff costs of £98! By 1932 the total receipts were down to £392 and staff costs had risen to £385. By 1938 the position was a little better with receipts of £563 and staff costs of £374. By this last year the total number of passenger tickets issued had, however, fallen to 545. After the Second World War use continued to be low and Probus & Ladock closed in December 1957, a pre Beeching casualty. In its latter days it was unstaffed. No trace can now be seen.

QUINTRELL DOWNS

OPENED: 2nd October 1911 (on the Newquay branch, Par – Newquay, originally opened for freight services in 1874 and passenger services in 1876).
CLOSED: Passengers – remains open as a request stop on the Par – Newquay branch.
Goods – 7th September 1964.

Quintrell Downs Platform (the suffix was dropped in January 1956) opened in early October 1911 at the site of an earlier east – west aligned goods loop and siding. South-east of Newquay, it was immediately to the west of a level crossing carrying the main road from St Austell to Newquay (A392). When the 300 ft long stone platform was built on the up (north) side of the line, serving what was then a small rural community, the track layout changed to a single main running line and two sidings on the down side. At this time an original small signal box was closed and replaced by a ground frame hut on the down side of the line close to the level crossing, which contained levers for the operation of the goods yard sidings, signals and a crossing gate lock.

When originally opened, a typical GWR pagoda style hut was provided on the centre of the platform. By the early 1920s the ground frame was moved to within a metal waiting shelter at the east end of the platform close to the gates. Photographic evidence indicates that this shelter was markedly different from the earlier

Quintrell Downs. Again looking west, some 40 years later in 1962, showing a shelter in a revised position at the east end of the platform acting as a waiting room and also housing the ground frame.

pagoda hut, in particular with an entirely different roof form. One source suggests however that it was an adaptation of the earlier pagoda. The nameboard on the new shelter stated 'Quintrel Down Siding East Ground Frame'. The frame remained in use until 1981 when the crossing gates were removed, being replaced by automatic barriers across which trains today move very slowly. Some sixteen years earlier the goods sidings were closed and removed, goods facilities having been withdrawn in September 1964. Today the shelter has been replaced by an open metal and glass structure. Tall lamp posts provide night time illumination. Quintrell Downs, now a request stop, serves a growing local community that has developed to the south-east.

REDRUTH

FIRST STATION

OPENED: 23rd May 1843 (with the commencement of passenger services on the Hayle Railway, Hayle Foundry Square – Redruth).
CLOSED: 16th February 1852.
REOPENED: 11th March 1852.
CLOSED: Passengers – 25th August 1852.
Goods: 1st May 1967

SECOND STATION

OPENED: 25th August 1852 (with the opening of the Redruth – Truro section of the West Cornwall Railway).
CLOSED: Passengers – remains open for services on the Plymouth – Penzance line.
Goods: 17th June 1912 (see text).

The first station at Redruth was the eastern terminus of the Hayle Railway, which opened for goods traffic in June 1838 and for passenger traffic in May 1843. Just under nine years later, it closed briefly while work was undertaken by the West Cornwall Railway which, by an Act of 1846, had incorporated the Hayle Railway in order to improve it and extend the line east to Truro and west to Penzance. After just under a month's closure, this first Redruth station reopened in March 1852. Sited on the western side of the town west of Coach Lane and south of Blowinghouse Hill West, it comprised a single platform beneath a wooden train shed with an adjoining stone goods depot. Five months later it closed permanently to passengers when Redruth's second station opened on a northeast-southwest alignment a half mile to the east. Sited close to the town centre and west of the short (47 yards) Redruth tunnel, it served trains on the extension of the West Cornwall Railway to Truro. The site of the first station was then expanded as a goods depot.

Redruth. A rare photograph of the station in the West Cornwall Railway era. The main wooden building is on the up side and beside it is the large wooden goods shed. Note the then simple shelter on the down side.

Redruth. The town's first station, the eastern terminus of the Hayle Railway, which opened for passenger traffic in 1843. After its closure in August 1852, the site became a goods yard (Redruth West or Old Goods). In this 1937 view the original wooden train shed and adjoining stone goods depot are still clearly seen. The yard closed in 1967.

The development of the second station was an involved process undertaken over a seventy year period. Originally of standard gauge, broad gauge tracks were added through the station in 1866 when the control of the line changed to an amalgam of Companies including the GWR. The gauge reverted to standard in May 1892. When the station opened it was a passing place on the otherwise generally single track line to Truro. The line west to Carn Brea was doubled in July 1897, east as far as Drump Lane in 1911 and Scorrier only in 1930. The main wooden building on the up platform had a low pitched roof and small projecting horizontal canopy. A plan of 1912 indicates that it contained from south to north, the station master's office, the booking hall, the ladies, a waiting room, a parcels office and cloakroom. Adjoining it to the south was a large wooden goods shed. Passengers on the down platform were initially served by a simple open shelter but this was subsequently replaced by a wooden waiting room with a wide canopy, and a gent's urinal at its southern end. The platforms were linked by a lattice girder footbridge north of the two buildings.

Over the years there was a series of minor improvements to the 1852 station facilities, in particular in the early 1860s. The trigger for a major change came in 1912 when a new goods depot was opened at Drump Lane about a half mile to the north. This resulted in the closure of the main goods facilities at the station itself, thus releasing land for station redevelopment. The Falmouth Packet of 21st June 1912 stated 'It is hoped that the removal of the goods depot to Drump will result in the company using the space thus left at their disposal in the provision of a station worthy of the trade and size of Redruth on which matter the company has several times been approached by the town.' Despite this pressure, major changes did not come until the 1930s when the 1852 station building was demolished and the present red brick structure incorporating the booking, waiting and toilet facilities was erected. It was a later version of a standard GWR design. The earlier downside wooden waiting room (which had replaced the original shelter) was retained plus an extension on its southern end. Both buildings have projecting platform canopies, the up side a gable roof style and the down side an upward extension of the roof. A corrugated iron hut was later added to the south of the main building. The 1888 lattice footbridge was retained. The station suffered bomb damage on 20th March 1941.

In the 1920s and early 1930s the number of passenger tickets issued per year always exceeded 100,000. For example, in 1923 the station issued 127,547 tickets and 889 season tickets; in 1935 the equivalent figures were 101,059 and 1015. In 1913 29 employees were based at Redruth and this figure rose to 34 in 1932 and 35 in 1938. This large labour force was under the control of a class one station master.

The development of goods facilities at Redruth was in a similar way to the station, an evolving story. As noted earlier, the first goods yard and shed were adjacent to the first station west of the town. Following the withdrawal of the passenger services

Redruth. Looking north-east in 1920 with the main 1852 wooden building on the up platform (left). Dominating the scene is the large Methodist Chapel. Note the fine lattice footbridge.

Redruth. Again looking north-east on 17th August 1968. The 1852 building on the up side (left) has been replaced by the substantial 1930s brick structure with its fine canopy covering the whole width of the platform. The earlier down side wooden waiting shelter is still there, plus a small extension at its south-west end. When seen in autumn 2008 the shelter had been renovated.

from this site, it was retained as a goods depot known either as Redruth West Yard or the Old Goods Yard. Its use continued until the beginning of May 1967, in latter years acting only as a coal depot. Some track was removed in 1960 and the rest was lifted on 14th February 1968. Most of the site is now used as a local authority car park.

At the second station goods facilities were provided on both sides of the line, the principal facility being the large black timber goods shed on the up side south-west of the 1852 station building. The shed had separate entrances for road and rail vehicles and a central loading platform. Also provided in the yard were loading docks, cattle pens and a 6 ton capacity crane. With the opening of the new goods depot at Drump Lane most goods handling facilities were removed from the station site, general goods facilities being withdrawn in mid June 1912. A dead end siding was retained on the up side together with a short spur which terminated in a bay platform and loading dock, created in 1915, on the site of the former goods shed. This could also be used by terminating rail motors. Sidings behind the down platform were lifted in 1914. All those on the up side, together with connections to the main line, were

Redruth. A party of Local Rifle Volunteers on the up platform in about 1900. Note the extensive display of metal advertisements on the end wall of the 1852 wooden building. Above the building the end of the large goods shed can be seen.

Redruth. Passengers waiting to join the train in about 1910. The caption on the original post card states 'The weekly exodus to South Africa', referring to out-of-work miners going to South Africa to work in the gold fields. Friends and family are gathered on the bank above to see them off.

taken out of use in 1964.

Facilities at the Drump Lane goods depot were extensive including six sidings and a large red brick goods shed (160 ft x 49 ft) with a gabled slate roof. A partially glazed canopy extended for 135 ft along the road side of the shed, giving good protection over the three side doors. Extensions to the building contained offices and mess facilities. The shed itself contained two hand cranes and a 160 ft long internal platform. Sidings in the yard served a loading bank and an end loading dock; there was also a 5 ton capacity crane. Drump Lane Yard closed on 7th October 1978 and the site has now been redeveloped for housing, the sidings being removed in the late 1980s. Prior to 1914 a signal box behind the north end of the down platform controlled movements at the station. This was succeeded by a 34 lever box at the end of the down platform which operated from 1914 to 1955.

Today the main up side building, dating from the 1930s, is in reasonable condition with booking and waiting facilities. A privately run refreshment room serves passengers at the north end. The down side timber structure, which was in a poor condition, has now been renovated to include a covered alcove with metal seats. A metal and glass shelter also serves passengers on this platform. The open footbridge, with a GWR monogram and 1888 date, remains. The site of the old goods yard on the up side is a car park. Two buildings stand on the site of the small down yard. The old signal box has gone.

RESPRYN

OPENED: 4th May 1859 (with the opening of the Plymouth – Truro section of the Cornwall Railway).
CLOSED: 26th June 1859 (to the public with the opening on the following day of Bodmin Road).
October c. 1864 (private use by Lanhydrock House).

This was a private station about three quarters of a mile west of Bodmin Road station serving Lanhydrock House (now National Trust property). In May and June 1859 it was made available for use by the general public pending the completion and opening of Bodmin Road on 27th June. It continued to operate as a private station for over five years until about October 1864.

ROCHE

OPENED: 20th June 1876 (with the commencement of passenger services on the Cornwall Minerals Railway, Newquay – Fowey).
CLOSED: Passengers – remains open as a request stop for services on the Par – Newquay branch.
Goods – 1st June 1964.

Sited close to the highest point on the line, the station opened when passenger services started on the Cornwall Minerals Railway in mid June 1876. Freight services had begun on the line at the beginning of June 1874. Originally known as Holywell, the station name probably changed to Victoria in 1879. Some sources suggest however that the name changed to Victoria when passenger services commenced, the name Holywell only applying to an early freight depot opened in 1874. Victoria is an adjacent hamlet just north of the line which at this point follows an approximate east – west alignment. A final change came from 1st May 1904 when the name Roche was adopted, relating to the village about one mile to the south.

In the early Cornwall Minerals Railway era there was only one curved platform on the up (north) side of the line, at the west end of which was the low wooden station building with an apex roof. A metal parcels store was a later GWR addition east of the building. Also under the auspices of the GWR, which had purchased the Cornwall Minerals Railway in 1896, a passing loop was added and a second platform erected on the down side. Passengers here were provided with a small wooden shelter. A small goods yard was also developed behind the up platform and in 1920 additional sidings were laid. On 3rd July 1936 the passing loop was lengthened to accommodate longer trains running to and from Newquay. Movements at the passing loop and in the goods yard were controlled from a small wooden signal box (24 levers) on the up platform east of the building and metal shed.

Passenger numbers were always low at Roche. In 1903 only 4,552 passenger tickets were issued; the figure rose to 6,238 in 1913 and 6,375 in 1923 but fell to 4,818 in 1933. In 1922 Roche had a staff of five and this continued into the 1930s. The goods yard accommodated a camping coach behind the signal box in the summer of 1963.

Decline, as at other stations on the line, came from the early 1960s. Freight facilities were withdrawn and the goods yard closed from the beginning of June 1964. Staffing ceased on 13th July. The signal box closed on 30th January 1965. From 3rd January the down line, down platform and all the sidings had been taken out of use. However seven months later British Railways decided to reintroduce use of the down line and platform and close the up side. The up line and sidings were removed in October 1965 and the station building and signal box demolished. The up platform was however left and today its remains are hidden by undergrowth though in November 2008 a small section of the west end ramp could be seen. Today the Newquay branch line trains continue to use the former down side platform on which stands a small wooden shelter. Access to the platform is via a rail level board crossing at the west end.

Roche. A view from the down platform in the 1960s. On the up platform is the low wooden building, a metal store and the small wooden signal box. The small wooden shelter serves passengers on the later down platform (left).

ST AGNES

OPENED: 6th July 1903 (with the opening of the Chacewater – Perranporth section of the GWR Chacewater – Newquay branch).

CLOSED: Passengers and Goods – 4th February 1963.

St Agnes station opened in early July 1903 when services started on the Chacewater to Perranporth section of the GWR line from Chacewater to Newquay. The remaining section of the line opened some 18 months later at the beginning of January 1905. The residents were disappointed that the station was sited about a mile south of the town centre. The topography of the area east of St Agnes,

St Agnes. Looking north shortly after the 1903 opening of the original station. An auto coach hauled by a locomotive stands at the single face platform behind which is the red brick building with a fine canopy.

St Agnes. A general view on 28th August 1948 looking south at the new layout following the major alterations of 1937. Note the island platform with passengers served by a wooden shelter. An angled footbridge links the platform to the earlier station building, which remains in use but devoid of a platform, platform side doors and a line side canopy.

in particular Trevellas Coombe, precluded an alignment of the line any further to the north en route to Newquay. Just to the north of the station was a road overbridge carrying a minor road to Goonbell.

When opened in 1903, the station comprised a north – south aligned single face stone curved platform on the down (west) side of the single track line. There was no passing loop. The main red brick building, with a large apex style wooden platform canopy and two chimneys, stood in the centre of the platform. From south to north it incorporated the parcels office/cloakroom, the booking office/general waiting room, the ladies' waiting room and the gent's toilet. The last had a separate entrance in the north wall of the building with a wooden screen. A feature of the station building was the large number of enamel advertisement boards. Passenger numbers at this 1903 station nearly halved between 1913 and 1933. In the former 17,085 passenger tickets were issued and in the latter 9,617. Initially four men were based here but three was apparently the normal level of staffing.

St Agnes. Looking down the station approach road towards the rear of the main building early in the 1950s. Note the full length canopy that was added on this side.

South of the 1903 station building on the down side, was a small goods yard with a stone goods shed through which ran a goods loop connected at either end to the main running line. On the north end of the shed was a small goods office. From this goods loop a short siding ran north terminating behind the south end of the platform. On the west side of the siding were cattle pens. A long siding ran north through the yard on its far west side terminating next to a weighbridge and office, the latter in the form of a GWR style pagoda hut. A large coal shed stood beside the southern end of this siding. At this time movements into and within the goods yard were controlled by a ground frame.

From 4th July 1937 a new station layout came into use. The station's platform canopy was removed and the single face platform demolished, the latter being replaced by a 300 ft long island platform south of the original to the east of the goods yard. The platform was served by a main down running line and an up side loop. Thus, for the first time, passing facilities were available at St Agnes, the loop having capacity for an engine, 38 wagons and a guard's van. The original station building remained in use being linked to the north end of the island platform by an angled footbridge and a rail level board crossing. The former had been removed by the early 1950s. A full length canopy was also added along the forecourt side of the building. Passengers on the island platform were provided with a wooden shelter, extensions of the apex roof forming narrow canopies on either side. The layout and facilities in the goods yard remained basically the same as pre 1937. Camping coaches were located in the yard between 1934 and 1939 and 1952 to 1963. From 1937 a 30 lever signal box sited off the south end of the island platform controlled movements at the loop and in the yard, replacing the original ground frame.

Passenger and goods facilities were withdrawn early in February 1963 when services ceased on the Chacewater to Newquay line. The island platform and goods shed were demolished and the tracks lifted. The station building survived however and after lying derelict for some years is now in commercial use in the appropriately named Great Western Railway Yard. One occupant of the building, when seen in March 2009, was 'Station Metalwork'. An ex-Devonport Dockyard four wheel diesel shunter (no.5200) stands above the yard.

St Austell. Looking west in the 1910s. A Bulldog Class 4-4-0 stands at the up (towards Plymouth) platform and a Pannier tank engine is at the head of a goods train. Note the 1890s massive goods shed (top left) which lasted until the early 1930s.

ST AUSTELL

OPENED: 4th May 1859 (with the opening of the Plymouth – Truro section of the Cornwall Railway).
CLOSED: Passengers – remains open for services on the Plymouth – Penzance line.
Goods – 6th May 1968 (see text).

The arrival of the railway enhanced the role of St Austell as the commercial and administrative centre of Cornwall's china clay industry. When opened in early May 1859 the station was on a passing loop on the otherwise single line; the track was doubled from Par to St Austell from 15th October 1893 and then west to Burngullow on 26th March 1899, both following the abolition of the broad gauge.

A plan dated about 1908 indicates that the main wooden building on the down side included a store, offices, the booking hall, a covered entrance way, a waiting room, refreshment facilities and ladies' toilets. By that date the original Cornwall Railway building had been extended east, as seen from the different canopy style. The gent's toilet was in a separate building west of the main building. On the up side was a wooden waiting room and toilets. A fine covered footbridge linked the two platforms from east of the down side main building to west of the up side waiting room. This was erected in 1882. The up side platform was extended west in 1971, replacing a short siding. The building on the down platform was demolished on 30th November 1999 and a spacious new tinted glass structure opened on 8th June 2000. A staff of 27 were based at the station in 1923; this figure rose to 40 for most of the 1930s.

The goods facilities at St Austell changed greatly over the years. The first yard and shed were sited north of the main line, west of the station, adjacent to a level crossing. These were replaced in the 1890s by a larger yard and what was described as a 'massive' goods shed south-west of the station on the down side. One long siding ran through this shed and two others, between the shed and the down platform, also served the yard, which had a 5 ton capacity crane. To the north of the station on the up side, a long goods loop ran behind the platform alongside which was a loading platform and cattle pens, the latter at the east end. Two other long sidings with buffers at the west end ran parallel to the goods loop, these were added in about 1910.

Reflecting the growth in demand for freight traffic at St Austell, a third, even larger, goods yard was opened about quarter of a mile east of the station on the up side on 2nd November 1931. From this point the down side yard was run down, the siding to the goods shed being lifted in 1932 and the shed itself removed. The new goods yard

St Austell. The road side elevation of the main down side building recorded on 3rd July 1963.

had seven sidings, one of which ran through a goods shed, and also had a loading bank for china clay. A 5 ton crane served the yard which ceased to handle general goods traffic in May 1968. However, certain complete loads were handled until about 1985, after which the sidings were lifted. The two remaining sidings in the second yard lasted until 1965 and 1979; their removal opened up the site for the development of a bus station, which has been enhanced over the years to make the station into a good public transport interchange.

St Austell. A view of the down platform buildings looking east taken from the west end of the up platform on 11th May 1968. The building has two sections indicated by the different style canopies, the original Cornwall Railway structure being at the west end with a plain horizontal canopy. The up side platform was extended west in 1971, the siding in the foreground being lifted.

The sidings to the north of the station remained for some years and were used by motorail services. The last of these operated to London in 1984, to Crewe in 1980, to Worcester in 1978 and to Dover in 1975. A small building at the west end of the up platform was for use by motorail passengers. The sidings were subsequently truncated and much of the site is now in commercial use.

The first signal box at St Austell was on the down side just to the west of the platform end. This was replaced in about 1899 by a larger 43 lever box, again at the west end, but this time on the up side adjacent to a level crossing. On 21st September 1931 the crossing was abandoned and replaced by a section of pedestrian footbridge relocated from St Blazey station, which had closed to passengers in 1925. The box itself operated until 22nd March 1980 and remains in place today, used by permanent way staff.

Today the station has a new role as the rail head for visitors to the Eden Project, some three miles north east of St Austell. The nameboard indeed states, 'Alight for the Eden Project'. The station facilities, including a buffet, are concentrated in the fine 2000 building on the down side. However, when viewed in autumn 2008, there was a contrast on the up side with the wooden building boarded up and no other shelter provided aside from the remaining platform canopy. The covered footbridge, sporting a fine GWR cast iron monogram, remained as did the pedestrian bridge at the west end.

ST BLAZEY

OPENED: Goods – 1st June 1874
Passengers – 20th June 1876 (with the commencement of passenger services on the Cornwall Minerals Railway, Newquay – Fowey).
CLOSED: Passengers – 21st September 1925.
Goods – 1st June 1964.

The standard gauge Cornwall Minerals Railway opened for freight traffic at the beginning of June 1874. Passenger services began two years later in mid June 1876. With its location close to Par Harbour and a number of early mines, and just to the north of the east – west Cornwall Railway between Plymouth and Penzance, it was understandable that the Cornwall Minerals Railway sited its headquarters at St Blazey, a settlement just to the north of Par. The extensive facilities included workshops, offices and an unusual locomotive shed. Built in 1873 of red brick, this shed comprised a half round-house with nine roads leading to a large turntable. This shed remained in use for 114 years, mainly servicing small tank engines operating china clay trains. It closed to steam in April 1962 but housed diesels until 1987.

When the Cornwall Minerals Railway opened to passenger traffic between Newquay and Fowey, there was no direct link to the Cornwall Railway which it passed under south of St Blazey and south-west of Par station. This link soon followed with the opening of the Par loop in January 1879. This ran from a point on the Cornwall Minerals Railway to the north of the workshops on a curved alignment joining the main line at Par station. For its first three years therefore St Blazey, just to the north of the convergence of the loop line and the north – south Cornwall Minerals Railway, only served trains running direct between Newquay and Fowey. It was then known as Par CMR or Par/St Blazey. With the opening of the loop the name changed to St Blazey and it also served trains running from Par to Fowey reversing at the station. Newquay to Fowey trains also sometimes called at Par, reversing at Par and St Blazey.

A substantial red brick building at the south end of the down (west) platform contained the waiting, booking, office and toilet facilities. In later years the building was rendered but no platform canopy was ever provided. On the up (east) side platform was a small wooden shelter, a coal store and a lamp room. A goods loop was laid in about 1910 behind the down side building, giving access also to a number of sidings to the north-west. These were principally used for the storage of china clay wagons. A long footbridge was also erected at this time, linking the south end of the platforms and also crossing the goods loop to link with the adjacent Par to St Austell road. An original Cornwall Minerals Railway signal box, south of the station on the up side, was replaced by a GWR 41 lever box at the south end of the down platform. It operated from 25th June 1908 and remains in use today.

St Blazey station closed formally in September 1925; workmen's traffic continued using the station until 29th December 1934. Passenger usage had been at a reasonable level: in 1903 15,972 passenger tickets were issued, this number rose to 21,162 in

St Blazey. Looking north on 1st June 1922 with the substantial red brick building on the down platform. An advert on the side of the small wooden shelter on the up platform states 'Watkins Pianos – Organs St Austell'. The station closed to passengers just over three years later.

St Blazey. A very early photograph of the mid 1870s with staff of the Cornwall Minerals Railway gathered in front of the station building. To the left is a CMR 0-6-0T locomotive.

1913 and 21,910 in 1923. In 1923 it is recorded that 53 staff were based at St Blazey, clearly most of these did not work at the actual station.

After the closure of the station to passenger traffic the St Blazey site continued to be very busy for many years for freight traffic until general goods facilities were withdrawn at the beginning of June 1964. The line south to Fowey was used however until October 1968 when it was closed, the alignment being taken for a road to carry heavy lorries transporting china clay to the quays at Carne Point (see Fowey text). There were many changes to the buildings and facilities at St Blazey over the years, too many to detail here. The station footbridge was dismantled and in 1931 a section was re-erected at the west end of St Austell station where it remains in use today. The station building itself was demolished in the early 1970s. The down platform survives today in good condition having undergone some refurbishment in 1997 for use by staff. (On 19th April 1984 it had been used by Newquay passengers due to a derailment on the Par loop line.) Remnants of the former up platform can also still be seen. The former locomotive roundhouse, now a Grade II listed building, was leased out for industrial units after its closure in 1987, the individual roads being separated by breeze block walls.

ST COLUMB ROAD

OPENED: 20th June 1876 (with the commencement of passenger services on the Cornwall Minerals Railway, Newquay – Fowey).

CLOSED: Passengers – remains open as a request stop for services on the Par – Newquay branch.
Goods – 7th September 1964.

The station opened in June 1876 when passenger services started on the previously freight only Cornwall Minerals Railway, linking Newquay and Fowey. For its first two years it was known as Halloon but from 1st November 1878 the name changed to St Columb Road, reflecting its siting some 2½ miles south of the village of St Columb Major. Closer to the south-east was the then hamlet of Indian Queens on the now A30 road. Laid out in an east – west alignment it comprised, from the outset, a passing loop and up (north side) and down platforms, with a goods yard behind the latter. By 1910 the goods yard had been enlarged and a large loading platform erected. Adjacent to the yard was a brick works. Between 1931 and 1933 the passing loop was lengthened by 60 yards to the west and 100 yards to the east in order to accommodate passing movements involving the lengthy excursion trains running through to Newquay.

The main station buildings were on the up side, the original low wooden structure with two chimneys standing towards the east end of the stone platform. Photographs indicate that at some time a west end brick extension was added to the earlier Cornwall Minerals Railway structure. A

St Columb Road. Looking east in the 1960s. The west end extension of the building on the up platform can readily be seen. To the left is the small wooden signal box. Note the opening in the front wall of the platform for the rods working the points.

view of 1922 also shows a large metal building behind the west end of the platform, probably used as a store. A small wooden shelter stood in the centre of the down platform. Inter platform movements were via a rail level board crossing at the east end of the platforms. A small wooden signal box on a stone base and with a slate apex roof stood at the west end of the up platform controlling movements on the passing loop and in the goods yard.

In 1903 9,341 passenger tickets were issued, this number rose to 15,040 in 1913 and 22,201 in 1923 but fell to 14,612 by 1933. During the 1930s nine or ten men were based at St Columb Road. Staffing ceased on 12th July 1964. On 3rd January 1965, in common with other stations on the line, there was major rationalisation when the passing loop, goods yard sidings and signal box were taken out of use. Goods facilities at the station had ceased in the previous September. The station building became derelict and was subsequently demolished, being replaced by a small hut. In recent years however, there has been significant refurbishment. A modern metal and glass shelter has replaced the hut and decorative metal railings have been erected along the rear of the former up platform. Remnants of the former down platform could be seen in November 2008.

ST ERTH

OPENED: 11th March 1852 (with the opening of the Penzance – Redruth section of the West Cornwall Railway).

CLOSED: Passengers – remains open for services on the Plymouth – Penzance main line and the St Erth – St Ives branch.
Goods – 1st May 1967.

Serving the village of the same name about a mile to the south-east, the station opened in March 1852 on the single track line between Hayle and Penzance. A passing loop was added in 1894. The line east to Hayle was doubled in 1899 but doubling to the west as far as Marazion did not come until 1929. The station became a junction from 1st June 1877 with the opening of the branch to St Ives, four miles to the north on the coast. At this point the name of the

St Erth. A general view looking south-west in 1962. On the 1894 down platform (left) is the original stone waiting room and the later timber shelter. The asymmetric canopy on the island platform provides shelter on the main up platform and the St Ives branch platform at which stands a train. In the distance is the standard GWR covered footbridge.

St Erth. A detailed look in about 1960 at the St Ives branch bay platform protected by the lower side of the asymmetric canopy. A 45 XX 2-6-2T locomotive stands on the short dock siding. Behind the bay buffers is the rear of the west end wing of the main stone building. To the left a train stands at the main down platform beneath the covered footbridge.

station changed from St Ives Road to St Erth. Much of the station's traffic over the years has been generated by the St Ives branch, with many passengers transferring from main line trains en route to the resort.

The original 1852 station was a small typical West Cornwall Railway Brunel style wooden structure on the north side of the single track. Major reconstruction took place in 1876/77 preparing for the opening of the St Ives branch. A down platform was added in 1894 to serve a new down side loop. Thus from the mid 1890s St Erth had three platforms: the main up and down and a dead end branch bay on the north side, this last at a slightly lower level than the up main. This platform layout remains the same today.

The main line platforms are some 500 ft long, including extensions at the west end in 1904. The branch platform was extended at the east end to 400 ft in 1900. During the steam era the branch bay included a run round loop with a short dock siding at the west end. This loop was used on the arrival of every train from St Ives as the branch line included inclines too steep for push – pull working. With the introduction of diesel multiple units on the branch the loop connection was lifted in 1969 but the parallel bay siding remains.

The main stone building on the up side is 'L' shaped with arched window and door apertures. The up main platform at its east end and the branch platform are covered by a large wooden canopy. Because the branch platform is at a lower level the canopy is asymmetric, angled so as to give maximum protection to both platforms. Another canopy protects passengers at the west end of the up platform. The main door in the west end wing of the building is protected by a small horizontal canopy. For some years a small porch at the entrance gave extra protection. At its maximum use the up side building incorporated a number of facilities including a booking office, general waiting room, ladies' waiting room, parcels office, station master's office and toilets for gentlemen and ladies. In addition the west end wing contained a refreshment room which was used both by passengers and by local farmers and traders when coming to the station with items for despatch by train. On the down platform passengers were originally only provided with a small gable roofed stone waiting room with a small horizontal canopy. A timber waiting shelter was later added to the west of this building. A feature of this down platform was the display of sub tropical flowers and palm trees. The platforms were linked at the west end by a standard GWR covered footbridge. Also at this end of the station a road under bridge replaced a level crossing in about 1893.

Before the First World War, St Erth handled about 30,000 passenger bookings a year and this level was maintained in the 1920s and 1930s. For example, in 1932, 28,851 passenger tickets were issued with season ticket sales totalling 158. In 1936 12 staff were based at St Erth.

In contrast to these large passenger figures, freight traffic was low, particularly compared with many

St Erth. The road side frontage of the main building in the 1950s. An open canopy on the up platform protects passengers at the foot of the footbridge steps (right). A small porch gives extra shelter to the entrance beneath the horizontal canopy.

other Cornish stations. The main goods yard was north of the station buildings, four dead end sidings trailing back west from the St Ives branch line. Two further sidings were sited in the V of the junction. Facilities in the yard included a 320 ft long loading platform. Finally, there were also two refuge sidings trailing back from the down line east of the station, one dating from 1936. There was an attempt to establish bulk movements of china clay from St Erth with a siding laid in 1927 for use by the Porthia china clay company but this failed to generate much traffic. More success came however when the buildings were taken over by a creamery from 1936 and St Erth became one of the GWR centralised bulk milk depots with rail tankers taking milk to London. This traffic ceased in March 1980. St Erth also handled large amounts of local flowers and agricultural produce sent to the Midlands and North. The main goods facilities ceased at the beginning of May 1967. A camping coach was stabled on the north side of the goods yard in the summers from 1953 to 1961; two were provided in 1962-64. Holidaymakers in the coaches used the station toilets. A GWR gable roofed 32 lever brick and wooden signal box, which remains in place today in the V between the up main and branch lines, was installed in 1894 to control movements at the station. It received a 69 lever frame in 1929 but only half of these levers were in use by the year 2000. All the main station buildings erected at the end of the nineteenth century survive today; this includes the covered footbridge. St Erth thus retains the character of a GWR junction station.

ST GERMANS

OPENED: Passengers – 4th May 1859 (with the opening of the Plymouth – Truro section of the Cornwall Railway).
Goods – 3rd October 1859.
CLOSED: Passengers – remains open for local services on the Plymouth – Penzance line.
Goods – 19th July 1965.

Sited within the settlement of the same name, St Germans opened for passenger services in early May 1859 at a crossing point on the otherwise generally single track line. Two Brunel type Italianate style

St Germans. The Cornishman approaches from the west. A party of Girl Guides is on the platform in front of the main up side building in 1954/5. The footbridge still retains its roof.

St Germans. A general view looking west on 11th June 1966. Note the bay window of the station master's office at the east end of the up side main building. The footbridge has lost its roof. At the extreme left is the signal box beyond the east end of the down platform.

buildings were provided. The main stone building, with a horizontal platform canopy, a bay window on the station master's office at the east end and a small canopy over the entrance door, was on the up (towards Plymouth) side. A similar style building, again with a horizontal canopy, served the down platform. A covered footbridge, with roofs over the steps to each platform, was erected in 1901 at the west end of the platform. It lost its roof in the early 1960s. In the 1930s nine to ten men were based at the station.

Following the completion of the double track deviation east of St Germans in 1908, freight facilities comprised a goods yard east of the station on the up side, with a goods shed and 2 ton capacity crane and also a goods dock behind the east end of the up platform. Two sidings served the yard, one running through the shed. Also, east of the station were two refuge sidings, one on each side of the main through tracks. The goods yard closed in July 1965 but the down side refuge siding lasted until February 1966.

St Germans. Looking south-east through the now open footbridge in 1962 showing the stone waiting shelter on the down platform and the signal box.

Train movements at St Germans were controlled for many years from a signal box beyond the east end of the down platform. The box closed on 6th May 1973 with the extension west of control by the new Plymouth panel. Limited functions at St Germans, acting as an interface between the panels at Plymouth and Liskeard signal box, were transferred into a room at the east end of the down side building. From 26th April 1998 this function also ceased, all movements then being controlled from Plymouth and Liskeard.

Today the station buildings, now listed, survive as excellent examples of Brunel style structures. On the down side the stone waiting shelter with canopy continues in use but the signal box has gone. When viewed in late 2008 the upside building had been taken over by Rail Holidays Ltd, though an open alcove with a seat still provides shelter for passengers. Holiday accommodation was provided in two railway carriages. One in the up side goods dock was a GWR travelling post office (no.84) built on broad gauge bogies in 1889 and hauled by the City of Truro locomotive when it broke the 100 mph barrier in 1904. The other carriage, also on the up side, was a LSWR luggage van (no.1353), built in 1906, and used as a home from the 1930s.

ST IVES

OPENED: 1st June 1877 (with the opening of the St Erth – St Ives branch).

CLOSED: Passengers – remains open for services on the St Erth – St Ives branch.
Goods – 9th September 1963.

St Ives opened at the beginning of June 1877 as the northern terminus of the branch line from St Erth, the last broad gauge Cornish branch to be constructed. Historically a fishing port, the arrival of the railway benefited this industry but it had a greater role in the development of St Ives as a holiday resort. The town became a popular destination for day trippers, church outings and Sunday school treats for Cornish residents as well as for long distance holiday makers from other parts of the country.

On a restricted site on the east side of the town overlooking Porthminster beach and beyond the north end of Porthminster viaduct, the station was aligned approximately north – south. It comprised a slightly curved stone platform on which stood a Cornish rugged granite building with a slate hipped

St Ives. An overall view looking south over the station site in 1962. In the foreground is the long curved platform and station building. The stone goods shed is seen above the building. The small 1877 engine shed, which had closed in the previous year, can just be seen in the centre left of the photograph.

roof, four chimneys and platform canopy. At the northern end was a lean-to section. Also provided was a wooden platform screen at the southern end of the building. In 1892 when the broad gauge was removed, the platform was widened with the result that its edge was no longer under the canopy. Alongside the platform were two parallel tracks including a run round loop. In the 1930s, in order to accommodate the longer trains terminating at St Ives, the platform was lengthened. This southern extension tapered to become very narrow but it was however still not long enough to accommodate the ten carriage

St Ives. Passengers are walking to catch a train to St Erth early in the 1960s when services were still steam hauled. Note the lean-to structure on the northern end of the stone building.

St Ives. Looking north along the curved platform in 1962. Note the wooden shield at the southern end of the building giving extra protection to passengers on the platform. A goods truck stands in the bay siding.

through trains from Paddington. Frequent arrivals at St Ives were carriages detached at St Erth from the Penzance bound Cornish Riviera Express. Passenger tickets issued at St Ives rose from 20,887 in 1903 to 46,862 in 1923 but fell to 23,844 in 1933. These numbers did not reflect the total numbers handled at St Ives with many travellers purchasing tickets at their starting point, often Paddington. A raised ticket platform was sited at the south end of the platform until 1st January 1903. For many years a destination for affluent visitors was the Tregenna Castle Hotel. One of the early visitors to the then castle was Sir Daniel Gooch, the GWR Chairman, who took rooms there in 1878. The GWR at first leased and then, in 1895, bought the building, sited in a commanding location overlooking the town, and converted it into a hotel. Staffing levels at the station varied both over the years and according to the season. It is recorded that 17 staff were based at St Ives for most of the 1930s. The station became partially unstaffed as from 6th May 1968.

Goods facilities, concentrated in a yard behind the south end of the platform, included a stone goods shed tucked in at the base of cliffs. The large rail entrance door aperture reflected its broad gauge origin; a siding ran into the shed through this door. A siding was also laid in about 1892 between this goods shed siding and a bay siding behind the south of the platform. However, this 1892 siding was short lived, being replaced by a loading platform with an 8 ton capacity crane. In 1938 this was downgraded to a 6 ton capacity version. St Ives engine shed (1877), to the south of the station and beyond the Porthminster viaduct was on the down (west) side of the single line accessed by a trailing siding. Adjacent to it was a water tank on cast iron columns with a coal stage beneath. Movements at St Ives were controlled by a signal box at the south end of the station under the cliffs to the west of the goods shed siding. The box was fitted with a 20 lever frame in 1903. Like many Cornish stations, for some years St Ives was the location of camping coaches. One coach was there in 1958/59 and two coaches in the summer season only from 1960 to 1964.

The Beeching Report recommended the closure of the St Ives branch but it was reprieved by the Minister of Transport because of the likely impact upon the holiday trade, in particular the difficulty of carrying large numbers of holidaymakers by replacement buses on the local roads. However, major rationalisation came from the early 1960s. The first to go was the engine shed, which closed on 8th September 1961 and was subsequently demolished. The track to the shed and the connection to the running line closed on 8th September 1963 and was lifted seven weeks later. The site of the shed is now overgrown. The station run round loop became redundant at the end of October 1963, with services being taken over by diesel multiple units. The loop was lifted, together with the goods shed and loading platform sidings, in January 1966. The signal box had ceased to operate two and a half years earlier on 8th September 1963 the day before goods facilities were withdrawn at St Ives. During the 1960s more and more of the station site was taken over for car parking, a rare facility in St Ives.

The last major change came from 23rd May 1971 when the original station building and platform became redundant, with trains now terminating at a new concrete platform erected in the former goods yard, a little to the south of, and adjacent to, the former site of the goods shed. The 1877 station building was subsequently demolished and today its site is used for more car parking.

With the success of the Lelant Saltings Park and Ride facility and the longer trains required to carry the large numbers of passengers, the new platform was doubled in length in 1979 with extensions at both ends, that to the south terminating at the north end of the Porthminster viaduct. At first passengers were provided with a large enclosed bus stop type shelter but today this has been replaced by a modern glass and metal shelter. A similar structure is sited behind the south end of the platform. Tickets and souvenirs of the St Ives branch can be purchased at a separate small building beyond the north-east end of the platform. Today a plaque at the station refers to the Riviera Project that sought, through the Cornwall Rail Forum, 'better stations for Cornwall'. The plaque, referring specifically to the St Ives Bay line improvements, states they were 'opened by Cllr Harry Isaacs, the Mayor of St Ives, in December 2004'.

ST KEW HIGHWAY

OPENED: 1st June 1895 (with the opening of the Delabole – Wadebridge section of the North Cornwall Railway).
CLOSED: Passengers – 3rd October 1966.
Goods – 7th September 1964.

About one and a half miles south-east of the village of St Kew, the station opened at the beginning of June 1895 with the start of services on the fifth section of the North Cornwall Railway from Delabole to Wadebridge. It was sited just to the south of a bridge that carried the railway over the main road from Camelford to Wadebridge. The use of the suffix 'Highway' rather than 'Road' for the station and the adjacent small community was very unusual. St Kew Highway served not only St Kew but also a number of other rural settlements including the village of St Mabyn, one and a half miles to the south-east. The station also acted as the rail head for more distant settlements to the west including the resort of Polzeath, St Minver and Rock to which road services provided connections. The large number of holiday makers travelling to Polzeath meant that most of the principal holiday trains to Wadebridge and Padstow called at this remote station.

On a north – south alignment, the station was on a passing place on the otherwise single track line. Up (towards Port Isaac Road and Delabole) and down stone built platforms ran alongside the two station loops, which were lengthened by some 50 yards at the south end from 11th October 1914. A rail level board crossing at the south end provided for inter-platform movements, there being no footbridge. As at the majority of stations on the North Cornwall line, the main station building was on the up platform. Of the standard North Cornwall Railway design, the two storey station master's house was at the north end with a single storey wing to the south. The building was constructed of local stone with a slate roof and, as at Port Isaac Road and Padstow, overhanging eaves. However, there was no extra slate cladding as found at some stations along the line situated in more exposed locations. The main station facilities of the booking hall and office, station master's office, parcels office and porters' room were in the single storey wing but the ladies' waiting room and cloakroom were in the ground floor of the house. The gent's toilet was in a small structure with a lean-to roof on the north end of the house. The station master's accommodation was fairly extensive but with no bathroom and with the W C in the backyard. An open front stone shelter served passengers on the down platform opposite the main

St Kew Highway. Looking south in 1963 with the main building incorporating the two storey station master's house on the up platform. A stone waiting shelter stands opposite on the down platform. In the distance is the 17 lever signal box controlling access to the small goods yard behind the up platform.

building. In 1928 4,706 passenger tickets were issued but by 1936 the total had fallen greatly to 1,497. Over the same period the number of tickets collected fell from 4,979 to 1,759. From 1927 overall control of St Kew Highway transferred to the station master at Camelford. However the station remained staffed until 6th December 1965 with porters and signalmen; the number had reduced considerably in the latter years.

The goods facilities at St Kew Highway were on a smaller scale than at some stations on the North Cornwall line, the principal role here being to meet the needs of the local farming community. The yard was on the up side of the line behind, and south-west of, the platform. Facing and trailing points gave access from the up side track and until 16th July 1939 there was also a direct connection with the down loop. One long siding, with a capacity of 15 wagons, ran through the centre of the yard alongside cattle pens and a stone built goods shed, with a canopy over the rail side entrance and a 2 ton capacity internal crane. A short spur from this siding terminated at an end loading dock at the south end of the up platform. The spur was lifted in 1964, the end loading dock having been removed in 1939. A headshunt ran south level with the goods yard alongside the main running line dropping south towards Wadebridge. Incoming goods at the yard included coal, foodstuffs and fertilisers, while exports were primarily sugar beet, corn, rabbits and pigs.

The signal box, a standard North Cornwall Railway square structure of the 1880s, had a stone base, multi-pane wooden sliding windows and a slate roof. Sited just off the south end of the up platform, it had 17 levers (3 spare) controlling the loops and the goods yard. Following the withdrawal of goods facilities in September 1964, the yard, together with the upside loop, were taken out of use from 21st November 1965. The signal box also closed. Until final closure of the station at the beginning of October 1966 the few trains used the former down platform.

Today St Kew Highway is unique on the former North Cornwall line in that all the main buildings are still in situ, including the only surviving waiting shelter. The station building itself is a house, the only significant change being the addition of a small conservatory on the former platform in front of the single storey wing. The trackbed between the platforms has been filled in, including an ornamental pond. The former goods shed has also been converted into a house. The original small community of St Kew Highway has expanded with new housing development, particularly north of the A39.

St Keyne Wishing Well Halt. Looking south from a road bridge at the waiting shelter in 1962. The nameboard states 'For St Keyne Well'.

ST KEYNE WISHING WELL HALT

OPENED: 1st September 1902 (on the Moorswater – Looe line originally opened for passenger traffic through this site in September 1879)
CLOSED: Remains open as a request stop for services on the Liskeard – Looe branch.

No facility was provided at this point when passenger services commenced on the Moorswater – Looe line in 1879 (for early history of this line see Looe text). However, by the turn of the century at a time when the link to the main line at Liskeard was under construction, there were petitions for a station, in particular from residents in the village of St Keyne about a mile to the west and also from other residents in the rural area south of Liskeard.

Sited on the west side of the line, the halt opened at the beginning of September 1902. Records indicate that the accepted tender included a masonry wall for the platform (200 ft long and 3 ft high). A photograph of 1952 shows however an old timber platform but by the late 1950s a more substantial structure was in place with concrete slab edging. Records also indicate that the original shelter was constructed of second hand material from the Moorswater area to the north and west of Liskeard. A contemporary article described the waiting shelter as being of wooden construction with 'a nameboard over the doorway'. All photographs show that it was clad in corrugated iron sheeting. Access to St Keyne Halt was by a path leading down from the adjacent road, near to a road overbridge. Entry to the

Saltash. A two coach steam rail motor from Plymouth stands at the down platform of the station following the major changes in the 1900s. Note that the covered footbridge is at its initial site east of the buildings. By 1910 it had been relocated west of the buildings.

platform was via a gate next to the shelter. Also on the platform were a wooden seat and an oil lamp. In addition to local traffic the station, until recent years never known as a halt, was used by visitors to St Keyne's Well, about a half mile south of the station. Restored by the Old Cornish Society in 1936, legend has it that St Keyne travelled widely in the sixth century before settling in Cornwall. She apparently blessed the waters of the well so that when a couple came to drink the water, the first to sip would be master of the home! It was a custom for newly weds to race each other to the well. It was a popular attraction even before the opening of the station but such was the importance for rail traffic that for some years the nameboard advised passengers to alight 'for St Keyne Well'. Indeed this traditional role has recently been re-emphasised as, in early 2008, the name was changed from St Keyne to 'St Keyne Wishing Well Halt'. From the early 1980s a further local attraction has been Paul Corin's 'Magnificent Music Machines', a museum of 'fair organs, pianos and orchestrons'. In 1997 the old platform shelter was replaced by a new brick structure with a sloping canopy supported by three stanchions similar to that now installed at a number of surviving small stations and halts in Cornwall. This stands at the north end of the platform.

ST LAWRENCE PLATFORM

OPENED: 26th October 1906 (on the Bodmin General – Boscarne Junction line opened through the site in September 1888).

CLOSED: 1st January 1917.

Sited to the north-east of the then hamlet of St Lawrence to the west of Bodmin, this single platform opened in late October 1906 on the Bodmin General to Boscarne Junction line opened eighteen years earlier in 1888. It was used by visitors to a mental hospital a half mile to the north-east. No details or photographs are available of this small facility which closed on New Year's Day 1917 just over ten years after its opening. This may have been a war-time economy but St Lawrence Platform never re-opened.

SALTASH

OPENED: 4th May 1859 (with the opening of the Plymouth – Truro section of the Cornwall Railway).

CLOSED: Passengers – remains open for local services on the Plymouth – Penzance line.
Goods – 9th September 1963.

Sited at the extreme east of the town, overlooking the River Tamar, the station's history has been closely linked with that of the nearby Royal Albert rail bridge, opened in May 1859, and the Tamar road bridge, opened just over 100 years later in October 1961. Saltash opened in May 1859 with the commencement of services on the Plymouth to Truro section of the broad gauge Cornwall Railway, a section that included the famous Royal Albert Bridge,

Saltash. A view east on 9th July 1960 showing a diesel hauled train to Penzance approaching the station over the Royal Albert Bridge. Note that the covered footbridge (right foreground) is in the post 1910 position. Work is under way on the Tamar road bridge which, opening in October 1961, had a major impact upon passenger use of the station.

at the west end of which was the station. Historians consider that the coming of the railway was the catalyst for the revival of what, in the mid 19th century, was a declining town.

From 1876 the GWR was subsidising a road service from Saltash to Callington using a four horse coach. This was reflected in some timetables with the station name given as 'Saltash for Callington'. From 1st June 1904 the GWR, using four motor cars, introduced a service to both Callington and Albaston. The station itself, on a north-east to south-west alignment, was rebuilt in 1880, with a stone main building with horizontal canopy on the up (towards Plymouth) platform and a stone waiting shelter on the down side. At this time a dock siding was installed at the south-west end of the up platform but this was abandoned during conversion of the tracks from broad to standard gauge in 1892.

In 1904 a steam rail motor service was introduced from the Plymouth area to Saltash. Its success, together with track alterations between the station and the Royal Albert Bridge, necessitated an extension and alterations to the up platform in 1906. Other developments around this time included redevelopment and extensions of the buildings on both platforms. Records also indicate a change in siting of the station footbridge, which had not been available in the station's early days. A map of 1905 shows a bridge to the north-east of the buildings but a 1910 plan indicates a revised position with a covered footbridge south-west of the buildings and signal box, a siting which continued until its demolition in the 1980s. The station was gas lit and for many years was adorned with palm trees.

An intensive service of steam rail motor trains was developed, running to and from Saltash, serving stations and halts in the Plymouth area, some as far east as Plympton. Auto trains took over from the early steam motors from 1909 and by the 1930s a suburban service of about 50 trains per weekday ran on this route. In addition some 30 through main line

Saltash. A detailed view of the up side building in the 1950s. Evidence of the westward extension of the building in the 1900s is seen in the varied form of the platform canopy. Note the large Wymans bookstall and the re-sited covered footbridge.

Saltash. The road side elevation of the up side building in the 1950s. The Western National bus has brought passengers to the station from other towns in east Cornwall for travel on to Plymouth by rail. Such bus services diminished after the opening of the Tamar road bridge in late 1961.

trains, serving the rest of Cornwall, stopped at Saltash. The overall number meant that, at that time, Saltash was the busiest passenger station in Cornwall. Staff numbers increased from 14 in 1903 to 21 in 1923; it was unstaffed from October 1971.

Regular steam working ceased in June 1961 and the opening of the Tamar road bridge later that year resulted in a major down-turn in passenger numbers at Saltash. Hitherto many bus services serving Cornish towns and villages had terminated at Saltash station, with passengers completing their journey by rail. Buses could now run through to Plymouth over the new bridge. The station became unstaffed from 11th October 1971 and the Plymouth to Saltash suburban services finally ceased in 1972. The footbridge was demolished with passengers having to use the road bridge south-west of the station. A highlight came in 1959 with a visit by the Queen to commemorate the centenary of the opening of the Royal Albert Bridge and in 1984 the Mayor of Saltash unveiled a plaque on the down platform to mark the Bridge's 125th anniversary. Celebrations were also held at the station on 4th May 2009 marking the 150th anniversary of the start of rail services over the bridge.

Saltash also had a role in goods traffic, this concentrated in a small yard on the up side south-west of the station. The yard included a dock siding, a small goods shed and a short loop siding. Limited space precluded expansion of the yard, which mainly handled flower and fruit products from the Tamar valley. General goods facilities were withdrawn in September 1963 but the track remained in place for train layovers until 1972. Movements at Saltash were controlled from a signal box on the up platform south-west of the main building. This box was closed and replaced by a ground frame on 2nd July 1973. It was subsequently demolished.

Today Saltash is served by local trains on the Plymouth to Penzance line. The main building on the up side still stands but, when seen in autumn 2008, was boarded up and fenced off from the platform. Ambitious plans, once put forward to convert it into a Brunel Heritage Centre, had not been implemented. Passengers travelling towards Plymouth are served by a small modern open stone shelter towards the south-west end of the platform. A similar open shelter stands on the down platform replacing the original building. Also on the down platform is a brick structure on which the 1984 plaque is displayed. The goods shed, which was in non rail commercial use in 2000, has now gone, the former goods yard being in use for housing and car parking.

SANDPLACE

OPENED: September/October 1881 (on the Moorswater – Looe line originally opened through this site for passenger traffic in 1879).

CLOSED: Passengers – remains open as a request stop for passenger services on the Liskeard – Looe branch.
Goods – 18th June 1951.

A short history of the evolution of transport in the Looe valley is set out in the text relating to Looe station. The Liskeard & Looe Canal transported both minerals from inland quarries to the coast and also sand and seaweed inland from the port of Looe for agricultural use. The name Sandplace reflects the location where barges both on the Looe River and on the later canal discharged their cargoes. When the canal was generally abandoned following the opening of the railway the southern section was retained as far as Sandplace until 1901.

In 1879 a 180 ft long goods loop siding was opened adjacent to the hamlet on the Liskeard to Looe road. It was on the east side of the valley line which had originally opened for mineral traffic in December 1860. This siding, as well as serving a local estate, was also the place where cargoes, discharged from the canal barges, were loaded on to open rail wagons. A building (65 ft x 12 ft), possibly a goods shed, was sited here. The siding remained in use until June 1951 and was lifted five years later. Today there is no trace.

Sandplace. Looking north at the shelter in 1962. The original timber face of the platform had by this time been replaced by concrete blocks.

In autumn 1881 a station was opened some 200 yds north of the siding on the east side of the single line, unlike other halts on the valley line. A detailed history of the line states that the station opened in September or October 1981 but the exact date is not given. It did not feature however in a timetable in December of that year. It had a 260 ft long platform and a timber frame corrugated iron clad shelter with a door. Access to the platform was via a gate in the fence alongside an adjacent road. Closure of Sandplace was proposed as early as 1907 but this was averted. A 1950 photograph shows a timber platform wall but by the early 1960s this had been rebuilt with concrete blocks.

In 1997 the original shelter was replaced by a brick structure with a sloping canopy supported by three stanchions. This is of a similar design to those now installed at a number of surviving small stations and halts in Cornwall. Today Sandplace is a request stop; currently the suffix 'halt' is not in use though it was from 21st September 1963 until 5th May 1969. When viewed in autumn 2008 two picnic tables were provided one each side of the shelter. Also on the platform were two cycle stands.

SCORRIER

OPENED: 25th August 1852 (with the opening of the Redruth – Truro section of the West Cornwall Railway).

CLOSED: Passengers – 5th October 1964.
Goods – 18th February 1963.

The station opened in August 1852 when services commenced on the West Cornwall Railway from Redruth to Truro. At its opening it was called Scorrier Gate. The suffix was finally dropped from 1st October 1896, though there is evidence it was not used between March 1856 and June 1859.

Scorrier, serving an adjacent small settlement of the same name and built on an embankment, was on a

Scorrier. Staff pose on the down platform (and tracks!) in the early 1900s. The original West Cornwall Railway building is to the left. The stone building to the right was added, probably in 1898, when the track was doubled. To the left is the 1902 signal box.

Scorrier. A general view looking east in 1963 from beneath the open footbridge. To the right are the original West Cornwall Railway building and the stone extension (nearest the camera). To the left is the up side stone shelter added with the platform in about 1898.

then single track section of the West Cornwall Railway. The one platform was on the down side. An up side loop and platform were added in about 1898. Both platforms were about 370 ft long.

An early wooden West Cornwall Railway building stood on the east end of the down platform. This was supplemented on its west side, probably in 1898, by a stone structure. Both buildings had wooden canopies, which were linked. A small stone waiting room provided shelter on the up side, also from about 1898. The platforms were linked by an open metal footbridge at the west end. In 1903 19,684 passenger tickets were issued; the figure rose to 24,925 in 1913 and 21,345 in 1923 but fell to 14,565 in 1933 and 11,199 in 1938. Over the period 1903 to the mid 1930s staff numbers fell from eight to five. The staff were controlled by a class 5 station master.

There were no sidings at Scorrier, though a limited amount of general merchandise was handled at the station itself. In 1938 it is recorded that a private siding to the nearby Wheal Busy mine was available for use a quarter of a mile east of the station. Scorrier's hipped roof signal box (25 levers) off the east end of the down platform operated from 1902 to 1930. The box was particularly important as, from 1913 until 1930, it was at the west end of a double track section of the line from Penwithers Junction, west of Truro. The section west on to Drump Lane, Redruth was doubled from 13th April 1930. Scorrier ceased to handle goods traffic in February 1963 and closed to passengers in early October 1964. Remnants of the down platform can still be seen.

Seven Stones Halt. A view east in about 1950 of the remains of this small halt built to serve the nearby Phoenix Park Pleasure Ground which operated from 1910 to 1914.

SEVEN STONES HALT

OPENED: 16th June 1910 (on the Bere Alston – Callington line originally opened through this site in 1908).
CLOSED: 1914.

Between Luckett and Latchley on the Bere Alston to Callington branch, this small halt opened in mid June 1910 to serve the nearby Phoenix Park Pleasure Ground, popular with visitors from Plymouth. This had been created on the site of the Phoenix Brick Works. On the south side of the single track, this stone platform was named after a small hamlet a half mile to the south. There is no record of a shelter being provided. Although the excursion traffic was heavy, the Pleasure Ground and the halt closed with the outbreak of war in 1914. Despite this, the halt appeared in a timetable until September 1917.

SHEPHERDS

OPENED: 2nd January 1905 (with the opening of the Perranporth – Newquay section of the GWR Chacewater – Newquay branch).
CLOSED: Passengers and Goods – 4th February 1963.

This isolated station, surrounded by only a farm and a few cottages, opened at the beginning of January 1905 when services started on the second section of the GWR Chacewater to Newquay line from Perranporth to the north Cornwall resort. That part of the line between Perranporth and Shepherds was wholly constructed by the GWR as

Shepherds. In this view of the up side platform and buildings in about 1910 the station master (centre right), two of his staff and a passenger pose on the platform, whilst the permanent way gang, the supervisor with a bowler hat, stand on the track.

an extension of the first section from Chacewater to Perranporth which had opened in July 1903. From Shepherds to Newquay the GWR upgraded earlier mineral lines. These lines included the J T Treffry mineral line from Newquay to East Wheal Rose lead and silver mine, opened in 1849. The Cornwall Minerals Railway took over the East Wheal Rose line and extended it in 1874 to serve iron ore mines at Treamble and Gravel Hill. The Gravel Hill line closed in 1888, the track being cut back to Treamble which carried public goods traffic until 1905 and minerals only until 1917. It then closed with the track being lifted for use in the war efforts. From 16th February 1926 the line to Treamble reopened for goods traffic and continued until 1949, though its official closure date was 1st January 1952.

Shepherds station was sited where the GWR line from Perranporth joined the earlier Cornwall Minerals Railway Treamble line; nearby were two old mines called Shepherds, hence the station name. Unlike the other two stations on the Chacewater/ Newquay line with passing loops (St Agnes from 1937 and Perranporth), Shepherds had a conventional layout of two platforms, one up and one down (towards Newquay), rather than an island platform. Aligned north-east to south-west, they were constructed of wood and, unusually for this line, this was the case throughout the station's life. The main brick building with two chimneys and an apex style platform canopy stood on the up (east) platform. Facilities included a booking office/ waiting room, a ladies' waiting room and gent's toilet, the last with an access at the southern end of the building protected by a wooden screen. On the down platform was a brick waiting shelter with a chimney and a small wooden canopy. Passenger volumes were never high at Shepherds: in 1913 5,474 passenger tickets were issued, the figure rose to 6,999 in 1923 but fell to 5,470 in 1933. A staff of four or five were employed at the station between the two wars.

A small goods yard on the up (east) side, north of the station, included a siding trailing back from the up line terminating adjacent to a cattle dock. A single camping coach was based in the yard during the summers from 1954 to 1961. The Treamble

Shepherds. A general view looking north-east in 1962. The main buildings and the signal box are on the up platform (right). Passengers on the down platform are served by a brick waiting shelter.

goods branch trailed to the west from the down line just beyond the north end of the down platform. Traffic movements around the station were controlled from a large brick signal box with multi-pane windows, a slate roof and chimney. It was on the up platform, north of the building and had 23 levers of which only 14 were used. At one stage a metal hut also stood at the north end of the up platform beyond the signal box. Shepherds closed for passenger and freight traffic in early February 1963 with the withdrawal of all services on the Chacewater to Newquay line.

The station site now forms part of a farmyard; the trackbed north of the station can still be identified. Sections of metal railings remain as a reminder of the railway past. A nearby house is named 'The Sidings'.

SHOOTING RANGE PLATFORM

OPENED: c.1885 (on the Bodmin – Wadebridge line originally opened through this site for passenger traffic in 1834).
CLOSED: After c.1947.

About one and a half miles south-east of Wadebridge, Shooting Range Platform opened in the mid 1880s to serve a nearby rifle range. It was not advertised or in a timetable but was used intermittently for many years. In 1909, for example, LSWR rail cars would call if not less than six wished to join or alight. Trains only stopped after receiving written authority from the army. Apart from an open platform, records indicate no other facility was provided. The exact date of closure is unknown although sources suggest it was still used just after the Second World War.

TRESMEER

OPENED: 28th July 1892 (with the opening of the Launceston – Tresmeer section of the North Cornwall Railway).
CLOSED: Passengers – 3rd October 1966.
Goods – 7th September 1964.

This remote station, opened primarily to serve the village of Tresmeer about a mile to the south-east, was actually sited in the small hamlet of Splatt. Its opening, with the completion of the line from Launceston, at the end of July 1892, was apparently a month behind schedule because of a landslip. A report in the *Western Daily Mercury* noted however

Shooting Range Platform. A view in 1950 of the disused facility which opened in the mid 1880s for users of the nearby rifle range.

Tresmeer. A general view looking north-east in the early 1960s showing the main brick building incorporating the two storey station master's house on the down platform (right). A brick built open waiting shelter and the 18 lever signal box are on the up platform.

that it was in time to be used for that year's Launceston Agricultural Society Show. For just over a year Tresmeer was a terminus station, the next section of the North Cornwall Railway opening as far as Camelford on 14th August 1893.

Tresmeer, on an approximate north-east to south-west alignment, acted as a passing place on the generally single track line with up (towards Launceston) and down stone faced platforms, some 2 ft 6 inches high. The short double track section through the station could accommodate about 24 wagons. The platforms and the double tracks extended north-east under a road bridge. Inter platform movements were via a rail level board crossing at the south-west end of the platforms.

The main station building was, unusually for the North Cornwall Railway line, on the down platform, a position only shared with Delabole and Launceston South. It was of a standard North Cornwall Railway design comprising a two storey station master's house at the north-east end and a single storey wing to the south-west. Unlike the majority of stations on this line, which were constructed of local stone, Tresmeer, like Egloskerry, the next station towards Launceston, was built of brick due to a lack of local stone in the immediate area. Unlike Egloskerry, the upper storey of the station master's house was not slate hung. The station facilities of the booking hall and office, station master's office, parcels office and porters' room were within the single storey wing but the ladies' waiting room and cloakroom were on the ground floor of the house. The gent's toilet was in a single storey structure at the north-east end of the house. The station master's accommodation was fairly extensive but with no bathroom and the W C in the back yard. To the south-west of the building on the down platform was a small corrugated iron oil and lamp store.

Passengers on the up platform were protected by a brick built open front waiting shelter with small windows at either end. Passenger levels at the remote location were never high: in 1928 4,835 passenger tickets were issued; by 1936 the figure had fallen to 1,748. Between these two years the number of tickets collected fell greatly from 4,567 to 1,745.

The goods facilities at Tresmeer were concentrated in a small goods yard on the down side behind, and south-east of, the platform. One long siding running alongside the goods shed was accessed via a headshunt running in a south-west direction from the down line. A spur from the siding led to an end loading dock at the south-west end of the down platform. The small brick goods shed, within which was a 40 cwt capacity crane, had a small horizontal canopy with a valance over the rail side entrance. The handling of livestock was important at the yard which incorporated the usual cattle pens found at most rural stations. This traffic was particularly heavy when the local Friday cattle market was held. A number of local traders had stores in the yard handling a variety of agricultural products; the export of rabbits was of some importance. For just over a year prior to the completion of line as far as Delabole, Tresmeer yard acted as the rail head for the export of slates extracted from Delabole quarry. In the 1930s the Southern Railway erected one of its standard fertiliser/feed stores for leasing to local companies.

Movements at Tresmeer were controlled from a signal box on the up platform south-west of the waiting shelter. A brick based structure with multi-pane wooden windows and a slate roof, the box had 18 levers. Economy measures operating from 28th October 1930 saw the single line tablet machine, telephone and telegraph equipment moved to the booking office to be worked by porters/signalmen.

East of the goods yard six cottages were provided for local railway employees. From 1927 control of the station passed to Otterham, the post of Tresmeer station master being abolished. The station remained staffed however until 6th January 1965. The goods facilities were withdrawn in early September 1964 with tracks in the yard being lifted by the end of 1965. The end dock siding had been removed in June 1964. The signal box ceased to operate from 14th November 1965 and from that date the loop was taken out of use and only the down platform was used until the station closed completely in October 1966.

Today the former station building survives, following renovation, as a fine house, one of the extensions being in front of the single storey section on the down platform. The trackbed between the platforms has been partly filled, with the platform acting as an attractive garden terrace. In the former goods yard the shed and a store are used by local businesses; the yard gate posts survive as do the nearby six Railway Cottages. A new bungalow has been built between the former station building and the goods shed.

Trewerry and Trerice Halt. Looking south at the concrete component platform with corrugated iron open shelter in the 1960s.

TREWERRY & TRERICE HALT

OPENED: 14th August 1905 (on the Chacewater – Newquay line originally opened through this site in January 1905).
CLOSED: 4th February 1963.

Sited just to the west of Trewerry Mill and south-west of Trerice Manor, a fine Elizabethan house now owned by the National Trust and open to visitors, the halt opened in mid August 1905 coinciding with the introduction of steam rail motors on the Chacewater to Newquay line. The section of the line through the halt had opened eight months earlier at the beginning of January (see Shepherds text). The first section from Chacewater to Perranporth opened in July 1903. On a north – south alignment the original halt comprised a wooden platform on the up (east) side of the single track line south of a level crossing. A GWR style pagoda hut served passengers. A wooden post and rail fence ran along the rear of the platform. By the 1920s the halt had been rebuilt with a concrete component platform on which was a corrugated iron open shelter. There were two seats, one in the shelter and one on the open platform. North of the level crossing a goods loop originally served the mill and was later used for coal deliveries. This closed in September 1948. The building by the level crossing was once a Cornwall Minerals Railway crossing keeper's

house. The halt closed when services were withdrawn on the line early in February 1963. Today a house has been built adjacent to the site, 'Trewerry Halt'. A garage stands on the original alignment beside the house. An original level crossing gate post survives. On another gate post is a faded notice 'Beware of the Trains'.

Truro. A detailed look in about 1910 at the eastern section of the down side building road side elevation. Note the elaborate iron work on the two towers and the raised clerestory over the booking office/hall roof. The large water tank was one of two that supplied a number of water columns at the station.

Truro. A comprehensive view of the full length of the down side building very soon after its completion in 1900. Note the large number of horse drawn vehicles and the Royal Mail cart (lower centre). To the right the western extension to the 1874 goods shed can be seen.

TRURO

OPENED: 4th May 1859 (with the opening of the Plymouth – Truro section of the Cornwall Railway).
CLOSED: Passengers – remains open for services on the Plymouth – Penzance main line and the Truro – Falmouth Docks branch.
Goods – c.1981 (see text).

Sited north-west of, and high above, the city centre, the station opened on 4th May 1859 as the then western terminus of the broad gauge Cornwall Railway. At its opening it was only used by trains of the Cornwall Railway but those run by the West Cornwall Railway transferred to it from Truro Newham station a week later on 11th May. The station, on an east-west alignment, was developed just to the west of the splendid Truro viaduct with its magnificent view over the city and cathedral. Truro station was later used by trains on the lines to Falmouth (from 1863) and to Newquay via Chacewater (1903/5).

At its opening Truro station was approached by single track lines from both directions, the tracks at the western end being of mixed gauge to accommodate

Truro. A view east in the 1920s from the lengthy footbridge beyond the west end of the station. To the right a train stands in the Falmouth bay platform 1 converted from a dock siding in 1912. The two trains stand at platform 2 (right) generally used for down main line trains and platform 3 (left) used by trains on the Newquay/Perranporth line. Up mainline trains generally used the outside face of the island platform 4 (far left).

the standard gauge trains of the West Cornwall Railway. There were three through tracks, one alongside a down side platform (161 ft x 14 ft) and two alongside an island platform (141 ft x 20 ft) on the up north side. There was also a short down side bay at the west end, used then as a dock siding. A third track ran between the two main up and down platform tracks. There were also two mixed gauge loop lines to the north of the station. This original Cornwall Railway stone built station building, erected by Olvers of Falmouth, was 130 ft long and featured an overall roof with two clear spans of 47 ft and 41 ft covering the three platforms. At that time there was a small goods yard with a stone goods shed on the down side east of the station and a wooden engine shed (100 ft x 38 ft) with a slate roof on the up side north of the station.

Into the twentieth century the basic track layout remained the same, although the down side dock siding was converted for use by Falmouth branch trains in 1912. The platforms, lengthened compared with the 1859 station, were numbered 1 to 4, number 1 being the Falmouth bay. Platform 2, the down side platform, was used by the down main line services from Paddington and Plymouth. Platform 3, on the south side of the island, was used by trains on the Newquay/Perranporth line and sometimes by incoming Falmouth trains; platform 4, on the north side of the island, was for through main line trains to Plymouth and Paddington. In 1912 platforms 2 and 3 were extended from 484 ft and 450 ft to 634 ft and 600 ft respectively at a cost of £398. Subsequent lengthening increased platform 2 to 650 ft, whilst platforms 3 and 4 were extended to 685 ft. Platform

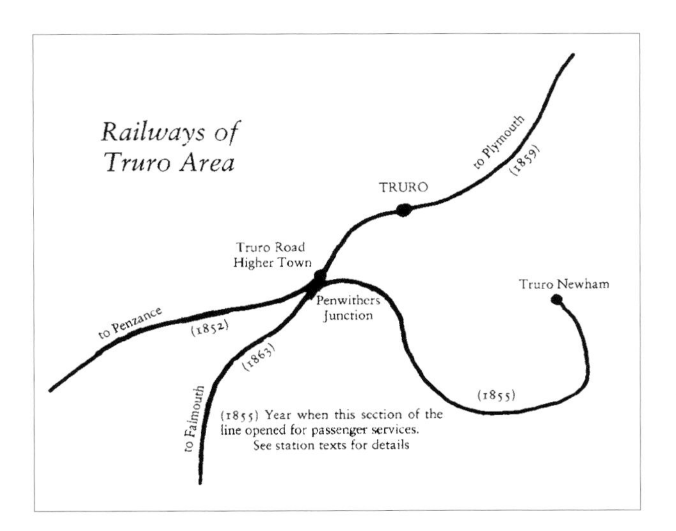

Truro. The road side elevation of the down side building in the 1930s. It remains very similar today except that a brick and glass extension was added in 1985 on the road side of the eastern section (right). This contains the booking office, which has been relocated from the centre of the building.

4 was served by a 1200 ft loop line which left the up main at the west end of the station and rejoined it at the east end. Up until 1st May 1897 there had been a ticket platform east of the station.

Beyond this north side up loop were four long parallel tracks; one was used as a carriage siding, whilst two others served as up and down goods loops which could be used for goods traffic by-passing the station. To the north again were a number of parallel sidings, installed by 1920, that were available for marshalling and storage. Six further sidings extended westwards on the up side providing additional stabling for carriages. At a cost of some £3000 these were used from about the end of 1913.

Extensive rebuilding of the station buildings themselves was authorised on 18th November 1896 at an estimated cost of £5,500. Extra costs of some £1,870 were entailed before the work was completed in 1900. This reconstruction involved the removal of the overall roof and erection of a typical late Victorian Great Western building on the down side. It comprised a long single storey brick structure with a hipped slate roof and two French style towers topped with elaborate iron work. In the centre of the roof was a raised cupola. This building included, from west to east, a bookstall, telegram office, refreshment rooms, waiting room/toilets, booking office and hall, the station master's office, another waiting room/toilets, a cloakroom, parcels office, inspector's office, porters' room and a boiler house. There were also two through passages from the road to the down platform. On the up side island two brick buildings incorporated refreshment rooms, waiting rooms and toilets. There was also a separate block of gent's toilets. Both platforms were covered by large canopies that were extended in 1936. Two horizontal canopies were sited above the road side entrances to the station. The platforms were linked by two plate girder covered glazed footbridges, one at the eastern end and one in the centre. No lifts were provided.

These buildings have basically served passengers until the present day, though the content of the down side building has changed. In 1985 a new travel centre was developed at the east end, this included the erection of an extension on the road side of the building. When visited in autumn 2008, the building included the new travel centre and booking office, a car hire office, toilets and a café. On the island platform the original two waiting room buildings were still in use, together with two smaller shelters, all under the large canopy.

As from 7th May 1971 extensive remodelling of the tracks at the station came into use. In particular the platform 4 through track was converted into a siding, being then known as the up bay. Platform 3 was now used solely for through up main line traffic. Falmouth branch trains that had sometimes used it were now confined to the down bay platform

1. These arrangements basically continue today but all track has now been lifted alongside the old platform 4.

Of all Cornish stations Truro has always been one of the best used by passengers, though St Austell has had higher use for freight traffic because of the china clay business. In the period 1903-1938 some 130,000 passenger tickets were issued per year at Truro; in 1913 the figure was 149,577, whilst in 1930 150,529 tickets and 417 season tickets were issued. By 1938 the figure had dropped to 108,930 but was offset by a rise in season ticket sales to 2,151.

Although not quite as important as passenger traffic, freight movements at Truro have been significant through the years. A goods yard on the down side beyond the east end of the station was accessed via a trailing connection from the down main line. It contained a number of dead end sidings, one of which ran into a large goods shed (1874) with a 240 ft long internal loading platform. The shed was extended west in the late 1890s rebuild. A further siding on the north side of the yard terminated beside a loading bay, whilst another to the south served a cattle loading dock. Three further sidings were available for wagon load traffic including coal and general merchandise. The yard included a 12 ton capacity crane in addition to a hand operated crane in the shed. General goods facilities ceased at Truro in about 1981.

A lengthy lattice open footbridge at the west end of the station replaced a level crossing in about 1876. This overlooked a large engine and workshop complex which was established in 1899/1900, replacing the first 1859 wooden engine shed sited north of the station. The stone engine shed section with a ridge and furrow roof had three tracks within and offices and a repair shop immediately to the north. The overall large structure also incorporated on the north side a carriage and wagon shop. A turntable was sited to the south-west of the engine shed, originally of 55 ft diameter, it was replaced by a 65 ft version in 1924. A diesel servicing point was added in a white extension to the shed in 1959. Steam locomotives ceased using it in 1962 and the shed closed in November 1965. The station was well supplied with watering facilities, standard Great Western water columns being sited around the station and yards. Large water tanks at the east end of the down platform and south of the engine shed fed these water columns.

In the steam era two Great Western style signal boxes controlled movements at the station, Truro West and Truro East. Both were brick and timber hipped roof structures with five paned windows. The 1897 West Box (49 levers) was to the north of the up goods loops and east of the engine shed. The East Box was erected in 1899 at the east end of the island platform, a new 51 lever frame being fitted in 1971. This box continues to operate today but the West Box closed on 7th November 1971.

Railway related employment has always been relatively high at Truro. In 1935 some 90 staff were based there, by 1938 this had risen to 98. In 1950 there was a grand total of 158 employees at the station and goods depot. In addition there were many other employees in the locomotive and permanent way departments.

Today Truro station continues to be a busy station and, when visited in autumn 2008, passenger use was high. The main line trains were using platforms 2 and 3 with the Falmouth branch shuttle at the platform 1 bay. Both covered footbridges remain in use. All track north of the former platform 4 has gone, with much of the former sidings site in use for car parking. The former engine shed site is today used, as it has been for some years, by buildings of Cornwall Farmers Ltd. A siding for fertiliser traffic originally served these buildings but this arrangement ceased in 1992. The goods yard only handled full loads after 1971. In late 2008 the former yard east of the station was being redeveloped for a mixed housing scheme, 'The Sidings'.

TRURO ROAD/HIGHER TOWN

OPENED: 25th August 1852 (with the opening of the Redruth – Truro section of the West Cornwall Railway).
CLOSED: 16th April 1855.

Truro Road/Higher Town was the original temporary eastern terminus of the standard gauge West Cornwall Railway, the eastern section of which opened from Redruth in August 1852. No details are available of the building, which was sited on a hill on the far west outskirts of the town. The station, officially known as Truro Road, closed formally with the opening of the West Cornwall Railway extension around the south of the city to a new terminus, Truro Newham, adjacent to the quay on the Truro river. Some sources suggest it was used again for a short while after the opening of the broad gauge Cornwall Railway at Truro.

TRURO NEWHAM

OPENED: 16th April 1855 (with the opening of the short extension of the West Cornwall Railway from Truro Road/Highertown).
CLOSED: Passengers – 16th September 1863.
Goods – 8th November 1971.

The West Cornwall Railway opened a station, Truro Road/Higher Town, on the western outskirts of Truro in August 1852. However the Company was anxious to have a terminus much closer to the town centre. Thus the Company directors resolved not to wait for the arrival in Truro of the Cornwall Railway from Plymouth but to erect its own station south of the centre by a quay on the Truro river. The standard gauge line from close to the 1852 station and Penwithers Junction around the south-west and south of Truro opened in April 1855, terminating at a typical Brunel style station building and goods shed. The station building itself was a timber structure with a hipped roof. An overall timber roof covered a single face platform, adjacent track and run round loop. Nearby was the wooden goods shed, quayside sidings, a 3 ton capacity crane and, in the early days, a small engine shed (1855) at the south end of the site. The last closed after the opening of the Cornwall Railway.

The anticipated financial return of the Newham

Truro Newham. The building that originally housed the offices when the station was in use for passenger services on the West Cornwall Railway between 1855 and 1863. Photographed on 14th August 1956, it survived for about a further 15 years until late 1971 with the site now redeveloped in an industrial estate.

Truro Newham. The wooden overall roof of the station that covered a single face platform and tracks. Photographed also on 14th August 1956, it was in use for goods traffic, a role it had fulfilled since 1863.

branch did not materialise and the West Cornwall Railway soon sought to negotiate access into, and joint use of, the Cornwall Railway's new terminus north–west of the centre which opened on 4th May 1859. On that date the new rail link from the West Cornwall Railway to the Cornwall Railway station was not quite complete and the arrival of West Cornwall trains was delayed by a week until 11th May. From then on virtually all West Cornwall Railway trains used the new Cornwall Railway station, at the west end of which mixed gauge was laid. This was never laid on the Newham line over which a very sparse passenger service continued until 16th September 1863; this comprised one train out in the morning and one back in the evening. This line to the quay remained open for over a hundred years used for freight traffic. In the 1930s a staff of three were employed at the station. The line eventually closed in November 1971; from 4th January 1965 the freight traffic had used a new depot on the site of the former engine shed.

The alignment of the Newham branch is now used as a footpath and the site of the station and goods depot has been redeveloped as part of an industrial estate.

Truthall Halt. Looking north in this photograph dated at about 1920. The GWR pagoda style shelter is at the south end of the timber face platform.

TRUTHALL HALT

OPENED: 3rd July 1905 (on the Helston branch which opened through this site in May 1887).
CLOSED: 5th November 1962.

Some one and a half miles north of Helston, Truthall was a late addition to the stops on the Helston branch, opening in early July 1905, some 18 years after the services began in 1887. In a remote rural area, it was provided to serve the villagers of Trannack and the residents of Truthall Manor. Named Truthall Halt at its opening, it became Truthall Platform in July 1906; at a later date in the British Railways era the suffix 'halt' was restored. Some tickets also referred to it as Truthall Bridge Halt. Sited on the down side of the single track line, the platform (84 ft long) comprised an earth filled structure with a timber (old sleepers) face and a cinder surface. At some point the original platform was shortened at its northern end to such an extent that, in its later life, it could only accommodate one carriage. Passengers for Truthall were advised at Helston and

Truthall Halt. Some 40 years later looking south in the early 1960s, the wooden platform has been considerably shortened and the pagoda shelter looks in a poor way.

Nancegollan to travel in the rear section to avoid the need to manoeuvre the train for passengers to alight. At the south end of the platform, close to a road overbridge, was a 20 ft x 8 ft corrugated iron GWR style pagoda shelter. There were no booking facilities, the train guard issuing tickets to passengers joining the train at Truthall. The guard was also responsible for lighting and extinguishing the platform oil lamps. No other facilities were provided at this remote halt, which closed with the withdrawal of passenger services on the Helston branch in November 1962. Freight services continued to use the line through the halt until October 1964 after which the track was lifted. The site is now overgrown.

Wadebridge. A faded but important photograph looking north-west in 1895. In the far distance, to the left of the carriage, is the station building (1888) on the single face platform. Nearer to the camera is the goods shed and to the left is the 1888 signal box beyond the south-east end of the platform. In 1899 this platform was lengthened and an island platform erected to the right of the carriage.

Wadebridge. Looking north-west in about 1912. To the right is the 1899 wide island platform. The wooden footbridge was erected in about 1910. In the distance is a steam rail motor.

WADEBRIDGE

FIRST STATION

OPENED: 1st October 1834 (with the commencement of passenger services on the Bodmin & Wadebridge Railway).

CLOSED: 1st November 1886 (for line re-building by the London & South Western Railway).

SECOND STATION

OPENED: 3rd September 1888 (with commencement of passenger services Bodmin Road – Wadebridge)

CLOSED: Passengers – 30th January 1967.
Goods – 2nd September 1978.

The town of Wadebridge stands astride the River Camel, the main part on the south-west bank linked to the suburb of Egloshayle by a long road bridge. Wadebridge was the location for some of the earliest developments in passenger train working in Britain. The staged development of its station facilities, was closely related to the evolution of the rail network serving north Cornwall. The first line was that of the standard gauge Bodmin & Wadebridge Railway, which ran south-east from the riverside quay through the town and via the River Camel valley to Bodmin and Wenford Bridge. A key role for this line was carrying coal and sea sand inland from the quay and ores and china clay from inland quarries to Wadebridge for export. Although historical accounts

Wadebridge. Looking north-west again on 19th July 1961. The 1920s concrete structure has replaced the earlier 1910 wooden footbridge. To the left is the original 1888 goods shed with its 1939 north-west extension (in a lighter colour) closing the gap between it and the station building.

vary a little on the exact date when passengers were first carried on the line, there is agreement that the official launch of such services took place on 30th September 1834 with public services commencing the next day. These limited services ran for over fifty years until, from 3rd September 1888, through trains were able to run from Wadebridge through to Bodmin Road on the main Cornwall Railway between Plymouth and Penzance. This followed the opening of the branch from Bodmin Road to Bodmin (GW) in May 1887 and the 1888 link to Boscarne Junction on the Bodmin & Wadebridge line.

In August 1882 the North Cornwall Railway, with the support of the London & South Western Railway (LSWR), obtained an Act for a line from Halwill Junction in Devon through Launceston to Wadebridge and Padstow. Subsequent Acts and Agreements authorised the reconstruction by the LSWR of the far north section of the Bodmin & Wadebridge Railway and the erection of a new station at Wadebridge. The

Wadebridge. The approach road and the exterior of the main building in 1910. To the left is the engine shed. To the right are the buffers of one of the two sidings that ran alongside the road.

Wadebridge. A general view looking south-east in the early 1930s. A T9 is standing with a train to Padstow. To its left is the island platform and at the far left is a glimpse of the 1895/1908 engine shed. Note the water column beside the engine.

LSWR legalised its ownership of the Bodmin & Wadebridge Railway on 1st July 1886. The LSWR had actually bought the Bodmin & Wadebridge Railway over 40 years earlier but Parliamentary approval was not obtained at that time. The purchase had been a purely tactical move with the aim of keeping the Cornwall Railway/GWR's broad gauge out of north Cornwall.

The next stage in the evolution of the network was the arrival of the North Cornwall Railway with the completion of its fifth section from Delabole to Wadebridge on 1st June 1895, thus completing the through route from Exeter. The North Cornwall Railway was operated by the LSWR and thus at Wadebridge the LSWR, after almost 50 years, linked up with the Bodmin & Wadebridge Railway, which it had bought in 1846! The last line to be opened was the final section of the North Cornwall Railway from Wadebridge to Padstow. Opening on 27th March 1899, the tracks ran north from Wadebridge taking over the inner siding of the quay complex.

The Bodmin & Wadebridge Railway ran south-east from Wadebridge Quay which was north-west of the road bridge over the River Camel. The small station building, on the up (north-east) side of the line was just to the south-east of an open level crossing with Molesworth Street, which led to the river bridge. The Company's workshops were on the down side of the line east of the station building, whilst the small engine shed was beyond the level crossing on the down side. These facilities lasted some fifty years until passenger services ceased at the beginning of November 1886 to allow construction of a new station by the LSWR. The tracks south-east of the Molesworth Street crossing were re-arranged and re-aligned and a new single face platform, on a north-west – south-east alignment, was opened on 3rd September 1888 catering for trains running through to Bodmin Road via Boscarne Junction. The 1888 structure was judged to be adequate to cater also for the arrival of the passenger trains on the North Cornwall Railway, in June 1895. Major changes came four years later however, when Wadebridge became a through station with the opening of the line on to Padstow. The original single face platform on the down side was extended at both ends to a total of 460 ft. An island platform was also erected opposite the original, served by the main up track and an up loop running alongside the outer face. When the North Cornwall Railway first ran into Wadebridge, trains joined the earlier Bodmin & Wadebridge Railway line east of the town at Wadebridge Junction and ran on a re-constructed single line to the station area. However, from 1907 a separate track was laid for the North Cornwall Railway trains with a scissors crossing just to the east of the station so that trains had access to all platforms. A further issue arose with the extension of the line to Padstow. Before construction a Board of Trade Enquiry was held regarding the proposed route of the passenger line over the level crossing at Molesworth Street, as hitherto it had only been used for infrequent freight traffic to the quay. Although not acted upon, one recommendation was a deviation of the route, the principal concern being the volume of vehicles and foot traffic using the road; on market days it was stated as being 45 vehicles, 35 cattle and 476 pedestrians! One witness said he had lost a horse, frightened by a train.

The main 1888 station building on the single face platform was a single storey dressed stone structure with a steeply pitched slate roof topped by three tall chimneys. An apex style canopy ran along three-quarters of the platform side. The building incorporated booking and parcels offices, waiting rooms and toilets. A bookstall operated for some years at the north-west end of the building. Until 1915 the LSWR and the GWR had separate ticket windows in the booking hall. The 350 ft long island platform, which came into use with the new layout on 12th March 1899, was wide enough to accommodate a large brick waiting room with a fireplace and chimney, the whole structure being covered by a large canopy. The three foot high platforms, originally supported by timber and iron struts, were gradually rebuilt in concrete pre-cast sections and finally in British Railways concrete blocks. Initially passengers crossed between the platforms using a rail level board crossing but an ornate open wooden footbridge was erected south-east of the main building and island waiting room in about 1910; this was replaced in the late 1920s by a concrete structure. Unlike at most North Cornwall Railway stations the station building did not incorporate accommodation for the station master. This was provided, as at Launceston, in a separate house. South-east of the station, it dated from the 1888 station redevelopment. Passenger numbers were high at Wadebridge. In 1928 63,686 passenger tickets were issued and 66,812 collected. In 1936 the

Wadebridge. The former main station building, photographed on 12th March 2009, in its role as the John Betjeman Centre for the Elderly. To the left a notice 'The Goods Shed' is on an extension of the original goods shed now in use as a youth centre.

equivalent figures were 47,739 and 59,860. By 1938 42,571 passenger tickets were issued but in 1944 the figure had almost doubled to 92,471. During the Second World War a number of trains arrived at Wadebridge carrying evacuees from the London area, in particular in 1939, 1940 and 1944.

Much of the freight traffic in the early days was concentrated at the riverside quay served by sidings of the Bodmin & Wadebridge Railway. At the station itself the principal goods facilities were in a yard behind and south-east of the down side platform. The yard included an inner siding which terminated in an 1888 stone goods shed sited immediately behind the south-east end of the platform. The shed, with a small canopy over the road side entrance, was doubled in length at its north-west end in 1939, closing the gap between it and the station building. The concrete block extension was not in keeping however with the original stone structure. Two further sidings with a 40 wagon capacity, ran alongside a loading dock and cattle pens. These were adjacent to the station's main approach road. In 1899 a further short siding was laid to a cattle dock. The goods yard, which could handle some 80-85 wagons at a time and had a 5 ton capacity crane, was used by a large number of traders serving both the town and the surrounding countryside. The transport of cattle from the local cattle market was important and the station and yard were particularly busy at the time of the Royal Cornwall Show held at Wadebridge in 1895, 1924, 1927 and 1957 and then permanently from 1960.

At the time of the station's redevelopment in 1895 – 1898 land to the north-east of the station, adjacent to the river bank, was infilled, the first structure from 1st June 1895 being a new two road engine shed, a timber building on a steel frame. At its west corner was an elevated metal water tank on a tall brick base. Access to the two road shed was only via a 50 ft turntable to the north-west; this was a problem if the turntable developed a fault. This shed was required to accommodate the larger engines now reaching Wadebridge via the North Cornwall line. Hitherto smaller engines had been serviced at the original Bodmin & Wadebridge Railway shed. From 4th February 1908 the engine shed was extended at its south-east end 'to accommodate the steam motor carriages' which had been introduced into the Wadebridge area particularly on the line to Bodmin.

Wadebridge. The original 1888 stone goods shed, viewed from the south on 12th March 2009, now in use as the Betty Fisher Centre. The photo shows the entry to the Rethink Arc organisation and the adjoining bus shelters.

At the same time the tracks in the engine shed were extended south-eastwards to join the up side loop line thus turning the shed into a more flexible through facility. The extension, in contrast to that at the goods shed, was in keeping with the original structure. The extended shed was well equipped to maintain engines some distance from the main shed at Exmouth Junction, 90 miles away, in Devon. The 50 ft turntable at Wadebridge was too small for use by Bulleid Pacific engines. These had to use a 70 ft table installed at Padstow in 1947.

All these developments were accompanied by changes to the signalling arrangements at Wadebridge. An 1888 box stood beyond the south-east end of the single face platform. Another early box was at Wadebridge Junction where the North Cornwall Railway line from Launceston joined the line from Bodmin and Boscarne. When the parallel extra line from Wadebridge Junction into the station opened on 12th March 1907, both these small boxes closed. Exactly eight years earlier on 12th March 1899 two new boxes had opened; Wadebridge West, adjoining the level crossing at Molesworth Street and Wadebridge East, a little to the south-east of the station. With the abolition of the old Wadebridge Junction box and the original station box in March 1907 the lever frame at the East Box was extended from 29 levers to 43 (10 spare) and that at the West Box from 20 to 29 (7 spare). The West Box contained a wheel operating the level crossing gates. Adjacent to the crossing and the box was a pedestrian footbridge for use when the gates were open for rail traffic.

Throughout the years Wadebridge station was well staffed supporting the passenger and freight operations. The station master's post continued until closure of the station for passenger services in 1967. At one time there were 140 men on the payroll though not all under the station master's personal control. After 1927 staff at Bodmin S R (North) and the halts came under his command.

The run down in operations at Wadebridge began at the beginning of October 1966 with the withdrawal of passenger services on the North Cornwall line from Launceston and through to Padstow. From early 1965 long distance services to Wadebridge and Padstow had ceased. Rail cars linked with Bude line trains at Halwill. Limited passenger services continued to and from Bodmin and Boscarne until withdrawal of services at the end of January 1967. The two signal boxes ceased to operate from 17th December 1967, the surviving points being hand operated. The engine shed closed in January 1967 and was subsequently demolished; also lost at this time were the surviving Bodmin & Wadebridge Railway workshops, the island platform and the signal boxes. The sidings at Wadebridge quay closed on 2nd April 1973 and all tracks beyond the level crossing were taken out of use. Many of the sidings at the station were removed in the mid 1960s. All freight services at the station ended at the beginning of September 1978.

Following this complete closure, all of the former station area has been redeveloped for various uses. The north-east section of the station site has been redeveloped for housing as has the original quay area. After some years of neglect the former station building has been renovated as the 'John Betjeman Centre for the Elderly', including a room of memorabilia of the Poet Laureate, who loved the North Cornwall line. North of this is a new library. The former goods shed is now the 'Betty Fisher Centre', named after its founder and opened on 1st October 1988. It is occupied by the 'Goods Shed Youth Centre' and 'Rethink Arc', an organisation providing community support services. The youth centre is in a recent north-west end extension of the original goods shed erected partly on the site of the 1939 extension which had previously been demolished. South-east of the old goods shed are bus shelters. The area formerly occupied by the Bodmin & Wadebridge Railway buildings is now a supermarket and car park. Through these new developments runs the appropriately named 'Southern Way', following the alignment of the main running lines. This road forms part of the Camel Trail, a cycle and pedestrian way established along the former railway from Bodmin to Padstow.

FURTHER READING

Anthony G.H., *Tavistock, Launceston & Princetown Railways*, Oakwood Press, 1971
The Hayle, West Cornwall and Helston Railways, Oakwood Press, 1968

Barton D.B., *The Redruth & Chacewater Railway*, Bradford Barton, 1966

Bastin C.H. and Thorne G., *The Railway Stations and Halts of Cornwall*, C.H. Bastin Publishing, 1994

Beale G., *The Liskeard and Looe Branch*, Wild Swan, 2000

Bennett A., *The Great Western Railway in Mid Cornwall*, Kingfisher, 1988
The Great Western Railway in West Cornwall, Kingfisher, 1988
The Great Western Railway in East Cornwall, Runpast, 1990

Body G., *Cornwall Railway*, British Rail/Avon Anglia, 1984
Railways of the Western Region, Patrick Stephens, 1983

Butt R.V.J., *Directory of Railway Stations*, Patrick Stephens, 1995

Clark R.H., *An Historical Survey of Selected Great Western Railway Stations, Layouts and Illustrations*, Oxford Publishing Co. Volume 2, 1979, Volume 3 1981

Clinker C.R., *Register of Closed Passenger Stations and Goods Depots 1830-1977*, Avon Anglia, 1978
The Railways of Cornwall 1809-1963, David & Charles 1963

Crombleholme R., Gibson B., Stuckey D., Whetmath C.F.D., *Callington Railways*, Forge Books, 1997

Dale P., *Cornwall's Lost Railways*, Stenlake Publishing, 2001

Fairclough T., *Cornwall's Railways*, Tor Mark Press, 1990
Cornwall's Railways - A Pictorial Survey, D. Bradford Barton, 1972

Fairclough T. and Wills A., *Bodmin & Wadebridge Railway 1834-1978*, Bradford Barton, 1979

Gough T., *The Southern - West of Salisbury*, Oxford Publishing Co., 1984

Hawkins M., *LSWR West Country Lines, Then and Now*, David and Charles, 1993

Jenkins S.C., *The Launceston Branch*, Oakwood Press, 1997
The Helston Branch Railway, Oakwood Press, 1992

Jenkins S.C. and Langley R.C., *The West Cornwall Railway*, Oakwood Press, 2002

Kidner R.W., *Southern Railway Halts*, Oakwood Press, 1985

Kingdom A.R., *The Plymouth, Tavistock and Launceston Railway*, ARK Publications (Railways), 2001

Leigh C., *GWR Country Stations*, Ian Allan, Volume 1 1981/1985, Volume 2 1984

Lund B. and Laming P., *Cornwall Railway Stations on Old Picture Postcards*, Reflections of a By-gone Age, 2007

McCarthy C. and D., *Railways of Britain Devon and Cornwall*, Ian Allan, 2008

Messenger M.J., *Caradon & Looe, the Canal, Railways and Mines*, Twelveheads Press, 2001

Mitchell D., *British Railways Past and Present*, Past and Present Publishing Ltd, Volume 17, *Cornwall* 1994, Volume 54, *East Cornwall* 2006

Mitchell V. and Smith K., Middleton Press
Branch Lines around Bodmin, 1996
Branch Line to Bude, 1994
Branch Lines to Falmouth, Helston and St Ives, 2001
Branch Lines to Launceston and Princetown, 1998
Branch Line to Looe, 1998
Branch Lines to Newquay, 2001/2003
Branch Line to Padstow, 1995
Plymouth to St Austell, 2001
St Austell to Penzance, 2001
Tavistock to Plymouth, 1996
Wenford Bridge to Fowey, 2000

Potts, C. R., *An Historical Survey of Selected Great Western Railway Stations, Layouts and Illustrations*, Oxford Publishing Company, Volume 4, 1985

Pryer G. and Bowring G., *An Historical Survey of Selected Southern Stations, Track Layouts and Illustrations*, Oxford Publishing Company, Volume 1, 1980

Quick M. E., *Railway Passenger Stations in England, Scotland and Wales*, RCMS 2nd Edition 2003, Supplement 2005

Reade L., *The Branch Lines of Cornwall*, Atlantic Publications, 1984

Robertson K., *Devon and Cornwall Railways in Old Photographs*, Alan Sutton, 1989
Great Western Halts, Volume 1 Irwell Press, 1990, Volume 2 KRB Publications, 2002

Roche T.W.E., *The Withered Arm*, Forge Books, 1977

Shepherd E.R., *Branch Line Memories (Devon and Cornwall)*, ARK Publications (Railways), 2005

Stengelhofen J., *Cornwall's Railway Heritage*, Twelveheads Press, 1988/1991, Revised edition 2003

Stretton J., *The Bodmin & Wenford Railway, Past and Present Companion*, Past and Present Publishing Ltd, 1999 (Re-print 2003)

Thomas D. St.J., *Regional History of the Railways of Great Britain*, Volume 1 *The West Country*, David and Charles, 1981

Tolson J.M., Roose G., and Whetmath C.F.D., *Railways of Looe and Caradon*, Forge Books, 1974

Vaughan A., *Great Western Architecture*: A Pictorial Record, Oxford Publishing Company, 1977

Vaughan J., *The Newquay Branch and its Branches*, Oxford Publishing Company, 1991
Rails to Newquay, Oakwood Press, 2008
An Illustrated History of the Cornish Main Line, Oxford Publishing Company, 2009

Waters L., *Great Western Railway – Then and Now*, Ian Allan, Volume 1 1994, Volume 2 2002

Wroe D., *The Bude Branch*, Kingfisher, 1988

Wroe D. and Others, *An Illustrated History of the North Cornwall Railway*, Irwell Press Ltd, 2008

Whetmath C.F.D., *Bodmin & Wadebridge Railway*, Forge Books, 1994

ACKNOWLEDGEMENTS

The author is very grateful for the permission to use photographs from the following collections: Lens of Sutton; pages frontispiece, 10, 12, 14 (top), 17 (top and bottom), 18 (top), 23, 24 (top), 25, 26, 27 (bottom), 28, 29 (top and bottom), 31 (left and top right), 35 (bottom), 37 (bottom), 40 (top), 41 (left), 43 (top), 45 (right), 46 (top and bottom), 47 (bottom), 51 (top), 52, 53 (top), 54 (top), 56 (bottom), 61, 62 (bottom), 65, 66, 67 (top), 70 (top), 73 (top), 79 (bottom), 80, 82 (top and bottom), 88 (top and bottom), 89 (top), 91 (top and bottom), 93, 96 (top and bottom), 98 (top and bottom), 99 (bottom), 100, 101 (top and bottom), 105 (bottom), 106 (top), 107 (top and bottom), 110 (top), 113 (top), 114, 115 (top), 121, 124 (bottom), 126, 129, 130 (top & bottom), 131, 132, 135 (bottom), 136 (top and bottom), 137 (bottom), 138.

Stations UK; pages 14 (bottom), 20 (bottom), 22 (left), 24 (bottom), 32, 33, 35 (top), 37 (top), 38, 39, 41 (right), 42 (top), 44, 45 (left), 48, 49 (top), 55, 56 (top), 59 (top), 60, 62 (top), 63 (bottom), 64, 69 (bottom), 71, 73 (bottom), 76 (left and right), 77 (bottom), 81 (bottom), 84, 86 (bottom), 89 (bottom), 92 (top), 97, 99 (top), 103 (top), 113 (bottom), 116 (bottom), 117 (top), 118, 119, 120, 125 (left), 127 (top).

Colin Caddy; pages 13, 16 (left), 74, 105 (top), 110 (bottom), 116 (top), 137 (top).

Roger Carpenter; pages 15, 16 (right), 57, 78, 79 (top), 108 (top), 111, 115 (bottom).

R.K. Blencowe; pages 18 (bottom), 86 (top), 90, 94 (bottom), 108 (bottom), 122 (bottom), 123.

Photos from the Fifties: Hugh Davies; pages 30, 42 (bottom), 95, 122 (top), 134 (top and bottom): Brian Connell; page 22 (right): David Lawrence; pages 27 (top), 117 (bottom), 128: Norman Simmons; pages 40 (bottom), 72, 94 (top). The remaining photographs were taken by the author or are from his collection where the copyright is unknown or unclear.